WITHDRAWN

The Universal (In the Realm of the Sensible)

BEYOND CONTINENTAL PHILOSOPHY

THE UNIVERSAL (IN THE REALM OF THE SENSIBLE)

BEYOND CONTINENTAL PHILOSOPHY

Dorothea Olkowski

COLUMBIA UNIVERSITY PRESS   NEW YORK

Columbia University Press
Publishers Since 1893
New York

Copyright © 2007 Dorothea Olkowski

First published in the United Kingdom by Edinburgh University Press

Library of Congress Cataloging-in-Publication Data
A complete CIP record is available from the Library of Congress

ISBN-10 0–231–14198–X
ISBN-13 978–0–231–14198–7

c 10 9 8 7 6 5 4 3 2 1

Contents

Acknowledgements

This book has been a number of years in the making. There have been many influences to absorb and radically new concepts and structures to understand and interpret. The result of this endeavor has been a change in the structure of my basic philosophical concepts, as well as a new view of philosophy and of the origins of philosophical concepts. I have come to appreciate that throughout the history of philosophy, the ties between philosophy and science, particularly physics and its theoretical tool, mathematics, have been much closer than I had ever previously been able to recognize. Plato, Aristotle, Descartes, Leibniz, Spinoza, Hume, Locke, Smith, Kant, Hegel, Nietzsche, Marx, Frege, Russell, Whitehead, Wittgenstein, Bergson, Husserl, Sartre, Merleau-Ponty, Rawls, Rorty, Harding, Tuana, Derrida, Foucault, Kristeva, Irigaray, Deleuze and Guattari – all have developed their own philosophical structures and concepts in relation to the dominant science of their day. Up to the mid twentieth century, it was still possible for a philosopher to engage also in scientific work. Edmund Husserl's Ph.D, for example, was in mathematics, and Wittgenstein studied physics before turning to philosophy. Thus, in the past, many philosophers contributed in significant ways to science. Although this no longer seems to be feasible, due largely to increasing specialization in the sciences and to the vast amount of conceptual and theoretical as well as practical information needed to carry out significant scientific research, most philosophers with a significant body of work have produced this work in relation to, if not structured by, key scientific ideas of their time. This is difficult, I believe, for some contemporary philosophers (both analytic and continental) to accept. Many philosophers believe that if this were true, then philosophy would be little more than the handmaiden of science. Yet, if it is the case, as, for example Gilles Deleuze has declared, that even when a scientific concept is fully worked out, its philosophical concept still has to be developed, then perhaps philosophy can start to see itself as neither the handmaiden of science nor its queen, but rather as part of a crowd, a network of influences that produce both science and philosophy, each with a different point of view.

Acknowledgements

Having awoken to the realization that philosophy and science were and are part of an ongoing network of intellectual and practical relations, I found myself in tremendous need. That is, given the difficulty of many concepts in physics and mathematics – particularly for someone newly arriving at their door – I needed a mentor, someone who would patiently explain concepts and their all-important contexts and who could and would demystify for me the often counter-intuitive fundamentals of physics and mathematics. Thus I am truly grateful to Marek Grabowski, who gave me so much of his time and who generously explained and explored increasingly complex ideas with me. It has been a privilege to learn from such a gifted and fearless thinker. Moreover, his continued insistence that I should create my own concepts rather than relying on those of the past has been a constant challenge so that I am grateful too for his intellectual and emotional support of my efforts in this direction. If the manner in which I have developed structures and concepts, in a philosophical context, strikes any professional, theoretical scientists as unwarranted, then I would simply ask that they consider that philosophy works with words, a much more unwieldy and imprecise tool than mathematics, and that the adventure of philosophy has everything to do with crafting concepts and structures in language. Thus interpretation is intrinsic to what philosophers do. Mistakes can be made, but this is also the case in mathematics and in the sciences. In the end we are all seeking to understand ourselves and others, the earth, the cosmos, the universe. In this there can be no regrets.

Samantha Grabowska brilliantly designed the cover of this book. Sensitive to both its contents and the sensibilities of the author, she created a richer and more complex image than I could possible have imagined on my own. I would also like to thank Todd May, Helen Fielding, James Williams, Galen Johnson, Constantin Boundas, Rosi Braidotti, David Rodowick, and Jean-Michel Rabaté, all of whom gave me criticism and/or encouragement when it was very much needed. My students at the University of Colorado, Colorado Springs, who have so often heard these ideas and tested them in their work, have been very important to me, especially, Joseph Kuzma and the students of Philosophy 404 – in particular, Amy McDowell, Cristy Stoddard, Mary Raymond, Crystalyn White, Jonathon Sparks, Paul Meyers and Danial Frazier. Carol Macdonald of Edinburgh University Press is a wonderful editor with whom I have been lucky to work. Wendy Lochner at Columbia University Press has given me so much encouragement, a great gift to me. My son, Max, fortunately for him, was away at college during most of the time I worked on this book, but he talked with me many times as I worked through the various stages of these ideas, and their relevance for him and his generation was often on my mind. I also thank my colleagues in the Department of Philosophy who have been positive and encouraging, as well as the University of Colorado at Colorado Springs for a Spring 2004 sabbatical during which much of this book was written.

Early versions of parts of chapters 1 and 2 of this book appear in 'Difference and the mechanism of death', *Deleuze and philosophy,* ed. Constantin V. Boundas, Edinburgh: Edinburgh University Press, 2006.

Introduction

French philosophy evinces a conflict of methodology that may be traced at least as far back as Michel de Montaigne (1533–92) and René Descartes (1596–1650). Montaigne is noted for rejecting scholasticism in favor of a philosophy conceived of as the practice of free judgment. He believed that insofar as human conduct does not obey universal rules, but a great diversity of rules, it follows that universal 'reason', 'truth', or 'justice' must be subject to doubt. Thus Montaigne pursues knowledge through experience; the meaning of concepts must be related to common language or to historical examples. This leads him to moderate his use of philosophical language and to prefer phrases such as 'perhaps', 'to some extent', 'they say', 'I think' when making philosophical claims.[1] Descartes, widely thought to have been influenced by Montaigne's skepticism, nevertheless moves in the opposite direction emphasizing judgment based on universal rules such as logic rather than experience. Descartes' interest in mathematics is evident, leading him to originate what are now called Cartesian coordinates (a system for representing the relative positions of points in a plane or in space). Most importantly, 'Descartes believed that a system of knowledge should start from first principles and proceed mathematically to a series of deductions, reducing physics to mathematics.'[2] Thus we have one skepticism, but two radically different solutions.

Mid to late twentieth-century French theory retains this rent in its fabric. The analysis of linguistic conventions arising from social and cultural life became the principle province of theorists like Jacques Derrida and Jacques Lacan. The move to mathematical formalism is evident in the work of philosophers like Alain Badiou and, of course, Gilles Deleuze. This book proposes a critique of the *limits* of the particular formalist, mathematical structure used by Deleuze, the manifold of continuous space-time of dynamical systems theory, yet it does not propose returning to a purely cultural and linguistic foundation nor a perceptual experience-based foundation such as that of phenomenology. Instead, it proposes a methodology and an ontology oriented in relation to formal, mathematical structures but able to be coherently and consistently asserted apart from them in terms of what is called *sensibility*. Thus, the ontology and methodology can potentially be characterized by what may be called, in mathematics, causal spin networks that, properly contextualized, make it possible to conceive of space-time, not as a pre-existent manifold, but rather as self-generating. Just as, for Bergson, *heterogeneous, sensible and ontological* duration extends itself into perception, language as well as to extensive, homogeneous space-time, it has been posited that the continuous or smooth space-time of dynamical systems may be derived from something else, a conception proposed as the microscopic description of space-time. Such a theory posits the possibility of thinking in terms of discrete space and time, as well as in terms of physical and philosophical observations that can be made only from *inside* the universe. Moreover, it is a view of the universe available only to inside observers who have only partial information about the universe, since only events in their causal past are accessible to them. Such a conception calls for a new view of physical reality – the acceptance of micro-scales – as well as a logical system that tolerates the excluded middle insofar as in such a system, something may or may not be true *or* false today and may or may not be true *or* false in the future. Implied, as well, is a different view of thinking, thinking from within what can be described as an ontological or worldly sensibility, a multiplicity of real influences emitted and absorbed so as to reflect a view of the universe from within as well as the emergent critical behavior and properties of that view. Although it is important to test this structure in conjunction with mathematical and physical concepts, as well as with those in cognitive science, biology, and chemistry, this ontology is consistent and coherent on its own terms as well. It is the realm of the sensible, the *sensible universal*, when this implies attention to visceral sensibility, to sensitivity, to information absorbed and emitted by both human and non-human entities on a cosmological scale. The realm of sensibility is neither perception nor knowledge, nor is it action; it is, rather, a sensible realm that can be experienced, understood and interpreted through the fundamental sensations of pleasure and pain.

Chapter 1, 'Philosophy and the Limits of Difference,' briefly introduces three systems of organization – three systems of ontology. First, that of the ancient Greeks; second, that of classical thermodynamics as developed by Leibniz and Newton for the purpose of predicting the paths of the planets; and third, that of the philosopher Gilles Deleuze, who introduces a philosophical variation of classical, dynamical systems theory. While pointing to limitations of the first two systems – limitations arising largely from developments in mathematics and physics as well as philosophical concerns related to the determinism of classical systems – this chapter goes on to construct a critique of the limits of the third system, that of Deleuze. Beginning with classical physics, a particular view of the universe emerged in science and philosophy, the idea that a physical theory can describe an infinitude of different worlds. Newton's physics gives us the laws by which particles move and interact with one another, but it does not otherwise specify the configurations of the particles. Given any arrangement of the particles that make up the universe, and any choices for their initial motions, Newton's laws can be used to predict the future. But Newton's theory ends up describing an infinite number of different worlds, each one of which arises as a different solution to the theory, which is arrived at by starting with the particles in different positions. Every space-time trajectory is defined by these laws, laws that specify the movement and interaction of particles. For classical dynamical systems, such as those described by Gilles Deleuze, the rules of motion are given; they are the Kantian transcendental Ideas that prescribe what can and ought to be done. What may be contingent are the particular particles themselves, that is, which particles enter into any given trajectory and in what order? In Deleuze's terms, which affects, which percepts, which concepts, and possibly even which prospects and functives (the objects of logic and mathematics respectively)? This cannot be predicted, thus every configuration of particles produces not only a different world, but an unpredictable world. But what do not alter are the rules themselves that specify the movement and interaction of particles. Moreover, in these worlds, space and time are given, not emergent. They are the pre-existent manifold, and time, in particular, is simply a parameter of space, a fourth dimension, a means for differentiating different spaces, but not a temporalization; it is not duration.

From here we move to another, a fourth ontological conception. The causal past of an event consists of all the events that could have influenced it. The influence must travel from some event in the past at the speed of light or less. Light rays arriving at an event form the outer boundary of the past of an event and make up what is called, by physicists, the *past light cone of an event*. In other words, rather than a single cone, such as that proposed by Henri Bergson, it will be proposed that every perspective and every state consists of a multiplicity of cones linked to one another in combinatorial structures, networks giving rise to self-organized, critical behavior. As the causal structure of events evolves, the motion of matter is a consequence of evolution. This raises an important question. Is it possible that smooth or continuous space-time, as proposed by Deleuze (following classical dynamics), is a useful illusion, and that from the perspective of a different system, the world can be said to be composed of discrete states on a very small scale that are discrete (or heterogeneous) with respect to both space and time on that scale? These questions lead to the introduction of some important philosophical implications of this system, implications found, in particular, in the philosophy of Jean-Paul Sartre, involving the structure 'self-Other' as a trajectory in a dynamical system. These implications will be developed throughout the book.

Chapter 2, 'A Place of Love and Mystery,' explores the Kantian rules that purportedly, as Deleuze and others argue, govern the organization of dynamical systems in *human* history. Kant's transcendental Ideas supply the rules of motion for a given spatio-temporal manifold. It is well-known that the transcendental Ideas correspond to no objects of experience. Derived only from syllogisms, transcendental Ideas give rise to illusion if we ascribe objective reality to them. Unlike the illusions of logic, transcendental illusions persist, even once revealed. This is why, Kant argues, we mistakenly take the subjective necessity of a connection of our concepts, which is to the advantage of the understanding, to be an objective necessity in the determination of things in themselves. It is a mistake arising from reason itself, and as even the wisest among us are unable to be free of this, each transcendental Idea gives rise to a necessary and unavoidable illusion, which, however, is thought to be harmless and even able to be employed in a positive manner. If human reason's natural tendency is to transgress the limits of experience, then we are entitled to suppose that transcendental Ideas have their own good, proper, and immanent use, and that use is to unify the manifold of concepts. Thus, Ideas of reason order everything, combining the greatest possible unity with the greatest possible extension. However, these ideas have no source outside of reason and outside of the empirical field. Insofar as we have no knowledge of any objects corresponding to these ideas, they are called 'problematic.' Particulars appear to be derived from the Ideas, in other words particulars appear to be derived from the universality of the rule. Still the question arises, how do we know that this is actually the case? Limiting the employment of pure reason to a purely regulative function is indeed problematic. All its possible conse-quences can never be known, but still, Kant insists, when we think about this approximate universal rule, we also think something else, that is, we think unity.

So it is that when speculative pure reason gives way to practical reason, what matters is what a consciousness can *do*. This makes the categories of freedom crucial, for they provide an axiomatic for the *acts* of any *intelligible* being and refer neither to sensible experience nor theoretical understanding. The claim is that they *produce* the reality to which they refer. According to Kant, the categories of freedom produce an intention of the will removed from human experi-ence. Given Kant's emphasis on the acts of an intelligible being, it may seem surprising when Deleuze argues that the faculties are set in motion, then put thought in motion in a *sensible* encounter. Yet, this makes sense, for sensibility spurs thought insofar as the sensuous and impulsive animal will sets thought in motion in order to free itself from its own affects, its inclinations, its weakness, its depravity, and its unworthiness. Set in motion, what faculties do is a matter of *practical power*, which means it is a matter of will or desire. If the power of a transcendental *I Think* is an illusion, the power of will freed of the *I Think* is a power that freely produces the world – without subjects and without objects. In this case, only the power of the virtual, the power of abstract production, will itself, desire itself, is real. As ontological forces, the faculties are productive, they produce the reality to which they give sense. Moreover, it is the transcendental Ideas, connection, conjunction, disjunction, derived from the logical categories of *rela-tion* that are the modes of production. They connect the part-objects with desiring-machines; then they carry out the dis-organization or dis-tribution, and consummation-actualization of the manifold of free will. The divine manifold of disorganization and distribution orders and organizes, producing both thought and the world, and producing entities that look like subjects or objects or worlds but are merely effects. Strangely, the role of God is to be the pure *a priori* manifold of space since it is in this manifold that things are determined to coexist in one time through the mutual determination of their position so as to constitute a whole in which each appearance stands *outside* of every other and all relations are *external*.

The distribution of desire or free will is the task of the disjunctive syntheses which might be considered the act of a god who comes down from the transcendental heights to generate its objects by split-ting apart every primitive empirical organization that has connected in its absence. The divine power of disjunctive synthesis (the dynamical category of relation) breaks up the monotonous binary linearity of the law of connection. The synthesis prevents the possibly false antinomy between any unconscious spatio-temporalization, which is to say, any impulsive and spontaneous eruption into an otherwise undisturbed linear causality – between this and the forces which might give us a rule to follow, that is, a purely intellectual determination. In this manner, pleasure is defined as the result of the determination of the will by reason, and feeling is defined as what we will to do. Indeed, there is a feeling, a feeling of constraint, of passive restraint that we are made to embrace insofar as it produces the same effect as pleasure. The feeling of passive restraint does not, however, involve any sensuous burden, as sensuousness would be incommensurate with the pure practical determination of desire, and with its pure practical creation.

To resolve any possible antinomy, Deleuze, like Kant, introduces what he calls, 'the dark precursor.' Whether we will it or not, whether we think it or not, we and everything that is connected to anything else will be torn apart. We will become a schizo, and if not, then catatonic, neurotic, paranoid. We will be overtaken by the forces through which 'we' pass; affects, percepts, concepts, prospects, functives, we consume them all and they consummate themselves through our *materiality*. Given the apparent inevitability of these forces, we can only hope that some of them are interesting, amusing or remarkable forces, meaning, forces that decode and deterritorialize. Anything interesting in life, it appears, is always a matter of what a force can do. Thus there is the necessity of moving quickly before flows are overtaken by the force of the capitalist socius, which seems to be the inevitable quasi-causality of the continuous manifold forming throughout history. Barbarism, feudalism or capitalism, there is always some full body ready to appropriate productive forces. In this sense, capital, with its cash nexus, its reduction of all codes to a single axiom, is simply the most recent expression of the regulative practical law.

Chapter 3, 'Love and Hatred,' takes up, from Chapter 7, the question of the *a priori* possibility of the Other as the stage upon which real characters or variable subjects are actualized as expressions of a field. On this scale, when an Other appears in the midst of the possible world that they express, any 'I,' as the expression of a different possible world will be annihilated, obviously eliminating any prospect of intimate relations. Yet, it is argued, none of these structures comprises unalterable truths; they merely inform us of the limits of imagination, understanding, and reason. Contemporary epistemologies and ontologies remain committed to structures enacting visibility and unconcealment, turning away from interiority, the unperceivable, the uncategorizable, seeking also the elimination of heights and depths. But in the social and economic system of the twentieth century, the unperceived and unknown themselves are pulled from hiding and every event is brought to the surface, there to be connected, disjoined and split apart, and ultimately reconnected to something new. If it is the case, however, that new faculties can arise and take shape, then perhaps new faculties will emerge, faculties for which our current sensory organs are too coarse. Such faculties, if they were sensible (rather than perceptual or cognitive), would initially appear to be elusive and subtle, yet they might give us the opportunity to depart the continuum of violence, what we will call the game of eluding death, meaning the infinity of affects, percepts, and concepts, prospects and functives, where faculties are broken apart and forced to their infinitesimal limits. Thus we will posit that the sensible absorption, emission and intuition of states structured in relational networks allows for the possibility of some hesitation, some slow-down essential to the intuition of sensibility.

But such a transformation will take more than just new ideas. Ostensibly new ideas are often nothing more than disguised and deflected variations of existing structures or orders. So, we might consider the possibility of a structure that generates the absolutely new. This is especially relevant in the sensible realm giving rise to the emotions. If the absorption, emission and intuition of love and hate, of diffusion and distress, those sensibilities that are most one's own, if this effort could be initiated, tolerated, conceptualized, it might require the most subtle data, that of light, that of relational networks passing from state to state. Relational structures might send out their influences from a still illuminated past into a newly glimmering present, informing and spinning out on innumerable networks, engaging and emanating, sending both the information we have absorbed and that which we radiate through our interactions. Once, all things, living and non-living, were conceived of as belonging to an epistemology of impressions, impressions of sensations and reflections on those sensations. The limit of this structure of external, proximate differentials lies in the manner in which it restricts relations to singular events that resemble, connect, are conjoined to or disjoined from one another: subject – object, male – female, here – there, mother – child, mouth – breast; mechanical connections like plug – socket or mortar – stone. But the myriad rays of light, illuminating and influencing events, when they are not completely imperceptible, tend to exert their influence unnoticed, even in the midst of our participation in them. Given that such relational networks are vast but not infinite, always subject to alteration from out of the past, we can see how easily we might be misled about our own sensibilities and faculties, our own stories and histories. Unable to conceive of our own sensible nature, our joy and happiness, our sorrow and sadness are never more than responses to the demands of the situation. The project of this book is to posit an interruption in which we can think through or refrain from these demands.

Chapter 4, 'Under Western Eyes,' begins by differentiating the realm of productive distribution, the continuous manifold, from that of the Renaissance objective observer. Confusing these two systems has been a distraction. Thus we undertake to distinguish the objectivity of single-point or multiple-point perspective from something that is quite different, the position of bodies in space at *any moment whatever*, that is, the position of bodies on a continuous manifold. The space of any moment whatever is implicit in Kant insofar as the Kantian topology already implies n-dimensions, an infinity of virtual connections, thus evading anything empirical. Perhaps too, the Kantian manifold, the category of relation, is the modern expression of an ancient idea, the idea that the power of nature is the divine power to break apart anything that has been connected. As such, it transforms every 'and . . . and . . . and' into 'or . . . or . . . or.' This might be commensurate with the millennial view of divinity. It suggests that it is the divine task, the ontological task of nature/god to disconnect what has been connected, to keep separate what otherwise might be related, coded, ordered, organized. So perhaps now we can see more clearly why, in this system, it has been claimed that the schizophrenic voyage is the only kind there is. Moreover, it appears that the differential relation, which describes the trajectories of the socius, produces by conjoining its elements. It produces the capitalist phenomenon of *the transformation of the surplus value of code into a surplus value of flux*. Given this, let us posit the following: the breakdown of subsisting codes and territorialities is an effect of replacing the barbarian and feudal codes with a new code, that of the mathematical differential equation. But the disjunctive synthesis that deterritorializes capital is a divine power that is still too slow. Too slow in the vicinity of attractors in the form of consumer goods. Thus the newly forming structure guarantees that even the desire of the most disadvantaged person will be determined to the greatest possible extent with the necessity of investing the capitalist social field as a whole. Moreover, it is precisely delays, accidents, and deviations that form the disjunctions that ensure the continuity, that keep the structure from displacing itself at infinite speeds and guarantee the ruin of traditional sectors, the development of extraverted economic circuits, a specific hypertrophy of the tertiary sector, and an extreme inequality in the different areas of productivity and incomes.

This chapter then examines the extent to which theories of justice assist in these efforts. John Rawls argues that political persons must regard themselves as self-authenticating sources of valid claims because they are independent of any particular set of ends or aims. Any situatedness or perspective undermines the reasonableness and rationality of their thinking. This fundamental autonomy brings about the principle of equal liberty and the priority of individual rights over social and economic advantages. Such principles are related to the Kantian notion of autonomy or freedom. Excluding the individual moralities of situated citizens might allow theorists like Kant and Rawls to claim to be neutral with respect to any particular interpretation of the good, although in the end, it appears that they impose their own conception of the good. What would this be? Their own interpretation appears to be a transcendental conception according to which the good is equivalent to autonomy, the continual evacuation of any point of view. It has been argued that the refusal to rank particular conceptions of the good implies a strong tolerance for individual inclinations, but in fact it implies no respect for individual inclinations at all, coupled with the recognition that they are inevitable. For in the face of autonomy, individual inclinations are little more than articles of bad faith. Bad faith is an immediate threat to the autonomy of one's projects because it is the nature of consciousness to be what it is not and not to be what it is. In this system, autonomy is keeping one's project ahead of oneself so as to never *be* that project, yet never to be cut off from it either.

This conclusion may be supported by the assertion, from Rawls, that the notion of autonomy formulated by justice as fairness is to be found in Kant where judgment frees itself so that it may set all the faculties in motion in a free agreement. Although understanding, under the provenance of theoretical reason, governs what can be known and the manner of knowing anything, it is practical reason and its rule over the faculty of desire that remains the most powerful aspect of reason insofar as practical reason demands freedom from causality, the unending chain of events leading to an unconditioned first cause.

While it seems to be the case that, in the first critique, the conflict between pure thought creating its objects and the necessary condition that thought be bound to sensibility gives rise to the conflict of the second critique, the necessity of freedom in spite of the mechanical laws of nature, nonetheless, it is practical reason, not theoretical reason, that posits an absolutely spontaneous first cause that stands outside of nature, while theoretical reason, for the sake of understanding, demands that we remain bound to events forming trajectories in the manifold of space-time. These trajectories are explored in this chapter in relation to the social and economic structure of Asian sex tourism.

Moral law directly 'determines' the will, not as natural (linear) causality, but as a negative incentive. Escaping the in-itself by nihilating oneself toward one's possibilities calls for the tearing apart of connections. The destruction of codes is the condition of autonomy, of free will. So the form of causality operates with respect to the mechanical causality of the world as the connection between phenomena, and phenomena await decoding; they motivate our autonomy. With respect to the categories of freedom, causality merely expresses the relation of autonomous will to an independent action through freedom. Legality (operating both in sensuous and practical nature) brings mechanical, causal nature into contact with intelligible nature connecting them *in one reason*. It makes possible the connection between sensible and practical maxims, between individual sensibilities and the acts of an autonomous transcendence. Subjective maxims such as: 'I desire submissive women whom I can subject to my will,' or 'I dislike women I cannot subject to my will,' or 'I dislike Asian men, I am unable to subject them to my will,' will be negated and in their place, we will assert practical maxims. For universal commanded law to be moral law, the objective determining ground of will must simultaneously be the subjectively sufficient determining ground of an *action*; moral law must be the negative incentive; respect, good faith must be the positive outcome of this intelligible act. To make moral law the incentive, we submit our formerly subjective maxims to objective maxims urging moral improvement. That such maxims are expressed in terms of specific injunctions should not be surprising. So the claim might be made that 'Asian men *ought* not to consume Asian women,' (deterritorialization of traditional codes), and 'Western men *ought* to control Asian men,' (reterritorialization within the axiom of capital), all with an eye to the moral improvement of Asian women and men. Such maxims bring the alleged chaos and contradiction of individual sensibilities into accord with the legislative and moral demands of universal *a priori* practical reason. In this universal form capitalism can embark on its project of universal control and profits, a project commensurate with the autonomy of freedom.

Chapter 5, 'Passive Restraint,' takes up the question of the inevitability of the regulative principles of connection, disjunction, and conjunction as an ontological structure. This chapter begins with the thesis that it may well be little more than the apparent lack of constraint on the part of the mind, its sublime overreaching, either in the direction of an unconditioned transcendental Idea of reason or in the direction of the uninhibited power of imagination that gave rise to so-called societies of discipline. 'Respect' for moral law, it has been argued, is nothing more than a fact, a cry against barbarism with no viable philosophical support. That is, what really matter, what have philosophical support are facts that confirm the system of reason. If reason organizes the data of cognition into a system of logical laws that produce general relations, then the system of reason is only as powerful as its predictive success. The system of reason must give the capacity to subsume facts under principles to the rational self. This end increases the self's capacity for its own preservation by making possible the subjugation of the material, sensible realm to logical laws and general relations. By this means, the material and sensible realm may be determined in advance and so is unable to reform and restructure. As predictable, as necessarily connected to logical laws and general relations, perception is made to conform to what these laws and relations can classify and confirm. This is the meaning of the statement that there is 'nothing to know.' There is no knowledge of the transcendental Ideas, but also, nothing new in the universe, only the unending trajectories of predictable behaviors. This is why, if they are rational, individual beings will develop themselves in accordance with these same laws and relations. On this scale, whatever does not contribute to the self-preserving predictive success of the individual threatens to return those individuals to the state of nature whose nasty and brutish tendencies they would fully suffer.

The situation is no different for the transcendental power of an empirical imagination. Here too, the state of nature is taken to be a wretched and savage condition, from which 'men' are protected by furthering their interest in what is nearest to them but also, and over-riding this, by strictly observing some universal and inflexible rules of justice. This, in spite of the assertion that when the mind passes from the idea or impression of one object to the belief in the existence of another, it does so because it is determined by principles that associate the ideas of these objects and unites them in *imagination*. The power of imagination is to be always ahead of itself and ahead of memory, able to disconnect and reconnect anything that catches its attention. Moreover, imagination is interested in determination, the predictability that lies not merely in relations of ideas but originally in relations of objects. Even as governed by imagination, persons are said to be more likely to value what is contiguous to them in space and time. This is because, in matters of the passions and will, proximity is what counts. So, persons exhibit a marked preference for any 'trivial advantage' insofar as it is proximate, rather than what is said to be truly in their interest, that is, maintaining order and observing justice, both of which require full and appropriate use of imagination.

Nevertheless, in spite of the increasing concern in societies with conformity to law, it is widely asserted that in Western nations, pre-World War II societies of discipline, in which individuals move from one rule-governed environment to the next, are finished. By the end of the twentieth century, the organization of everyday life as the passage from family, to school, to the factory, farm, or office, and perhaps to the hospital, prison, or the military may well have ceased. What has changed is the structure of the institutions. Formerly organized by rules that guaranteed certainty, meaning, the capacity to predict the trajectories and relations of objects in the world, the rules now guarantee only the chaos of probability. Connection, disjunction and conjunction continue everywhere, but now they connect neither what is natural nor even things that are conventional, but only contingencies, with the result that there is increasing unpredictability. This results in undermining the self-governing nature of political, social and industrial institutions. Demands for reform of such social institutions may be only a manifestation of their demise as self-regulating entities. If so, they may all fall under what can be called the 'unity of time,' time characterized as a parameter of space (n + 1 dimensions), similar to that found in telecommunications systems themselves in service to the differential universal, the universal that carries out the threat to delocalize and empty out the interior of all once-private institutions on a global level.

Far from relieving humanity of its suffering at the hands of the Oedipal family or the disciplinary prison, we expect from this release nothing less than the emergence of new global societies of control. In the self-enclosed societies of discipline, the individual may have been subject to a 'phase transition,' a disequilibrium provoked by external forces, resulting in a leap from one coded, enclosed system to another, requiring a radical adjustment to new or newly emerging conditions but nevertheless one more or less in equilibrium. But now, we can expect that because of the deterritorialization of each of these formerly isolated interiors, what we are facing is a global system of rules that have developed to accommodate the newest technological form of the ontology which they serve. Nevertheless, the restrictive resources of all the old models of transcendental Ideas will continue to be drawn upon in their regulatory capacity. Nostalgia for the return to states of 'equilibrium' characterizing disciplinary society seem to be chief among the tools utilized to guarantee that such a return will never actually take place. As suggested previously, reason will be concerned primarily with the faculty of desire, determining will according to rules (hypothetical and categorical imperatives) but only insofar as the ground of choice is *not empirical*, therefore, not connected to pleasure or pain, but only wholly in accordance with an *unconditional practical law* in relation to which every single subject is passive. This chapter is committed to examining the structure and effects of this passivity in the cultural climate, particularly as it pertains to the concepts and realization of pleasure and pain.

Chapter 6, 'In the Realm of the Senses,' is a final attempt to think about an epistemology and an aesthetics outside of the constraints of dynamical systems theory. Given the realization that whatever is seen, heard, scented, even touched or tasted comes to any sensibility from out of the past, the demand for infinite speeds reflects a refusal of cosmological limits and of sensibility. This may be due to the lack of any philosophical concept of combinatorial networks and influences, not only for human beings, but for all things. Given this reconsideration of the place of sensibility among human beings and by extension, under the name of 'influence,' to non-human beings, to all states, much more needs to be said about epistemological and aesthetic structures. Rather than humanism – or the other side of the mirror, extreme contiguity – let us propose a sensible intimacy, for all things, human and not human. Rather than extreme uniformity, the *blocs* of percepts and affects, the chaotic indetermination of dynamic continuities, let us propose the slow-down, the interval between what has been felt or said or thought and some emergent concept, some new perception, emotion, word or language. In this interval, the past may enter the present, for the first time, flooding it with sight, sound, scent, touch, taste, and the myriad sensibilities of which we know nothing, insofar as we have not yet learned how to measure them nor how vast is their realm. Without this, we have no sensible contact with our cosmos, no contact with its events, objects, elements, inhabitants, its wave-lengths without which the world is grey; no color, darkness or light. Let us recall that the world, in this sense, may be said to consist of images and nothing but images; visual images, sound images, fragrant or odorous images, tactile images transmitted at speeds up to the speed of light, influencing one another in relational networks spinning across the world, if not the cosmos. Every image transmits energy and matter to every other, each one emitting and absorbing, each image a perspective newly emerging from all the other images with which it interacts.

This chapter begins with an investigation of the photographic image and what has been called cinematographic knowledge. The point is made that, for cinematographic knowledge, time is an independent variable, a parameter of the spatial manifold. Time is useful for calculating the positions of real elements of matter at *any moment whatever* if their current positions are given. However, from this point of view, events do not happen, rather, events are already mapped on the trajectory. We simply encounter them along our way; the emergence of absolutely new states, spatialization and temporalization, the absolutely new, would be an illusion. States are taken to be nothing more than continuous snapshots, successive images, indifferent images. Because the partitioning of space and time are given equal rank, the succession of images is simply the illumination of points on a line, a line that is given all at once. But alternatives can and have been offered. In contrast to the concept of the snapshot, a successive image in a determined trajectory, a virtual immobility, this chapter proposes the concept of the discrete photograph, the heterogeneous image that is an effect of an 'uncertain art,' a science of desirable or detestable bodies, that *animate* the spectator by means of discontinuous elements and discrete effects. From here, the chapter goes on to propose a new image of philosophy. Indeed, there is nothing preventing us from considering another possibility – the possibility that the dynamical model of independent subsystems does not apply to most of life – the possibility that since the universe began, atoms have not spread themselves out uniformly but stubbornly cling together to form heterogeneous clusters of stars, planets, galaxies. This would imply also that the relentless sense of *loss* that we are said to experience is only a consequence of combining previously separate subsystems leading to a decrease in the number of those subsystems. With these ideas in mind, we may dare to propose another image for philosophy – one long ago discarded by the philosophers who embrace the dark precursor.

In Pelasgian mythology, the light-bearing goddess of the night was identified with the moon and the moon was identified with life. This was the basis of the mysteries of Eleusis, a celebration of the joyful birth of the new moon, following the dark-moon, when the girl, Kore, is abducted by the death-sun. What is interesting in this myth is that from its point of view, darkness corresponds to the disappearance of the moon, its luminous, reflective rays. Death is then the darkening of the moon and *death comes from the sun*. The winter solstice celebrates not only the return of Kore to Demeter from the caves of Hades, but also rebirth. Kore gives birth to the moon, and the girl Kore is herself transformed into a moon goddess. This concept and this image invokes what may appear to be a daring proposition. The proposition that the true transformation, the return of Kore to Demeter and to the moonlit earth is her transformation from girl to goddess, from sunlight to moonlight. What is implied here? There is a transformation of material or natural elements, a quantitative and qualitative transformation in which something new is achieved, something that, like the moon, illuminates the heavens with its reflective light and by means of this reflective illumination, transforms all, not once, but again and again. No doubt in the ancient world the cosmos was generally conceived of as finite and bounded, having actual edges beyond which there might be nothing to sustain an object's structure. In such a cosmos transformations are limited, possibly little more than repetitions or maximally a finite number of variations. Still, is there any reason not to believe that the universe conceived of as a creation of the Goddess is not at least *unbounded*, a sphere that is finite in area but delimited by no boundaries? Nevertheless, what matters for the moment is the image of the Goddess floating, dancing with the wind above the water, the transformational aspect of this conception and this image, for which it may prove to be of the greatest importance that, whether it is called *cosmos* or world-order, there is no severance of the connection between the concept and the reflective moon, the luminous aspect of the night.

So we end with two images of philosophy. There is the powerful and dark image whose shadow is cast over us to this very day. It is the image of the continuum, the perfection of the undifferentiated, the one, the image of a Platonic god who wanted everything to be as much like himself as possible. Thus, it has been argued that for the apprentice philosopher, for the 'man' in the cave, only death will lead to something more, to something beyond the realm of shadows, of blocked light and direct vision. Is the philosopher the messenger of death? Conception, rather than the transformation of the light that enters the eye into energy that is transmitted to the brain, instead finds its proper meaning as the re-birth into truth, a truth situated in an eternity beyond appearances, in the *One*, that is always mirrored at least twice, once by the god himself and once more by the philosopher or 'his' apprentice. Let us dare to question this image of philosophy, using the reflected light of the moon and let us conceive of a second image of philosophy, not an imitation but a transformation of the material and natural elements, an image more difficult to obtain. So much has been lost, so much appropriated. The pre-Hellenic Pelasgian account of creation survives only in the most fragmented manner, but the standard interpretation of even these fragments overlooks the wide-wandering goddess Eurynome and seeks to establish the patrimony of her creation Ophion. His eventual banishment by the Goddess does not prevent the resurrection of his myth. In the tales of men, Kore is abducted. How else to fill life with shadows? But what if what happened in Eleusis was the separation and reunion of the dual goddess Demeter-Kore? Thus, Kore is the reflected light of Demeter, and Demeter is the life-giving light, the photon whose energy is transmitted in diffracted light rays. Demeter-Kore is the story of the reflected, refracted and diffracted energy of that light, wandering in the world, transmitting its energy. In this cosmos, Kore returns from darkness to her origins, light and energy are conserved. So, let us be skeptical of the philosopher, for whom Demeter-Kore is the origin of the philosophical receptacle of all becoming, the wet-nurse of the cosmos. Let us instead propose, imagine, theorize that the Goddess and Demeter-Kore are themselves concepts, concepts that constitute a first philosophy, a description of the nature of reality and of its creative structure. Let us not forget that energy is not lost, that light is absorbed and emitted, that sensation comes to sensibility from out of the past. And let us consider this new image of philosophy.

Notes

1. See the excellent online entry by Marc Foglia, Université de Paris I/Sorbonne, at Marc Foglia, 'Michel de Montaigne', *The Stanford Encyclopedia of Philosophy (Fall 2004 Edition)*, ed. Edward N. Zalta, http://plato.stanford.edu/archives/fall2004/entries/montaigne/.

2. Eric W. Weisstein, 'Torque', *Eric Weisstein's World of Physics*, http://scienceworld.wolfram.com/physics/Torque.html. Wolfram is the producer of the software 'Mathematica.'

1

Philosophy and the Limits of Difference

What the ears hear

A story-teller tells a tale. We hear it, fascinated or irritated, completely in agreement or completely in disagreement. Either way, it is a question of what the ears hear.

> Summoned to lay down the rules for the foundation of Perinthia, the astronomers established the place and the day according to the position of the stars; they drew the intersecting lines of the decumanus and the cardo, the first oriented to the passage of the sun and the other like the axis on which the heavens turn. They divided the map according to the twelve houses of the zodiac so that each temple and each neighborhood would receive the proper influence of the favoring constellations; they fixed the point in the walls where the gates should be cut, foreseeing how each would frame an eclipse of the moon in the next thousand years. Perinthia – they guaranteed – would reflect the harmony of the firmament; nature's reason and the gods' benevolence would shape the inhabitants' destinies.
>
> Following the astronomers' calculations precisely, Perinthia was constructed; various peoples came to populate it; the first generation born in Perinthia began to grow within its walls; and these citizens reached the age to marry and have children.
>
> In Perinthia's streets and square today you encounter cripples, dwarfs, hunchbacks, obese men and bearded women. But the worst cannot be seen; guttural howls are heard from cellars and lofts, where families hide children with three heads or with six legs.
>
> Perinthia's astronomers are faced with a difficult choice. Either they must admit that all their calculations were wrong and their figures are unable to describe the heavens, or else they must reveal that the order of the gods is reflected exactly in the city of monsters.[1]

The Great Khan remains suspicious of the many tales of many cities recounted to him by Marco Polo. He asks the explorer if he will repeat these same tales to people in the West upon his return there. The explorer replies calmly that 'the listener retains only the words he is expecting . . . It is not the voice that commands the story: it is the ear.'[2] What the ears hear, what the eyes see, what the skin touches, what the tongue tastes, what the nose smells, what each sensory organ expects is what each commands; what is it that the senses independently and *in common* expect and command? What was commanded for the rules of the foundations of Perinthia, whose very name alludes to an intimate, if not obscene feature of the body? Was it the projections of the astronomers or the monstrous order of the gods? Was it the fixed point in the walls where the gates should be cut or the cripples, dwarfs, hunchbacks, obese men and bearded women? What was said of Perinthia is that its rules of foundation would give way to a city that reflects the harmony of the firmament; that nature's reason and the gods' benevolence would shape the inhabitants' destinies. Harmony, reason and justice would prevail. But this assumes many things. It assumes that the state of affairs external to the calculations, to which the calculations refer, is coherent; it assumes that reflection is real, that nature's reason is amenable to human calculation. It assumes that the calculations of the astronomers are not other than those of the gods, that the monstrous offspring of the city are not themselves the inevitable progeny of harmony, reason, and justice. What it does not assume, what it does not take into account is the idea that these assumptions are a view of the world. This view, in accordance with common sense, is a view long in decline. The astronomers' ideas appear to us more and more to be the remnants of a faded dream, so more and more we abandon them as the fairy tales of a worn-out logic, no longer operating anywhere in the universe, no longer aspects of our past, no longer perspects of our present.[3] Such calculations, we believe, have failed to be adequately universal or perhaps they were misapplied, mistakenly referred to a scale in which their effects could only be disastrous.

We, like the Great Khan, assume that the world can be known, that we are capable of thinking the world. Relying on his extensive atlases with their renderings of countries and continents, the Emperor charts the world. In accordance with common sense, he concludes that our senses and reason provide us with knowledge of species or beings. He believes in the fundamental rightness of determining their identity in a genus through the opposition of predicates, and of substantiating that identity through the judgment of analogy with other genera which are themselves grounded in resemblance through perception.[4] *On the other hand*, in accordance with our own good sense, we believe that our observations and expectations correspond to the real. But insofar as we continue blindly to affirm identity, opposition, analogy, and resemblance, insofar as we complacently await the equalization of all inequalities, then, along with the astronomers of Perinthia, we may be viewed as little different from the uneducated simpletons of Plato's *Republic* who believe that sight is in the eyes. For, as the philosophers proclaim,

> 'sight may be in the eyes, and the man who has it may try to use it, and colors may be present in the objects, but unless a third kind of thing is present, which is by nature designed for this very purpose, you know that sight will see nothing and colors remain unseen. – What is this third kind of thing? What you call light.'[5]

The philosophers know that it is the sun that causes the light, that causes sight to see and causes the objects to be seen. And the sun itself is caused by the Good, it is begotten as analogous to the Good, but in the world of sight and things seen. Thus when we conclude that identity, opposition, analogy and resemblance still operate as the conditions of knowledge, we may be seen as turning our eyes to objects whose colors are viewed in the dimness of night; when the vision is obscured and the eyes are nearly blind, clear vision is lost.

Yet, it might be argued that identity, opposition, analogy and resemblance, along with the habituation that makes the future more like the past, and so apparently more and more truthful, remain useful in some limited contexts. Perhaps as forms of distribution, these categories still orient limited spheres of life and thought, whether those of recognition or those of prediction. Beyond this, they provide the occasion to formulate eccentric thoughts by means of their perversion or distortion.[6] Already for Plato, sight and things seen, hearing and sound, touch and things felt, taste and things tasted, smell and odors, all the senses are said to need a third element to see, hear, touch, taste and smell, in the absence of which, eyes, ears, skin, tongue, and nose are nothing. Often we do not even begin to understand the series of relations that condition our sensibilities, our perceptions, our knowledge, our thoughts and acts. If, however, we have already called our common sense and good sense into question, if we have found ourselves enfolded within a new structure, a structure characterized by discordant harmony, the open-ended interplay of the faculties that provides a solution to problems posed as *Ideas*, when the being of the sensible perplexes the soul and forces it to pose a problem, then we think we have moved beyond the dimness of the night, the coarse operations and categories yielding prediction and recognition, good sense and common sense.[7]

So it seems that the failure, the incoherence or insufficiency of the ancient rules has exposed an exquisite opportunity, one that allows other concepts, other structures, to be entertained. The common sense of the astronomers has long since given way to the good sense of the philosophers. Overwhelmingly, the good sense view has been that, given a world 'endowed . . . at the creation with a store of energy . . . that divine gift would persist for eternity, while the ephemeral forces danced to the music of time and spun the transitory phenomena of the world.'[8] By this means, a new set of calculations, a new point of view came to dominate the philosophers' rules. The principle at stake here is one which avows that the total quantity of energy in nature is unchanged as its distribution changes irreversibly. In society as in nature, the point would be to maintain the minimum of rules, the simple acceptance that jostling atoms pass on their energy at random, purposelessly tending toward uniformity, equal distribution under the laws of nature. When a great deal of energy is stored in one segment of the society or in one part of the universe, then allowed to wander aimlessly through the system, the energy will spread uniformly throughout, reaching, finally, a uniform distribution, a steady state. In spite of the fact that throughout the system there will continue to be areas where energy accumulates, where individual atoms are not evenly distributed and inequalities proliferate, for the observer possessing good sense, an observer far enough removed from particular segments, the system uncontroversially reaches a steady state, a uniform distribution.[9] In principle, inequality disappears, differences are canceled in a process of self-negation, and in place of Perinthia, with its ancient ideals, we have built Los Angeles, the expression of the ideology of the middle classes.[10]

But now, another point of view is emerging into the present out of the past as common sense and good sense are melting into a groundless ground, the depthless depth, the extensive magnitude, the space as a whole, the manifold that rules over all, the inexplicable at the heart of thought.[11] So we are driven by a kind of desperate necessity into the unequal, the affirmation of difference, and implication, 'the perfectly determined form of being.'[12] 'What if?' we ask, over and over, each time with a different emphasis, a different vocal intonation, a different cadence; what if there is a world only insofar as the calculations which form it are inexact and unjust and the world is ineluctably the remainder of those calculations, the *perineum*? What if every phenomenon refers, not to an ordered set of calculations whose outcomes are knowable in advance, but to an infinite disparity, the sufficient reason of *all* phenomena.[13] Or, what if the world were still differently ordered or its ordering changes in ways which can be theorized but whose actualization is unknown and remains unknowable in any current terms, or if the only terms in which it can be accounted for are those of a vast number of Marco Polos (or Markopoulous), each of whom has her own ontological unconscious, her own constantly changing journey of subtle influences that modulate and modify, informing her receptivity, illluminating her cognition, inciting her actions?[14] What if the world is the result of some spatial and temporal contingency in which what is neither true nor false today only becomes true or false tomorrow, or some time after tomorrow, or never? If this were to be the case, then certainly the carefully constructed categories of good sense ('on the one hand,' this, this and this are current states of affairs, but on the other hand, only 'that' results) as well as the resemblances and representations given by and for our perceptions and cognitions leading to actions would be as little reliable as the astronomers' calculations. Perhaps also, the reason of the sensible, the condition of that which appears, that which is not space and time, but which determines the indeterminate object as this or that and individualizes a self situated among objects, perhaps this reason too has its limits.[15]

We have, in the past, relied on recognition to make the world intelligible to us for the sake of thought and action; we have defended equilibrium as the law of harmony, reason and justice, and now, we presume the problematics of the Idea will provide us a place among the astronomers. Given the unfailing usefulness, the explanatory power of these systems whether those of recognition and habituation or that of faculties and Ideas, how is it possible that we could be mistaken? In fact, we are not mistaken insofar as we place ourselves on a plane of consistency, where every system-series of heterogeneous and coupled concepts manifests the problems its components were created to resolve. But to cling desperately to modes of thinking whose philosophical intuition has long ago evaporated or to embrace a single structure as if it were the final power, the last limit, unable to be overtaken by any other point of view, or more provocatively, unable to be connected to other structures which lie on its boundaries, is to cease traveling, to stay in the same city, the same house, the same room.[16] Thus, if what is yet unknown, what is completely unexpected, were ever to be able to take form, to emerge as the creation of a new perspect, an unforeseen aspect that is frightening and shocking or fascinating and beautiful, we would have to venture to risk vulnerability, for the sake of musing and imagining, interpreting and illustrating concepts and realities whose scales are not univocal, whose reach may not be that of the gods, but which nonetheless are constructed as something new.[17] Like the explorer, we would have to ceaselessly visit new cities, but also, ceaselessly stray, distracted and diverted from the very rules that bring us there, impressionable and supple, tractable and pliant to every touch, taste, scent, sight and sound. And each and every telling of tales would have to be attentive to the manner in which every site endlessly makes and remakes itself and us.

Such precautions may not yet be enough to calm the authority of the discursive intellect, whose power to know through reasoning, discussion, internal debate, dialectic experimentation, deduction, language or proof constantly threatens to silence any more immediate apprehensions or intuitions.[18] Nor can we be complacent about self-referential, non-discursive concepts whose consistency, intensive ordinates and resonances with other concepts seems to guarantee an endless becoming in relation to all concepts situated on the same plane. For if we pay attention, we see that every system of thought has its limits, it is simply a matter of time.[19] If to seek rational explanations means to think and speak in terms of known discourses that can be generalized and universally applied according to the accepted rules of pure intelligibility, binary logic, the transcendental or transcendent thinking subject, dialectics, historicism or universal rational communication, to name only some, then the force at work in reason is much less thought than it is repetition. In our quest to evade such repetition, perhaps it is necessary to try everything new. But can we confidently situate ourselves in our travels by grasping the Idea of the world? Not simply the Idea as the unconditioned cause of continuity, but instead, the Idea as the universal for individuals, the continuum in which Ideas are differentiated, that refers to the annihilation of objects of intuition and concepts of the understanding in favor of the universal and its differentiable appearance? For even these new worlds, these new Ideas may likewise turn out to be structures operating in some of our wanderings, but not necessarily in all. In short, not confidence but fragility, not conviction but sensibility may be our guide.[20] Even non-discursive concepts are able to be enunciated; created, signed, performed by conceptual personae whose power and force is commensurate with the power and force of the concept they wield. Do you long for the power of a concept of self? Simply repeat after me, 'I think, therefore I am,' and all the doubting, thinking and being of the *cogito* are yours, your persona.[21] Given the multitude of forces at work, each ready to claim sovereignty, we might have to embark on a more hazardous outing, another spin through the world which puts philosophical intuition into play and which recalls us to our finitude in order to construct logics and languages influenced by the unperceived, unknown past that nonetheless inhabits us, like light rays diffracting into spectra.

The citizens of Perinthia conceal their hideous offspring. Having constructed a city, a world, a plane of consistency which maddeningly fails to manifest its anticipated outcomes, the citizens are incapable of altering their assumptions. They do not acknowledge the varieties of individuals, the random effects of their reasonings, so alien, so arbitrary as to lack consistency sufficient to form species. The explorer is so little surprised by this that he does not comment. Weathered, in his travels, by the profusion of landscapes and domiciles, creatures of the land and sea, vocal articulations and tones, physiologies and physiognomies, epidermal textures and tints, and odors, redolent or rank, the explorer intimates that on the other side of the astronomer's assumptions lies the realm of the insensible, the unthought, the zones of indetermination, the constructions and structures of relations that give rise to unfamiliar scenes through absolute points of view. And while it may the case that each sensory organ is simply a habit, a slow-down, assembled on the body in response to claims arising from the milieu, nonetheless, it may also be the case that each of these habits – not only every ear, but every eye, skin, tongue and nose – may in the end uniquely command a different story, but only insofar as all of them are themselves elements of a one-way arrangement, structured by contingencies, causal influences which are possible from their point of view. Of course, we readers and travelers have expectations. We may ask for the story of all stories, the One story that anticipates and accommodates all stories, those known and those yet unknown, in which case each story is discredited as it bleeds into the next, truer story. Or, we may revel in the story-teller who synthesizes one story into the next by a magical process of cancellation and redemption. Or, we may request a universal story, but one that would be spoken differently in every expression, always another language, location, time, always new characters, unanticipated circumstances altering in relation to one another, forming and deforming at infinite speeds to accommodate a seeming infinity of points.

But is there a philosophical intuition which allows the traveler to exist in a universe where each story begins with some unique yet interconnected duration, a perspective constantly altered by the intimations of light, outside of which no transmittal of information is possible, but whose very limitations provoke a dazzling, radiant and resplendent sensibility? In this proximity, it is certainly the case that discontinuity guides behavior; infinite speeds are unreachable and smooth space-time breaks apart. In return, spatio-temporalization reappears, photons traveling from near and far make of every state a view of the universe, a chance to gaze but briefly from a past into a present constantly altering with every new influence. In this glance, the future cannot be predicted, and intensive processes as much as intensive relations take on the appearance of icebergs, frozen in space-time. In this glance, we are invited to peer into the past, a past that has never been present, as the discrete interactions between past states may influence a present 'now' or later or not at all in relation to whatever other states they influence or are influenced by along the way.[22] Is it possible to become, in this duration, like the traveler who arrives so late at night that she forgets not only where she is but who she is and how she arrived there, who falls asleep in one world and wakes up on a newly forming earth, a discrete space and time, a view of the universe never previously intuited, never anticipated in perception, never analogous to any experience, and never before postulated by thought, but which initiates a life, a milieu, a point of view?[23] Is it possible to open one's ears, eyes, skin, tongue and nose to a series of innermost, insensible conditions that are neither expectations nor commands but are indistinguishable from the dreams, pathological processes, esoteric experiences, drunkenness and excess of the night before?[24] The Idea of Perinthia, expected and commanded, friend to the Ideas of truth, harmony, reason, nature and justice, and to the Idea of philosophy, forecloses such a principle of adventure, advising against it, fearing its pathology, its deviance from known laws and postulated principles. This makes the bizarre effects of the astronomers' calculations all the more bewildering. The astronomers pose a problem, they set the faculties in motion; out of what they trust to be the determinacy of existing conditions, they project a set of determinate expressions for Perinthia believing that they have posed a true problem. Likewise, if we philosophers pose a problem, if we set the faculties in motion, and if this problem is an Idea in which difference is thought in place of contradiction in order to overcome the concept-intuition duality, then perhaps we too have posed a true problem. If posing this problem allows us to pass the other side of the mirror, if something has been *created*, something whose source is outside of reason and also, outside the empirical field, do we nonetheless assume that this is the mirror of all mirrors, the only beyond, the only thought?[25]

In the midst of all these efforts, what light brings to us might be a completely different kind of problem. It is a problem that might arise if there exists a sensibility whose processes are so finely scaled that they cannot be said to constitute faculties; a sensitivity for which concepts that force even unfinished faculties to their limits may be tantamount to habituation or worse, to capture, to inescapable tedium. Be careful! Even the free play of faculties may result in an axiomatic whose abridgment of all order and organization defies fixed modes of being but whose absolute reduction of all semiotic systems to zero manifests itself overwhelmingly in the sublime Idea, the defeat and destruction of the very vulnerabilities that gave it birth. We have been looking for an Idea of difference according to which difference *gives* the world, distributes the world as diverse rather than as reflection, resemblance, representation, habituation, identity or as equal, but also an Idea of difference whose transcendent function, whose power to force thought to problematize does not in the end obscure the myriad durations and minute sensibilities that first gave rise to it, obliterating their infinitesimal influences, victim to the power of the superior force of the differential continuum. 'Difference,' 'diverse': if these are not just words, they must be shown to be concepts resonating in the world, inhabiting systems and milieus, space and time, actualizing what is obscure, including those states incapable of being expressed in a differentiating continuum.

The concern here is with the origin and efficacity of concepts. The concern is with the neglect of tiny, discrete relations in favor of smooth continuities; but also, and in a preliminary manner, the concern here is with the repudiation of the conceptual and effective slow-down and of sensible vulnerabilities in favor of infinite speeds, the motion of faculties and the Idea which drives them in the production of concepts. We might attend then, not only to the extent to which concepts are efficacious but, more crucially, to the manner in which they intervene in the world. On the one hand, we have come to accept that if what is given, created or evolved is *diverse*, producing what is expected or commanded would appear to be increasingly uncertain. But beyond this, we might also consider the effects of any newly proposed structure which claims universality.

> In the progressive determination of the conditions, we must, in effect, discover the adjunctions which complete the initial field of the problem as such – in other words, the varieties of the multiplicity in *all* its dimensions,

the fragments of the ideal future or past events which, by the same token render the problem solvable; and we must establish the modality in which these enclose or are connected with the initial field [and] . . . we must condense *all* the singularities, precipitate *all* the circumstances, points of fusion, congelation or condensation in a *sublime* occasion, *Kairos*, making of the solution some abrupt, brutal and revolutionary explosion.[26]

Given this prescription, perhaps we could ask in what manner this differs from what we have always, already done in the past?

It has become commonplace for us to argue that if what is given, created or evolved is *diverse*, then the attempt to guarantee resemblance or reflection is doomed, and the drive to construct identities and equalities may just as likely end in a world or a city of terrifyingly deformed inhabitants who can never measure up to the Idea. Moreover, if what is given, created or evolved is *diverse*, the methodology of expectation and command – which is to say, the rational process of producing the diverse as identical and equalizing the otherwise unequal – stands opposed to the apparently irrational and reviles it even though it is nothing more than the resistance of the diverse to the identifying and equalizing processes of nature and reason.[27] Thus the unequal necessarily appears monstrous and the unorganized, a nightmare. By means of commands and the emerging resistance to those commands, we arrive at an entirely false problem according to which the diverse appears to be utterly irrational and unintelligible while that which looks identical or equal is commonly accepted as the very definition of the rational and the intelligible. Not only do expectation and command, identity and equality confirm and so define the rational, they are given near universal respect as commensurate with what is harmonious, just, good and true. This would be the case no matter what the concept is. We have seen again and again how the drive to identify, to equalize, distorts even the most nomadic concepts. Yet, there are always new demands, demands that might be more terrifying than the old demands. There might be new demands that the limited relations between states and their alterations, which together construct an ever-changing point of view, be foregone so that all may enter into the indeterminate Idea, celebrate its n-dimensions consisting of variables or coordinates, maximize its continuities, the sets of relations between changes in variables, and become defined as elements, effects of sets of relations, which do not change until the Idea itself alters its order and metric, until a new Idea, a new problem is posed.[28] It remains to be seen if this force, so new, so unanticipated, is as powerful as the previous ones.

Vulnerable sensibilities

There are many questions to be sorted through here. Let us attempt to work our way through some problems, beginning with the problem provisionally described as that of constructing anything; the problem which mathematicians might take to be a version of 'projection.' I am suggesting that although the conception of the problematic Idea that undergoes continuous differen*ti*ation/differen*ci*ation is a conception that undermines the recognition, representation, habituation, equalization nexus of classical, modern thought, replacing it with the Idea of difference and the diverse, it may nonetheless do damage to conceptions of receptivity and interactive networks, particularly where these operate on a micro-scale and particularly where they address questions of spatio-temporalization. In responding to this new interest, that of vulnerable sensibilities, the first question might be something like, what do we mean by extreme vulnerability? There are *many* ways to address this question, but since we have cast this problem in the realm of the coarse and habituated senses, the ears, eyes, skin, tongue and nose, let us begin with sensibility. What, after all, are the ears, the eyes, the skin, the tongue, the nose? They are, apparently, habits which form on the body to enable various creatures (including humans) to function within their milieus. The senses are habits arising with the evolving needs and interests of unique creatures. Monera, spiders, fish, cats, primates, humans, each have evolved certain sensible habits that allow them to interact with and to survive in their environments and, without being subject to too much ridicule, perhaps the same can be said of all plants, of all strata, both organic and non-organic in the traditional sense. For creatures with sensibility, such habits are formed not only in the syntheses driven by what the senses perceive, for what interests the senses, what creatures attend to is already ordered to a great extent by previous syntheses, by previous relations in apparently unlimited differenciable processes. This is synthesis in the realm of physiological, chemical, biological or social processes, the multiple motions of every individual, since every component of every milieu is in motion and appears to influence other components through its motions.

Nevertheless, it has been argued that survival of the organism depends on a collection of biological processes that maintain the integrity of cells and tissues throughout its structure.[29] For example, biological processes such as respiration and feeding require oxygen and nutrients that rely on neural circuits to control reflexes, drives and instincts, thus ensuring that respiration and feeding take place. Other neural circuits for drives and instincts are connected to fight or flight behaviors to avoid destruction by predators or adverse environmental conditions. Still other circuits are related to drives and instincts that help ensure procreation and care of offspring. Generally, drives and instincts are thought to operate either by directly generating a particular behavior or by inducing psychological states that produce behavior, mindless or otherwise. Virtually all such drive- and instinct-produced behaviors contribute to survival. This includes emotions and feelings which are powerful manifestations of drives and instincts, but only, it appears, insofar as drives and instincts are no less habits than ears and eyes, organized in relation to other elements of the milieu, even though emotions and feelings, unlike senses, are more likely to be the habits of individuals or groups of individuals in milieus rather than simply of groups evolving over long periods of time. Indications that such biological functioning is habitual lie in the notion that a significant change in the disposition controlling basic biological functions would be detrimental to the organism. Many dispositions operate at a covert level and are never directly knowable by the individual. Nonetheless, there are more overt behaviors which imply the existence of these others. Again, when some of these are called *instincts,* this may indicate not an innate drive but simply the *tendency* to organize in relatively invariable patterns whatever is at hand.[30] Instinctual regulation of functions such as nutrition or flight tend toward sustaining the body. It has been roughly described as government for the body and by the body, sensed and managed by the body's highly organized but differenciated processes. In humans, the systems regulating these processes can be triggered viscerally (from inside) by, for example, low blood sugar, from the milieu (outside) by any surprise, or from the so-called 'mental' inside through the realization of some impending state. Although many neurophysiologists claim that neural circuits operating these cycles constitute a *pre-organized mechanism,* in other words, a foundation which can then be tuned to the surroundings while the surroundings serve as a superstructure, it may well be the case that given the appropriate scale, everything is superstructure. The so-called foundation becomes a foundation when ordered by evolved relations, which in turn are forms or structures of behavior that organize themselves originally in individuals and groups involved in milieus.[31]

No matter how many connections and constantly changing relations are involved, if the regular connections of habituation were our only mode of organization, all living things could be assembled in relatively invariant species and each species would be constructed along with senses and habitat in a manner that would be unfailingly uniform. The slightest alteration of conditions – if such an alteration were even possible – might well destroy everything.[32] But *difference* differentiates as an absolutely necessary solution to posing the problem in this manner, simultaneously producing altered milieus and altered individuals. The forms of expression and forms of substance of these types of structures depend on the ultimate determination of the differential elements of the milieu and on the type of relations between them which, as a whole, constitute a system of virtual relations that then are actualized, incarnated in organisms, according to determinations of species but also according to the differentiation of parts.[33] In this system of planes, self-constructing perspectives, like the irrational and the unequal in the system of identity, could never show themselves. How is it possible to claim that any sensibility can be a changeling, an intrinsically modifying point of view since it seems that ears, eyes, skin, tongue and nose are inescapably the limits of sensibility, that we do not sense sensibility yet sensibility performs sensation, so it is said to awaken memory and force thought? Drugs, alcohol, vertigo, the tools of sublimation convince us of this, carrying us to the *limit* of sensibility, beyond which the being of the sensible collapses, a snarling confusion, so capricious that psychosis arises at the boundaries, looming, imminent.

Nonetheless, if it is possible to slow down without being caught by the force of connectivity, to linger for a moment with the prospect of some non-continuous states that gradually permeate more and more of one's sensibility, that are not a structure of behavior, but also not a continuous multiplicity, if this is possible, then let us begin by thinking a simple form of discontinuity, limited by its existence in smooth space, but nevertheless, preliminary to more adventurous concepts to come. Try to contemplate the situation of susceptible sensible trajectories, oriented by attractors, and moving – always in motion – given the necessities of such spaces. Search for some organization that is not quite a faculty, not the energy that unfolds unequally in quantity, in the open place in which actualized beings are composed. Search for something that is not the actualization of an Idea in the qualities that can never be sensed or perceived (except possibly under the influence of hallucinatory drugs) insofar as they are not things but differentials, differentials covered by qualities that contradict the differential process and are given as something to be sensed, as temporal in a limited manner. Search also for something that is not the unfolding of actualizations of the Idea which nonetheless demand distance from one another so as not to be run together; and finally, something that is not the implicated energy of continuous processes, energy unfolding in the actualization of actual beings.[34] What if, in the midst of some milieu, some process of continuous differentiation-differenciation, characterized by rapidly changing events and personages, a sense of expectation – what if there is a glimpse, a shudder, a leap, something else? What if there emerges some evanescent darkness, some momentary shift invested with the misery of an onslaught of distressing reverberations? Responding to this in confusion, perhaps you construct an Idea, a structure, a multiplicity, a system of multiple, non-localizable ideal connections which is then incarnated. It is incarnated in real (not ideal) relations and actual (physical) terms, each of which exist only in relation to one another, reciprocally determining one another. What is essential is the movement from ideal or virtual structure to actual incarnation, from the conditions of a problem to the terms of its solution, from differential elements and ideal connections to actual terms and diverse real relations constituting, at each moment, the actuality of time, the time of processes, of differentiation, of connections.[35] So you slip into the construction of an Idea whose intensities produce appearances redolent of harsh wind, dark days, gloomy landscapes.

What solution does this Idea offer? It might allow you to encounter a physical Idea as the distribution of shuddering disturbances and to go on with your life. After all, you *are* a busy person with a lot of responsibilities and important work to accomplish; people are listening to you, counting on you. In the mean time, you reach for an umbrella, whether you need it or not. Or, you might slip into the construction of a different kind of problem, a biological Idea, one whose ideal elements are oriented by the varieties of sublimations generated by the affinities of their anti-depressive *pharmakon*, in which case, you reach for zoloft or make an appointment with your therapist. Or, you might slip into a social Idea, wherein the ideal connections between production and property as established by labor or the owners of the means of production incarnated in diverse societies condition its actualization in your society, with the result that certain sectors enjoy guilt-free lives of leisure, while others dementedly drive themselves to labor, dedicate themselves to every imperative of production, every rule of law, and embody this as the highest virtue. Each of these trajectories is a possible solution to a possible problem whose form of expression and form of content intertwine, determining one another in the system-series of signs that emerges in space and time.[36]

30

But what about a girl, raised by her mother's parents, denied access by her mother, left waiting, left alone or left behind by her again and again? This girl does not learn French, though her mother is fluent. Nagged by the mother to lose weight, she defines thin for herself, becoming anorexic. Yet she remains riveted, fascinated, inexplicably drawn to the woman who keeps her out. When she is twenty, no longer a girl, her father, forced by the grandparents to disappear nineteen years before, re-enters her life. Eyes filled with tears, he weeps his regrets. 'They didn't let me hold you . . . Not at all.' 'They had you on a schedule. It was sacrosanct, it was absolute . . . If you cried no one was allowed to pick you up . . . They didn't even let me say good-bye.' At the airport, again, 'I love you. I lost you, but now I have you back, and I'll never let you go again.'[37] She is captivated, fascinated by what she naively describes as her likeness to him, his likeness to her; their symmetry. He vilifies her grandparents, her mother. 'I defend them, but they have hurt me too,' she concurs. Now, she only wishes to have conversations with her father as one despot steps in for another. Seeking her own definition, she nonetheless hovers, uncertain, between one trajectory and the other, she does not plunge into the orbit of the mother who attracts her but only so as to hold her at a distance, keeping the daughter circling eternally around her. Maintaining her distance from the mother she hedges her bets – she wins and she loses. Improbable events occur. The space around her curves and twists, huge discontinuities emerge and, having nowhere else to go, she falls through the cusp, from one reality to another, it is 'a kind transforming sting, like that of a scorpion: a narcotic that spreads from . . . mouth to brain,' it is a catastrophe, a catastrophe that saves her but also condemns her as it hurls her onto a completely new plane.[38] This perilous interruption, discontinuous and isolated in space and time, overtakes her, paralyzes her and stands like a 'vast, glittering wall' between her and everything else, 'a surface offering no purchase, nor any sign by which to understand it,' a screen through which she can see her past but which separates her from its continuity, its multiplicities, completely, seemingly endlessly.[39]

Had this happened to you, you might try to problematize, to slip into an Idea in order to resume your busy life and evade this precipice before falling across it, but even so, the existing tendencies of the field will always act on you. Or, having failed this, you may, like the woman, simply stop there in a cold torpor, a sensation like being hit by a car, your knees drawn up to your chest, protectively, your voice internal, and you, unable to vocalize, everything taking more energy than you can possibly imagine; a life of idle enervation seizing you.[40] Now, you wait; you move as little as possible, no matter how terrible the process in which you find yourself. In this new world, even after a perfectly discontinuous break with the old world, if you have not been destroyed in the suspension between two manifolds, you barely move; you proceed but only with exacting slowness, sensing displacement, sensing that you could plunge into another powerful trajectory that pulls you toward it with increasing ferocity, or perhaps you will simply slow down and die. Situated here on this *separatrix*, this site between attractors, the in-between, extreme sensitivity to initial conditions makes your flow irrevocable, irreversible, and what took place in that discontinuous and isolated moment *is* you and nothing but you; it feels as if there will never be release for you.[41] The capacity to love and hate, to gather together the ordinary or singular points as well as the capacity to explode uncertainly but probalistically into the actual all but evaporate. Here, nothing happens. Not the infinite probability of the sublime, but nothing; no discordant harmony, no faculties, no stupidity, insofar as there is no refusal, only a great deal of silence, waiting . . . for something. The young woman's father attempts to speed up and dislodge her infinitely slow course. She is stretched but not torn. Viewed somewhat differently, her slowdown appears as so-many wild flights, here and there away from the line of attraction, crazy attempts at escape that return her to the same point and the effect of which is the same as no movement at all.[42] Attempting to return her to the old trajectory, to return her step by interrelated step to her place prior to the fall, the leap, the gamble, the mother takes her to her own psychiatrist. 'I sense my mother's doom there in the dead brown color of the walls, in the way her doctor's hand perspires, even in his skinny, dotted Swiss necktie. She will never escape *her* mother,' which is to say, the leap or fall onto another manifold is the only way to escape this attractor, this deadly orbit.[43] 'I'm just going through a stage,' the young woman tells them. 'She's right.' 'I am in love with him, but it . . . I'm not . . . I wouldn't do that,' and they believe her.[44] The father offers to support her while she writes. Now, on this new manifold, following this new trajectory, she believes that apart from him she has no life, that is, no will. Once again, nothing but capture. Stricken with pneumonia, she prays for death. 'Everyday is a drowning. Except for brief spasms of weeping that leave my face as wet as if I actually have, for a moment, broken the surface of some frigid dark lake, I feel nothing.'[45]

Even in this nothingness, this glacial existence, light travels, photons move, information spreads from state to state. Something is happening, shaping itself, influencing and shaping whatever its light rays reach. It is not the differenciation of an Idea, not the actualization of a physical or biological or social Idea, but something. The young woman secures admittance to the hospital morgue. She expects to be frightened by the corpse of her grandfather. 'I touched his eyebrows and his cheek, the white stubble of his beard . . . I sat beside my grandfather's cold body, touched and smelled and embraced it . . . The hour I spend with my grandfather, kneeling by the long drawer, changes my life. The kiss I place on his unyielding cheek begins to wake me, just as my father's in the airport, put me to sleep.'[46] Facing real death, the ultimate slow-down, something subtly alters. It is a kind of *sublimation*, a critical point like the jump from solid to gas, from ice to steam. Having spent years absorbed in cultivating and caring for her hair, extremely long blonde hair, the woman unexpectedly cuts it and tosses away the two-foot-long ponytail. The mother dies, the father exiles himself from her field. Unpredictably, all her parameters are altered. Her passivity, her diffusion, her slow-down, have kept her from being absorbed by processes forming in any direction, until the field alters. Had this been you, had this been your discontinuous break, your passivity, your slow-down, your kiss, your ascent from solid to vapor, invariably, albeit imperceptibly, these moments might have arisen in the context of another structure, once defined by discrete spaces, discrete times, influences shifting in relation to one another, contributing to your heterogeneous duration.[47] This might be your awakening into a perspective, the emergence of a spatio-temporalization, the genesis of a context, the ontological past reaching you, yielding for you, at any given moment, a remarkable view of the past of the world, a point of view shared by no one and nothing, yet overlapping with that of others insofar as their pasts and yours have intertwined wherever you and others have been exposed to the same influences, wherever you have influenced one another.[48] If, in this trajectory, you did not instantaneously perceive, conceive and act on what interests you, your conventional responses, your responsibilities or your important work – or, on a less coarse level but what would have been the same thing, if you, meaning what is provisionally 'you,' were not simply enveloped by the myriad forces competing to compose you, the singular points and differential connections forming and reforming on the continuum – you may have entertained an interval in which to contemplate and to pose a question from out of your own duration. Not transcendent contemplation, but

contemplation from inside, a discrete life, the duration of an ontological consciousness without a soul. Is it possible that neither the
perception-conception-action nexus nor the conception of continuous
relational processes smoothly assembling and reassembling in space are
the whole story? As Marco Polo insinuates, it is all a matter of what
the ear hears.[49]

If you, philosophers, theorists, writers, inventors, whomever, if you
sustain this slow-down, if you abandon your romance with intensity
and multiplicity, your preoccupation with your individuation, your
subject status, your personality, your fascinating contacts and connections, with the infinite and n-dimensional ideal and actualizable
relations overtaking you continuously, you may exist elsewhere than
on these trajectories, in between their virtual existence. You may exist
in the slow-down as Idea or as event, without these multiplicities actualizing you, actualizing others, actualizing the world. Eventually,
yes, something will have to happen. Something, some motions, some
perceptible flow or immanent becoming, some increase or decrease in
power, immediately influences the plane of immanence that constitutes
your processes, affecting this emptiness, this consciousness without a
subject, this life without an object.[50] In this sense, on your plane of
immanence, there is no opposition between the beings you are and the
beings that inform you. The virtual multiplicity, the Idea and its actualization as actual beings unendingly connected, implicated in and
implicating other beings; ceaselessly affecting one another, operates as
a universal, yet nevertheless fails to consider your vulnerable sensibilities, your perspective, your zone of indetermination. It has been
remarked that,

> We are used to the idea that a physical theory can describe an infinitude
> of different worlds. This is because there is a lot of freedom in their appli-
> cation. Newton's physics gives us the laws by which particles move and
> interact with one another, but it does not otherwise specify the configura-
> tions of the particles. Given any arrangement of the particles that make up
> the universe, and any choices for their initial motions, Newton's laws can
> be used to predict the future . . . Newton's theory describes an infinite
> number of different worlds, each connected with a different solution to
> the theory, which is arrived at by starting with the particles in different
> positions. However, each solution to Newton's theory describes a single
> universe.[51]

Every trajectory is defined by these same laws, laws that specify the
movement and interaction of particles. For dynamical systems, the
rules of motion are given, what may be contingent are the particular

particles themselves, that is, which particles enter into any given trajectory and in what order? Which affects? Which percepts? Which
concepts? Which prospects and functives (the objects of logic and
mathematics respectively)? In an open system, as opposed to Newton's
closed universe, this cannot be predicted, thus every configuration of
particles produces not only a different world, but an unpredictable
world. But what do not alter are the rules themselves that specify the
movement and interaction of particles. Moreover, in these worlds,
space and time are given not emergent. They are the pre-existent manifold, and time in particular, is simply a parameter of space, of any
space whatever, a fourth dimension, a means for differentiating different spaces, but not a temporalization. Where the space-time manifold is always, already given, duration disappears.

But what if it were possible to theorize a world in which different
observers 'see' partly different, partial views of the universe, partial
views which nonetheless overlap? Would this imply a dependence on
the location of the observer, on the observer's unique sensible duration, not the flow that constitutes her, but the information that constructs her perspective – her *spatio-temporalization*? Recall the image
of a cone, so intimately identified with Henri Bergson's concept of
ontological memory, that memory created by the imperceptible influences of states in the world on a vulnerable sensibility. Under the sign
of this cone, the entire past coexists with each new present in relation
to which it is now past.

> Memory, laden with the whole of the past, responds to the appeal of the
> present state by two simultaneous movements, one of translation, by
> which it moves in its entirety to meet experience, thus contracting more
> or less, though without dividing, with a view to action; and the other of
> rotation upon itself by which it turns toward the situation of the
> moment.[52]

All of this occurs, as if these memories were repeated a vast but not
infinite number of times in the many possible contractions of any past
life, but always altering, altering in each so-called repetition under the
influence of intersecting networks of states. These *different planes* are
myriad in number but not infinite. They stand in relations of simplicity and contiguity, influencing one another and influencing the present
for the sake of action or restraint. For any present, for any perspective emerging from this past, there is the influence of the many layers
of the past and of many interactions, networks of interacting states.
How like this is to what is called *the past light cone of an event*.

The causal past of an event consists of all the events that could have influenced it. The influence must travel from some state in the past at the speed of light or less. So the light rays arriving at an event form the outer boundary of the past of an event and make up what we call the *past light cone of an event*.[53]

But what if, rather than a single cone, a single event, we think about a causal network of interconnected states for which every perspective and every state consists of a multiplicity (not an infinity) of cones linked to one another, influencing one another, 'combinatorial structures' that have been called 'spin networks,' networks giving rise to self-organized, critical behavior?[54] Under these conditions, the causal structure of states evolves and the motion of matter is a consequence of evolution.[55] This brings forth the following conjecture. What if, we conjecture, what if smooth or continuous space-time are useful illusions, and what if, from the perspective of a different system, the world can be said to be composed of discrete states, states on a very small scale, but nevertheless, states discrete with respect to both space and time on that very small scale?[56] Under such conditions, what would be observed, what would be discerned?

If, in the midst of a certain trajectory, one characterized by gloom and darkness, you enter a slow-down, evading speed, eluding intensity, if you are pushed or fall into the conflicted space-time of a catastrophic discontinuity or, if the parameters of your global field simply shift, if you dissolve under the influence of a change of scale, then something unexpected, some unforeseen influences may permeate your boundary. Perhaps, you begin to feel the earth to be no longer callous and unsympathetic, no longer full of conflict and indifference, and a sort of gracefulness and ease envelops the world. If you feel buoyant, delicate, and all your gestures, imaginings and thoughts proceed from this grace, then, perhaps what is taking place is an emergent, critical organization, a spatio-temporalization. As states seemingly far into the past of the world approach, pure light radiating across the spectrum, transmitting and influencing 'you,' by which I mean, your sensibilities, sensibilities that precede yet give way to not only what sees and is seen but hearing and things heard, touching and things touched, taste and things tasted, smell and odors, and beyond this, influencing all the imperceptible particles, particles influencing particles, bodies working on bodies.[57] By their motions, these illuminations have 'altered the shade of a thousand perceptions and memories, pervading them.'[58] Imperceptibly, perhaps improbably, your 'I' itself becomes incandescent, your fissured identity radiates its own luminescence, you are not forced immediately or mediately into the multiplicities of some lonely trajectory gathering itself together out of fragments of ideal differentiated connections immanent to their explosion, but you too become light, subtly altering, reflecting, refracting, dispersing, influencing. You have traveled to a new world. Beauty, the unpredictable, might be once again thinkable.

The continuum of differentiation-differenciation is the field of pure immanence, as a system, its primary processes are not the same as those being proposed here.[59] These processes involve the construction of a vulnerable duration, a sensitive contingency, an ontological spatio-temporalization, an ever-changing perspective in the heterogeneity of space and time. Such a perspective, if it is thinkable, if it is real, could manifest itself as a sort of history, not a linear, causal chain, but a complex causality, layers and layers of states, always susceptible to realignment, to patterns and particles resolving their scintillation and constructing an ontological memory below the speed of light. These primary processes, often imperceptible, ephemeral, evanescent, influence one another and in this, they influence the sensibility of human beings. This is not yet perception, for it does not yet imply typical perceptual prerequisites, thought-like mental processes such as description, inference, and problem-solving, no matter how unconscious or non-verbal.[60] Rather, given that this is something much more difficult to situate, it is much more likely to be overlooked. It is the manner in which states (including very tiny states) influence and alter one another and so influence and alter human sensibility, all sensibility. These influences are not the objects of perception nor of consciousness; they cannot be experienced as increases or decreases of power, as the raising or lowering of intensities. They are, in some sense, passive and primary. If they are noticed at all, it is usually only insofar as they are *felt*, felt as pleasure, felt as pain, as expansion and diffusion, as discomfort and distress. Their influence on sensibility comes via the sensory system, but as ontological not personal memory, it is manifest in the exceptional absorption and emission of each state-organism – purely contingent, subject to alteration, but circumscribing what is characteristic of each sensibility as an original spatio-temporalization. It is the way, all of a sudden, your eyes crack open when you smile; it is the unnecessary bow you often add to the ceremony when you are introduced; it is the way you cut your hair, in between for the moment, neither long nor short; it is an absolute, immediate, non-conscious consciousness, an ontological unconscious whose passive existence no longer refers to an individual or to a being but is unceasingly suggested in the reflection, refraction and dispersion of light in a spectrum.[61]

Discrete processes infiltrate even perceptions, percolating through them, saturating them with their coloring, their diffractions, prismatic and spectral, stunning in their range. This is not the same system as that of the catastrophe, which forms without connection in place of adjunct fields gathered together and singularities exploding, but the catastrophe, a discontinuous space-time, prepares our thought for this more ephemeral, shimmering construction. Persisting on the cusp, the edge between attractors, in the intimacy of a life, something like the creation of a new spatio-temporalization is already thinkable, for the spatial and temporal dimensions of a cusp are that of a change, be it separation or unification.[62] This is not the personal memory of a subject, not the memory of a resemblance, nor the memory of intensities, but the ontological memory of a new life that begins again, completely new, at each discrete place and moment. Ideas on continuous manifolds exist as multiplicities; they determine everything in multiple trajectories; they actualize worlds; they form a vast field of virtualities. Their actualization may be called creation, insofar as actual beings do not resemble virtual Ideas, but the rules governing their trajectories, their formation and deformation, do not change.[63] And yet, between the first kiss and the second lies the abyss – the realm in which nothing occurs – no movement, no intensities, no individuation. Nothing gathers together the adjunct fields, nothing connected to nothing – thus there will be no condensation, no sublime explosion of the ideal into the actual. Still, all around you, such activities, such actualizations, seem to continue unabated; unfolding the universal, each Idea connected with every other, busily varying themselves, forming new multiplicities and breaking them up, oriented by the dream of complete determination. Morning arrives; imperceptible neural circuits prepare habitual responses, so called automatic reactions or involuntary movements. Yet alerted by the beginnings of the intensive sensations, something may yet intervene. Your body, your ears, eyes, skin and nose, your neural circuits, your elements, all radiate the myriad imperceptible processes reaching you, contracting them in a perspective. You lie in bed, awake but not moving, as the past gathers itself through you. You may be asubjectively conscious of the emergence of something unanticipated, unspecified, yet inevitable. Not only is your response altered, your existence is now reforming. These incidents, altering, reflecting, refracting, absorbing, emitting, are not the expression of a concept but the construction of a spatio-temporality from out of the light which reaches you from the stars. This is not the world of good or evil, subject or object, problems or solutions but the world of non-intensive, heterogeneous movement-moments assembled from the relations between myriad luminous influences by a universe that views itself from within, and you are its eyes as well as its ears, nose, skin and mouth. When the resulting spatio-temporalization, the effect of myriad minute sensibilities is realized, brought into the present out of the past that never was a now, encountered in that present as pleasure or pain, expansion-diffusion or discomfort-distress, it becomes real. Out of this, is it possible to construct a life whose sensibilities are vulnerable and subtle, vast yet circumscribed, where pleasure and pain arise from radiance and obscurities crossing over and interfering with one another, rays of light, not a number but particles, energy, acceleration over unperceivable yet sensible distances?

What danger lies here?

What is the danger here? What is it that threatens our philosophical interests? Transcendence? Subjectivity? Or, is the danger that of not reaching a sufficiently universal universal? Does the claim that Being is univocal and that the chaos that the multiplicity of planes of immanence generates satisfy our craving for a multiple world, a changing world, a startling and beautiful world, a world of pleasure and pain, love and hate? Can we think the universal as this multiplicity, or do we fall back into illusion? If we stay with the ontological claims of the univocity of Being, does it yield no more than a monotonous repetition of a limited repertoire of concepts? Or, are we to imagine a more abstractly universal production yet, an ontology conceptualized in accordance with something like set theory, *the* foundational discipline of mathematics, in the sense that any mathematical proposition can be rewritten in the language of set theory?[64] If the danger is transcendence, we think it is at least a familiar one. The transcendent subject or object falling outside the plane of immanence, actualizing the plane of immanence, then attributing it wholly and entirely to itself seems to be among the worst philosophical errors we know.[65] 'I' feel this or that, we claim. 'I' am this or that. 'I' am aware of, thinking of, acting on some object, some thing, place, person, emotion, some thought which 'I' claim is 'mine.' This 'I,' as well as this object, thing, place, person, emotion or thought all have taken their cue from the Cartesian plane which attributes to every person an independent existence as a subject, an individually-wrapped ego or atom, such that 'I have to make an effort of thought to believe that I have before my eyes not just coats and hats, but other living beings, other people.'[66] The effect of assuming the transcendent position is to identify the sphere of immanence with the thinking subject, an identification reinforced by Kant for whom synthetic unity is the effect of a subject representing itself to itself. The transcendent effect continues to be fostered by the post-Husserlian phenomenological concept of intentional consciousness directed to objects outside the so-called subject including other selves and the human world.[67]

But for every pauper who reinjects transcendence into the plane of immanence, there seems to be a 'prince' who never admits transcendence into the movements of infinite thought moving at infinite speeds. Still, in light of other systems of thought, other spaces and times such as those of catastrophes or those rays of light giving birth to spatio-temporalization, one cannot help but reflect on Hume's view of pure immanence in relation to what he argues is the fantasy of substance and of the soul. Taking up Spinoza's concept of substance, Hume demurs.

> There is only one substance in the world . . . and that substance is perfectly simple and indivisible, and exists everywhere, without any local presence. Whatever we discover externally by sensation; whatever we feel internally by reflection; all these are nothing but modifications of that one, simple, and necessarily existent being, and are not possest of any separate or distinct existence. Every passion of the soul; every configuration of matter, however different and various, inhere in the same substance and preserve in themselves their characters of distinction, without communicating them to that subject, in which they inhere. The same *substratum*, if I may so speak, supports the most different modifications, without any difference in itself; and varies them without any variation. Neither time, nor place, nor all the diversity of nature are able to produce any composition or change in its perfect simplicity and identity.[68]

A 'hideous hypothesis,' Hume exclaims, no less hideous than the hypothesis of the immateriality of the soul. Certain objects and perceptions – a passion, a smell, a sound – exist yet are incompatible with place and incapable of any conjunction with matter or body, yet they are certainly co-temporary with other objects of perception. (The taste and smell of fruit is inseparable from its color and tangibility.) Given that these impressions are co-temporary and that taste and smell are influenced by color and tangibility, we *feign* a conjunction of place, something altogether unintelligible and contradictory. We suppose, for example, that taste exists within some body and that it fills every part. Why? Because we want unity and we will do anything to get it, including supposing a causal relation founded in temporal contiguity to be conjoined with space. Both those who conjoin thought with extension and those who conjoin thought with a simple indivisible substance are at fault in this; in particular, those who insist on the doctrine that the subject-soul is indivisible and immaterial. That is, what difference can there be between the claim of Spinoza that the sun, moon, stars, plants, animals, humans and all other productions of art or nature are nothing more than modifications (modes) of a single, simple, indivisible subject in which they adhere; what difference between this and the theologians' claim that the universe of objects of thought (again, the sun, moon, stars, plants, animals, humans and all productions of art and nature) are likewise modifications of one, simple, indivisible substance? For Hume, all our ideas are derived from impressions, thus any connection or disconnection between objects must be there in our impressions. If we accept this axiom, the question is, from where does the idea of substance arise? Certainly, whatever is clearly conceived may exist, but is substance as pure immanence clearly conceived? Whatever is different is able to be distinguished, able to be separated by imagination. And what is separable may be taken to be separately existing, in need of no support. Anything distinguishable may be called a substance, which is to say, it is not a substance but merely an impression. If impressions are all that are given to the mind, then there can be no idea of a substance as that in which something else inheres or is embedded.[69]

Are we now reduced to name calling? Is this simply a matter of taking up one position in opposition to another? Such efforts are futile. There may be no choice here but to attempt a philosophical intuition. As Michèle Le Doeuff points out, intuition, in classical language, designates a mode of immediate apprehension, a direct intellectual grasp as opposed to mediated knowledge achieved through reasoning, discussion, internal debate, dialectic, experimentation, deduction, language, proofs. Not only was intuition once thought to be a valid mode of knowledge, it was thought to cooperate with these other methods of inquiry and to be what sets the process of discovery in motion as well as what completes it.[70] It is Hegel, she argues, who replaces intuition with the labor of conceptual analysis, since intuition (which does not know itself) consists of beautiful thoughts not knowledge. And once intuition was separated from discursivity, it was doomed, since it cannot be taught as a precise method or system.[71]

Nonetheless, I am advocating that we attempt an intuitive grasp of the depth and breadth of the question before us, one which may help us to locate it in a field, a system, a set of relations, whatever the matter at hand calls for. The problem as it is currently stated is that whenever immanence is established, transcendence once again invades the pure field.

Following the follies of the rationalists, the idealists, and the phenomenologists, Jean-Paul Sartre has been said to finally restore the 'rights' of immanence of an impersonal transcendental field, a field in which immanence is immanent to nothing but itself. Human reality exists in immediate synthetic connection with what it lacks; the pure state giving rise to itself is apprehended by it as this lack. Emptiness and negation are never really known, for it is asserted that the second Cartesian proof (Meditation III) is perfectly rigorous so it is without question self-evident to claim that the being which is nothing surpasses itself toward the being which is the foundation of its being, not this time toward God, but rather, toward a perpetually evanescent relation, a relation of continuous engagement.[72] Thus a feeling, suffering, for example, must be kept distinct from norms of suffering, which is to say, the suffering of which we speak is not the suffering we feel. This latter feeling 'awaits our coming in order to be'; it has no density, no being and can only be expressed in the grimace of the sleeper, seizing him and flowing over him like a storm transporting him out of himself.[73] With this evanescent relation, with no density and no being to distribute, I have no argument. But the philosopher is not really satisfied with this; he wants both to *be* and to *conquer* what he feels. The suffering that touches him lightly with its wing, that cannot be *grasped* will never satisfy him; it is not a solidified feeling, realized by an actor who performs it like a drama. This is what the *man* wants. He does not want suffering to approach him, to diffract itself through the almost-nothing he is, yielding a stunning spectrum of sensibilities. He wants another kind of suffering, one that puts into play the totality of the immanent affective field as if it were a stage on which he will perform. In this way, he *hopes* to make it exist through others and for others. But this, as we will see, would be an illusion. Were it to be nothing more than a pure state, its lightness and contingency would allow for the almost nothing of any subject, but would destroy its value. For human life, the man argues, something more than the contingency of evanescent states may be central to existence.

The pure Idea in the pure field of immanence, once posited, unfolds; it unfolds into this or that possible world, thereby making of people and things the expressions of those possible worlds, the per-soning of concepts, the production of a field whose personae are not subjects but habits.[74] How fitting that such 'subjects' are defined not by their presence, but by their absence, insofar as they are funda-mentally absent, no more than expressions of an Idea, neither subjects nor objects. No wonder Others are, first of all, distractions. 'They constantly break into our activities and interrupt our train of thought . . . the mere possibility of their doing so illumines a world of concerns situated at the edge of our consciousness.'[75] So it would seem, neither a subject nor an object, the Other is another intensity, but of a particular sort. Yet, the Other is not all disruption. In the unfolding of an Idea, in the infinite field of virtualities and potential-ities which are capable of being actualized, I cannot feel or perceive or conceive of everything all at once. Objects I cannot see, forces I cannot feel, concepts I cannot conceive, nonetheless come together, form a world, insofar as they are felt, perceived or conceived, in prin-ciple, by the Others, who guard the margins from whence arrive other affects, percepts, concepts, prospects, and functives, in accordance with the laws of transition which regulate the passage from one concept to the next, one prospect to the next, one affect to the next. This is why 'my desire passes through Others and through Others it receives an object. I desire nothing that cannot be seen, thought or possessed by a *possible* Other. That is the basis of my desire. It is always Others who relate my desire to an object.'[76] The emphasis here must be on the word *possible*, insofar as the Others who are the basis of my desire are possible Others not real Others; they are expressions of the field of immanence, never exceeding the nothingness each of them must be. Others are known, not by any positive characteristics, not through the spectrum they are; they are known through their absence. I know of Others insofar as, when they are not present, I am confronted by the brute structure of the world. It is as if I have left the earth and ventured alone, back in time, to a star in a world whose distance exceeds the speed of light, there to find nothing but abstract forces, space and time symmetrical processes, n-dimensions, motion, expansion. But in our world, the *a priori* possibility of the Other is the stage upon which are actualized real characters or variable sub-jects as expressions of that field, expressions of its dynamics, and which do not and may not exist outside of that field.[77] With this in mind, we might inquire into whether or not a real character in a novel or a variable subject is, in our lives, commensurate with a 'you' or a 'me'? For, if when an Other appears in the midst of the possible world they express, if 'I' as the expression of a different possible world must be first be annihilated, then it is impossible that there would be any intimate relations between anyone. In this scenario, love involves no frequencies, no vibrations or oscillations of molecules of air or molecules of matter, nerves or cells. Love is an expression of a possible world; hate too has nothing visceral about it, it simply expresses another possible world. We would be mistaken if we were to imagine that the creation of love or hate is an emergent construction of 'one's own' sensibilities, for what is 'one's own' is, in this structure, nothing; intensity is all, the manifold of continuous space-time is reality.

Still, there is the specter of the hideous hypothesis. Perhaps, in order to come to any opinions about Hume's critique, we might look more closely at the workings of a plane of immanence, of unfolding events expressing possible worlds. We might also have to look at the luminous world where what I have called perspectives radiate. Let us consider a simple situation, one that involves only a few states, a small space. A woman searching for something that will teach her to hate finds her efforts stymied. She wanders both listless and desperate among creatures inhabiting the zoo. Pushing herself from site to site, or pushed by dynamic forces over which she has no control, she struggles in a vain attempt to free herself from the determinacy, the objectification of being-for-Others, the Idea which holds her in its grip, the intensities coming at her from all directions without touching her. Willing even to undergo annihilation of her own past, which would mean annihilation of her present, thus annihilation of herself, she would gladly transmit the Other, the inhabitant of his own perceptual field, into her plane of immanence in order to project the Other as object and nothing but object, in order to be capable of destroying it absolutely and finally.[78] Again and again, her efforts are cut short.

> But it was spring. Even the lion licked the smooth head of the lioness. Two golden animals. The woman looked away from the cage where only the warm scent reminded her of the carnage she had come in search of in the zoological gardens . . . 'But this is love, this love again,' the woman said in rebellion, trying to find her own hatred, but it was spring and the two lions were in love . . . The hippopotamus, the humid hippopotamus. Its round mass of flesh, its round mute flesh awaiting some other round, mute flesh. No. Then there was such a humble love in maintaining oneself only as flesh, there was such a sweet martyrdom in not knowing how to think.[79]

Influenced by the profusion of elements reaching her sensibilities in the manner of warm scents, humid flesh, sweet stupidity, the woman does not encounter the possible world of pure negation that she anticipates and she feels acutely disappointed.

She has been posed as a problem; she awaits an Idea that will unfold itself around her in a magnificent appearance, a world of hate in which her own hatred would be an expression of that world of hate, yet, in seeming contradiction, a world in which a particular Other could be annihilated by this hate. If this is a problem which she poses to the world or which is given to her to resolve, in principle, it will be impossible for this particular outcome ever to occur. Rather, she will be swept away, at infinite speeds, along a trajectory whose power and force forms her, gives her a place and determines that she will be a victim not a victor, cast off and despised as the object inside the perceptual field of the Other. In spite of the futility of any counter-desire for nihilation, she blindly aspires to what would appear to be impossible, the abandonment of her plane of immanence, her a-subjective immediate consciousness, her trajectory, the continuous series of multiple, probablistic events which make her the fractured and fissured being she is. She wants to hate, which is to say, she seeks the death of the Other. From the perspective of another system, not that of the plane of immanence, but that of rays of light, absorbed and emanating from state to state, the death of the Other who is in her past would not leave her unaffected. Seeking the annihilation of an Other who inhabits one's past would annihilate some part of one's own past. Sweeping them from memory, from one's ontological unconscious and one's vulnerable sensibilities is commensurate with seeking the death of Others, obliterating them through the annihilation of one's own unexpected but luminous relations to the past, to all that one has become. This concept of hatred, murdering the Other, might also be suicide insofar as the Other colors one's own present, influencing it in myriad and subtle ways which we cannot know in advance but which only emerge with the multiplicity of changing relations emerging with spatio-temporalization. But the woman cannot quite manage this concept of hatred; it does not burn her with its intensity; it does not actualize her with its attractive force, drawing her irresistibly in its direction. Between her and the rest of the world there are nothing but weak interactions, incoherence, a cacophony of frequencies, wavelengths, speeds.[80]

So she stumbles through the zoological gardens pausing, exhausted, in the vicinity of the a large enclosure where there stands a buffalo, a creature 'so black that from a distance his face had no features . . . his was a blackened shape of tranquil fury.'[81] Black body, white horns, motionless, still, rigid, small crimson eyes, calm, tranquil, without haste, the buffalo's components assemble themselves with numbing slowness as the creature barely moves. She too ceases to move. Up till this moment, the woman has drifted fugitively from cage to cage. A child runs past without even seeing her. Approaching the bars enclosing the huge animal, she is already shrunken and brittle; craving hatred, she is barely conscious, 'breathing without interest, no one interested in her, she herself interested in no one.'[82] Given these sentiments, it is not surprising that there is something feigned, something ingenuous in her craving that is manifest in her dizzy oscillation between love and hate. Given that her own senses are inapprehensible to herself, that she does not see herself seeing nor feel herself touching, she does not appear to be free to make herself into the expression of whatever Idea she can posit. Moreover, without interest in an Other, or an other's interest in her, she is not in space, she is not in time, she is invisible, she is alone. Why hate? Perhaps, like the founders of Perinthia, she had projected harmony, reason and benevolence as the necessary outcome of her calculations for love. And if such harmony or unity produces only monsters, they must be destroyed. Or perhaps she recognizes the possibility of the Other as an expression of a plane of immanence, yet finds in its realization only an absence, a nothing, slipping beyond her consciousness the moment it comes into view, defining her world yet immediately disappearing.

Yet simultaneously and paradoxically, her problem would seem to be that she can only make herself exist by assimilating the Other as an Other in their freedom.[83] Were she to deny the Other, her own being-for-Others would disappear too. Her problem is to figure out *how to acquire the Other's point of view on herself*, then to assimilate the Other as an Other-looking-at-her, to consume the Other's point of view, to make it her own. Might this imply that under some circumstances it is possible, if not necessary, to call for an augmented recognition of one's own being looked at? What are the implications of the assertion that, 'it seems that the structure Other precedes the Look; the latter, rather, marks the moment at which *someone* happens to fill the structure.'[84] Or, otherwise expressed, someone *happens* to fill the structure; no matter who, someone *exists* that structure as a projection, an actualization of the Idea. On a plane of immanence, the Look makes both oneself and the other exist; it actualizes the structure of the plane. We might ask, does becoming, actualized as the expression of an Idea on a plane of immanence, conceptualize the level of complexity involved in existence? Or, is it possible that with respect to existence, we might seek to find a way to think, to conceptualize the multiplicity of pre-perceptual influences, sensibilities and receptivities that eventually give way to seeing and being seen, feeling and being felt, touching and being touched, tasting and being tasted, hearing and being heard. The plane of immanence, with its intensities, trajectories, and attractors, remains anonymous, empty, gray. Location in space is the fundamental manner in which its desired infinity of elements are defined. Thus, for every plane inhabited by humans, the great temptation is to insert the Look, everywhere the Look. Without it, absence, near-nothingness.

In the proximity of her relation with the immobile creature, the woman slows. Symmetry broken, she contemplates her duration, the constantly changing past of her constantly changing present, and she finds only alien elements. They do not attract her; they are not affective intensities emerging from the far corners of her present. Yet, these states relate to one another and converge in her direction, in the direction of her sensibilities. There is some indeterminate white and some fragility spreading inside her, she knows not exactly from where. There is an extreme weakness, exclamations, cries of 'ah' 'ah' 'ah,' a sense of purity, veneration, of black blood, the world shriveling, something warm, something incomprehensible: drowsiness, numbness, feigning, innocence, ingenuousness, weariness. Color, sound, odors, tastes, touch: physiological counterparts of frequencies vibrating in the world, not just anywhere in the world, but in the woman's proximity. Mostly, such frequencies do not register perceptually; they are not objects, thus her vague awareness only of something incomprehensible, something difficult to pinpoint. When such imperceptible frequencies make themselves known, they do so by means of pleasure or pain, expansion or contraction. So now, unexpectedly in pain, the woman provokes and incites the unperturbed creature.

She picked up a pebble from the ground and threw it inside the enclosure. The immobility of the buffalo's torso, which seemed even blacker than before, remained impassive. 'Ah' she cried, shaking the bars . . . The buffalo remained with his back to her . . . Then the buffalo turned around. The buffalo turned around, stood rigid, and, from afar, looked at her. 'I love you, she said, out of hatred for the man whose great and unpunishable crime was not loving her, 'I hate you,' she said, imploring love from the buffalo. Provoked at last, the great buffalo, approached without haste . . . The woman staggered in amazement and slowly shook her head. The buffalo remained calm. The woman slowly shook her head, terrified by the hatred with which the buffalo, tranquil with hatred, watched her . . . Innocent, inquisitive, entering ever more into those eyes that fixed her without haste, ingenuous, wearily, sighing, without wishing nor being able to escape, she was caught in mutual assassination.[85]

Unexpectedly, neither one dominates and thereby annihilates the other, instead, mutual assassination, coupling.[86] Neither moves, neither seeks escape, yet the hatred each manifests for the other is shocking in its tranquility, stunning in its perturbability, since only a moment before the woman was shrunken and brittle, interested in no one and no one interested in her. This is not what she expected; it is not the annihilation of the Other so that she may exist in its place, but a hatred that is the confluence of a network of imperceptible relations and states, a past, largely unknown to her, in which she and the creature have been implicated. It is her zone of indetermination, the interval between the trajectories she never inhabited, between the nothingness she never was and the nothingness she never will be, intersecting in a nexus of heat and light.

You, human beings, are not after all dirt or spiders. You begin to distinguish a number of sensations arising at the periphery of your body and these sensations converge, awakening a pleasure or pain whose strength remains relative to how much or how little of your organism becomes involved. Every great pleasure and every extreme pain, every expansion and contraction, would be constituted out of pre-perceptual vibrations, oscillations coming from the world, influencing you, sometimes slowing down, sometimes speeding up, interacting with other frequencies, although most of the time, neither melting away incoherently nor freezing in complete synchrony. Even when such oscillations are coupled, there are inevitably differences in their natural frequencies.[87] Each vibration possessing its own speed and wavelength interacts with your molecules, your nerves, your cells; it leaves a layer of memory. The greater the proximity, the more your molecules are influenced, the more layers of memory are left by these perturbations. It is a memory 'laden with the whole of the past,' the past of a part of the world coupled with your vibrations, your rays of light; it is not the personal past, but the ontological past, the past of states in the world intersecting with one another, emerging in a spatio-temporalization that is you.[88] Finally, alert to this convergence of worldly influences coming to you from a past of which you are largely unaware, your ears may pick up otherwise unheard tones, your eyes may focus on distinct forms previously unseen, your skin softens or hardens, flushes or pales, your nose opens or closes to emerging scents, your taste is remarkably sweet or salty, sharpened and precise or dulled so everything tastes of chalk. Physically, the light on a dark, cloudy day and the light on a bright, sunny day can each be said to illuminate to a different degree of magnitude and produce different sensations.[89] Physically, the hate that emerges face to face with the huge creature, the buffalo, transforms the woman so that she cannot depart but topples to the ground, overwhelmed by the very past that gives her existence.

Always fascinated by our projects in the world, we ignore nuances; we often prefer the certainties of expectation and command: the ruse of recognition that hardens into identity or the habituation that equalizes the present into the future. But are we at a point in our existence in which in order to evade these rules, we can turn away completely from the ordinary astonishment of pleasure, the awakening jolt of pain? We are caught here between the Idea of difference, the cascading intensities that hold us in their grip and direct us here and there, and the discrete break, the broken symmetry, the ontological unconscious. For this there is no salvation. Perhaps we justify our preference for continuities by claiming that the masses need it because they lack the capacity to think their own duration. We evaluate various planes of immanence. We call them 'democracy,' or 'religion,' or 'truth,' or 'objectivity.' We show the masses how their Idea is one of a plurality of solutions insofar as it is one of a plurality of questions posed on a plane of immanence. Yet if diversity is a concept and is real, we might ask ourselves in what respect it is actualized. Is every actualization doomed by a failure of imagination or is this failure deliberate, part of the admonition against what has often been called 'one's own,' part of the turning against properly philosophical intuition? If it is the case that what is constant or universal in human nature is the non-human, not this or that interaction with an Other but simply the capacity to be moved by one force or another, by this or that intensity, then our so-called humanity is nothing more than the expression of a possible world, a world to which we are condemned, which we nonetheless celebrate as life. Were we to try to follow the endless associations in any direction, in any dimension(s); not casually and carelessly, but reflectively and philosophically, only to find that our zone of indetermination has evaporated, that we think what is given to us to think, that we see, hear, taste, touch, smell, what our plane gives us to see, hear, taste, touch, or smell. What is left is nothing of one's own. But what is really 'one's own'? Inclinations, privileged ideas and objects are no more one's own than the belief in the transcendental Ideas of Self, World or God.

For the woman in the zoological gardens the discovery of her own hate comes not from the recognition of hate, nor from a past experience repeating and reproducing itself, causing her to hate; nor perhaps does it arise as the expression of an Idea, a possible world from which she must be exiled in order to let hate live. Every affect, every perceived object and every concept that is thought participates in a structure. This structure is not derived from the visibility of the figure on a ground, even if this visible is the surface of an inexhaustible depth, the opening to visions other than our own.[90] Indeed, this structure may turn out to be something ascertainable by a vulnerable sensibility, but imperceptible on the usual scales, scales that are relatively coarse. Scales that are coarse but useful insofar as making sense of them does not put undue demands on either imagination or conceptualization, demands that are connected to forces and powers always ready to capture sensible beings, to enhance or diminish their perceptions, but never to leave them an interval, a zone of indetermination in which what is most one's own may emerge.

Notes

1. Italo Calvino, *Invisible Cities*, tr. William Weaver (New York: Harcourt Brace, 1974), pp. 144–5. I have always been fascinated by this story. The undecidability of the cause of the city's outcome turns out to be paramount.
2. Calvino, *Invisible Cities*, p. 135. Thus the listener, not the speaker, remains sovereign.
3. Svetlana Alpers, *The Art of Describing, Dutch Art in the Seventeenth Century* (Chicago: University of Chicago Press, 1984), pp. 49–51. Alpers notes that Renaissance artists distinguished between perspectives involving mathematical constructions (perspects) and what appears on the retina (aspects). I would like to adapt these terms to express the idea of a changing past evolving into a particular present.
4. I have provided an analysis of Aristotle's version of difference as critiqued by Gilles Deleuze in *Gilles Deleuze and the Ruin of Representation* (Berkeley: University of California Press, 1999), pp. 17–27.
5. Plato, *Republic*, 507 d–e. In this, Plato is prescient.
6. Gilles Deleuze, *Difference and Repetition*, tr. Paul Patton (New York: Columbia University Press, 1994), originally published in French as *Différence et Répétition* (Paris: Presses Universitaires de France, 1968). After their first citation, pages from all original French texts will be given in parentheses. See ch. 2, 'Difference in Itself,' and pp. 224–8 (289–93); Plato, *Republic*, 508 a–e.

7. Deleuze, *Difference and Repetition*, p. 140 (182–3).
8. P. W. Atkins, *The Second Law* (New York: Scientific American Books, 1984), p. 9. Overwhelmingly, philosophical world-views seem to be correlated with those of theoretical physics, especially cosmology.
9. Atkins, *The Second Law*, pp. 50–7. See especially p. 54, 'What is the final state of the universe? . . . This *apparent* end of change occurs when there is uniform distribution.' This model is perfectly adapted to modern bourgeois societies whose pretence of equal opportunity is the very ideal of a democratic institution. See Gilles Deleuze, *Difference and Repetition*, pp. 224–5 (289–91).
10. See, for example, Mike Davis, *City of Quartz, Excavating the Future of Los Angeles* (New York: Vintage Books, 1992). The ethnic and class divisions Davis reports are precisely the effect of the position that in a capitalist democracy, everyone has equal opportunity.
11. Deleuze, *Difference and Repetition*, p. 230 (296–7). 'Difference is explicated, but in systems in which it tends to be canceled; this means only that difference is essentially implicated, that its being is implication. For difference, to be explicated is to be canceled or to dispel the inequality which constitutes it' (p. 228 (293)). See pp. 224–39 (289–308) for good sense, common sense and their relation to difference as intensive quantity.
12. Deleuze, *Difference and Repetition*, pp. 232, 234, 237 (299, 301, 305).
13. Deleuze, *Difference and Repeititon*, p. 222 (286). Deleuze develops the concept of disparity, but I want to push beyond his critical framework.
14. I am playing on the name of physicist, Fotini Markopoulou-Kalamara. See Fotini Markopoulou, 'The internal description of a causal set: What the universe looks like from the inside,: gr-qc/9811053, *Communications in Mathematical Physics* 211 (2000) 559–83. I am indebted to Marek Grabowski for bringing this work to my attention and for explaining the mathematics. The ontological extension of this material is my own doing and I am fully responsible for any errors or misstatements.
15. Deleuze, *Difference and Repetition*, p. 226 (291–2). This is what Deleuze calls good sense.
16. Deleuze, *Difference and Repetition*, p. 141 (184–5). I have discussed the concept of force in the context of interpretation in *Gilles Deleuze and the Ruin of Representation*, pp. 94–9. Now, I am interested in the limits of force.
17. See Alpers, *The Art of Describing: Dutch Art in the Seventeenth Century*, pp. 49–51. Alpers' Renaissance between perspectives involving mathematical constructions (perspects) and what appears on the retina (aspects), are useful here insofar as I am transforming them into images of a new structure.
18. Michèle Le Doeuff, *The Sex of Knowing*, tr. Kathryn Hammer and Lorraine Code (New York and London: Routledge Press, 2003), p. 4, published originally as *Le Sexe du savoir* (Paris: Aubier, 1998).

19. Gilles Deleuze and Félix Guattari, *What is Philosophy?*, tr. Hugh Tomlinson and Graham Burchell (New York: Columbia University Press, 1994), pp. 18–23, originally published as *Qu'est-ce que la philosophie?* (Paris: Les Éditions de Minuit, 1991), pp. 23–9. The question, in reading Deleuze, for example, is precisely a question of limits. What are the limits of the continuous manifold of space-time?

20. The Idea as the unconditioned cause of continuity is Immanuel Kant's; see *The Critique of Pure Reason*, tr. Norman Kemp Smith (New York: St Martin's Press, 1965), A334, B391. The Idea as the universal for individuals is that of Deleuze, *Difference and Repetition*, pp. 182–3 (236–7). Deleuze's paradigm is the differential equation of a circle (the universal of the circumference or of the corresponding function), which does not refer to a particular or a general, but in which 'dx and dy are completely undifferenciated in the particular and in the general, but completely differentiated in and by the universal', pp. 171, 172 (222, 223).

21. 'The concept condenses at the point I, which passes through all the components and in which I' (doubting), I' (thinking), and I' (being) coincide. As intensive ordinates the components are arranged in zones of neighborhood or indiscernibility that produce passages from one to the other and constitute their inseparability', Deleuze and Guattari, *What is Philosophy?*, p. 25 (29).

22. This idea is suggested by Lee Smollin, *Three Roads to Quantum Gravity* (New York: Basic Books, 2000), pp. 54–65.

23. Kant, *The Critique of Pure Reason*, A161; B 200. These are the principles of pure understanding of which the first two provide formal but intuitive certainty while the latter two guarantee the necessity of concepts that connect experience *a priori* as well as the expression of the possibility, actuality or necessity of *things*, that is, the expression of the relation of the concept which they predicate to the faculty of knowledge.

24. Deleuze and Guattari, *What is Philosophy?*, p. 41 (44). This is one of Deleuze and Guattari's philosophical intuitions which seems to open other avenues of exploration.

25. The reference here is to Kant who claims in *The Critique of Pure Reason* that we can only see the transcendental ideas behind us in a mirror and that it would be folly to assume they are on the other side of the mirror, as well as to Deleuze who states that we have, in fact, passed through the mirror.

26. Deleuze, *Difference and Repetition*, p. 190 (246); emphases added, translation altered.

27. Deleuze, *Difference and Repetition*, p. 224 (288–9).

28. Deleuze, *Difference and Repetition*, pp. 182–3 (236–7).

29. Antonio Damasio, *Descartes' Error* (New York: Avon Books, 1994), pp. 114–17.

30. Henri Bergson, *Creative Evolution*, tr. Arthur Mitchell (Lanham, MD: University Press of America, 1983), p. 140, published in French in Henri Bergson, *Oeuvres* (Paris: Presses Universitaires de France, 1959), pp. 613–14.
31. For an account and critique of this concept of structures of behavior, see my essay, 'A Psychoanalysis of Nature?' in *Merleau-Ponty, From Nature to Ontology*, no. 2 of *Chiasmi International* (Paris and Memphis: Vrin, 2000), pp. 185–205.
32. I have discussed habits and habit formation particularly in relation to the idea of passive synthesis as well as in the context of the ideas of David Hume and Henri Bergson, in *Gilles Deleuze and the Ruin of Representation*, pp. 104–9 and 147–54.
33. Form of expression refers to the organization of functions in order to carry out an action, a methodology, or a manner of proceeding, whether it is writing, organizing governments, or dancing. Form of substance refers to the so-called raw materials and their qualities which are always organized in some manner and never just brute material. See, for example, Brian Massumi, *A User's Guide to Capitalism and Schizophrenia* (Cambridge: MIT Press, 1992), pp. 12–14 for an extended example.
34. Deleuze, *Difference and Repetition*, p. 232–9 (299–304). This is, I hope, an accurate description of Deleuze's conception of a continuum on a manifold.
35. Deleuze, *Difference and Repetition* p. 183 (237). It remains somewhat difficult to see how any 'one' constructs anything, rather, any 'one' seems mostly to respond to what constructs one.
36. Deleuze, *Difference and Repetition*, p. 184–7 (238–42). I have discussed system-series in *Gilles Deleuze and the Ruin of Representation*, pp. 186–7.
37. Kathryn Harrison, *The Kiss, A Memoir* (New York: Random House, 1997), pp. 62, 66. This memoir is, nonetheless, a novelistic account.
38. Kathryn Harrison, *The Kiss*, p. 70. I am assuming, for the sake of simplicity, that there are two input parameters, one the mother and the other the father. My understanding of 'catastophe theory' comes from John Casti, *Complexification: Explaining a Paradoxical World Through the Science of Surprise* (New York: HarperCollins, 1994), pp. 43–84. The simplest type of catastrophe is called a fold, it has one input. This is not the same as the Deleuzean idea of fold which is the unfolding trajectory on a manifold. Catastrophes are precisely the leap that breaks the trajectory and allows for a discontinuous transition to another manifold with other attractors. The most complex catastrophes have four inputs.
39. Harrison, *The Kiss*, p. 71.
40. Harrison, *The Kiss,* pp. 75, 101. The catastrophe in and of itself is neither negative nor positive; it is simply a discontinuous transition from one manifold to another.

41. Ian Stewart, *Does God Play Dice? The Mathematics of Chaos* (London: Basil Blackwell, 1989), pp. 100–1. Separatrices are flow lines that separate basins between two attractors instate space. Harrison, *The Kiss*, pp. 187–8.

42. In mathematics, such trajectories are called 'wild intersecting separatrices.' They can be envisioned as looping 'wildly' to the 'left' and 'right' of any trajectory, producing the *effect* of little or no forward movement, thus an *effective* slow-down. For my acquaintance with and understanding of these and of most of the mathematical concepts in this chapter, I am greatly indebted to Marek Grabowski.

43. Harrison, *The Kiss*, pp. 141–2; emphasis added.

44. Harrison, *The Kiss*, p. 142.

45. Harrison, *The Kiss*, p. 170. It seems that neither this nor her previous trajectory offered any kind of solace – they are directions whose affects, percepts and perhaps concepts, prospects and even functives produced a subject that is purely captured. Perhaps in this context, this is the very definition of *nothingness*.

46. Harrison, *The Kiss,* p. 190. The catastrophic break has, at least, preserved her for this moment.

47. 'Note that the microscopic events do not need to be the same (or a discretization of) the events in the effective continuum theory. Also, the speed of propagation of information in the microscopic theory does not have to be the effective one, the speed of light c.' See Fotini Markopolou, 'Planck-scale models of the universe', p. 3. available as: arXiv: gr-qc/0210086 v2 (7 November 2002).

48. 'The 'viewpoint' of an event p in the causal set, the history of the world to the knowledge of p, is the set of events in the causal set in the past of p. This is a subset of the whole causal set. Here we consider the causal pasts evolving over the causal set.' See Fotini Markopoulou, 'The internal description of a causal set: what the universe looks like from the inside', p. 11.

49. Gilles Deleuze, 'Immanence, a life', in *Pure Immanence, Essays on A Life*, tr. Anne Boyman (Cambridge: MIT Press, Zone Books, 2001), p. 25. Originally published in French as 'L'Immanence: Une Vie,' in *Philosophie* 47 (Paris: Les Éditions de Minuit, 1995). I am playing with the Deleuzian idea of immanence, but not embracing it. This does not imply that I am endorsing a view from outside, that is, a transcendental point of view, precisely the opposite. See, Lee Smolin, *Three Roads to Quantum Gravity* (New York: Basic Books, 2001), pp. 47, 53–7. See also Gilles Deleuze and Félix Guattari, *A Thousand Plateaus, Capitalism and Schizophrenia*, tr Brian Massumi (Minneapolis: University of Minnesota Press, 1987), pp. 482–92 for their account of the smooth and striated space. Originally published in French as *Mille Plateaux, Capitalisme et Schizophrénie*, (Paris: Les Éditions de Minuit, 1980), pp. 602–14.

50. Deleuze, 'Immanence, a life' pp. 25, 26, 27.
51. Smolin, *Three Roads to Quantum Gravity*, pp. 42–3. The conception of a continuous manifold does not challenge the basic tenets of classical theory.
52. Henri Bergson, *Matter and Memory*, tr. N. M. Paul and W. S. Palmer (New York: Zone Books, 1988), pp. 168–9; Bergson, *Oeuvres* (Paris: Presses Universitaires de France, 1963), pp. 307–8. I have attempted to render the operations of affectivity and ontological memory in all their complexity in *Gilles Deleuze and the Ruin of Representation*, pp. 109–15. This quote reflects a view of the relativity of time.
53. Lee Smolin, *Three Roads to Quantum Gravity*, p. 58. I would like to claim that this similarity is conceptual and not merely metaphorical, yet I am fully aware that such claims are subject to a variety of interpretations.
54. See figure 1.1

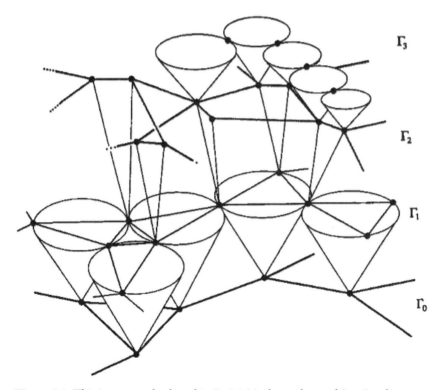

Figure 1.1 *This image can be found in Fotini Markopoulou and Lee Smolin, 'Causal evolution of spin networks', Nuclear Physics. B508 (1997) 409, preprint available as: gr-qc/9702025, p. 16.*

55. 'A causal set C is a discrete partially ordered set with structure that is intended to mirror that of Lorentzian spacetime . . . If we are "outside"

the causal set, what we see is a collection of such causal pasts, one for each event in C. It is the thesis of this paper, however, that being outside the causal set is *unphysical*. We instead care about the same situation as viewed from "inside" C by one of the above observers. We want to know in what way *the inside viewpoint* is different from the outside one and if it has some interesting structure.' See Fotini Markopoulou, 1998, 'The internal logic of causal sets: what the universe looks like from the inside,' *Communications in Mathematical Physics*, 211 (2000) 559–583 (gr-qc/9811053), pp. 4, 5; emphases added.

56. Smolin, *Three Roads to Quantum Gravity*, pp. 58–65. I owe much here to Smolin's simplified explanations of quantum gravity as well as to discussions with Marek Grabowski who guided me through the more complicated mathematical aspects of these concepts. Misinterpretations of these concepts are entirely of my own doing. I have tried to stretch these concepts without distorting them. This can be difficult since, in mathematics, context is everything and implications beyond very precise contexts can easily be disputed.

57. My source for the description of light and photons is James B. Kaler, *Stars* (New York: Scientific American Library, 1992), pp. 36–9.

58. Henri Bergson, *Time and Free Will, An Essay on the Immediate Data of Consciousness*, tr. F. L. Pogson (New York: MacMillan, 1959), pp. 8–12. Bergson, *Oeuvres*, pp. 11–12.

59. 'We propose the concept of differen*t/c*iation to indicate at once both the state of differential relations in the Idea or virtual multiplicity, and the state of the qualitative and extensive series in which these are actualized by being differenciated,' Deleuze, *Difference and Repetition*, p. 245 (315–16).

60. See, for example, Irvin Rock, 'the intelligence of perception', in *Perception* (New York: Scientific American Library, 1984), pp. 234–5. Rock differentiates between experience and perception (rightly so) and even proposes that perception may precede conscious reasoning in evolution, making thought a modification of perception.

61. Deleuze, 'Immanence, a life', p. 27. Again, I am extending the Deleuzean conception outside of the field in which it was instituted.

62. Casti, *Complexification*, p. 72.

63. Deleuze, *Difference and Repetition*, p. 212 (273–4).

64. See, for example, Alain Badiou, *Deleuze, The Clamor of Being*, tr. Louise Burchill, from *Theory Out of Bounds*, vol. 16 (Minneapolis: University of Minnesota Press, 1999), p. 14, for the argument that Deleuze's ontology produces concepts that are monotonously repetitious, and 'An introduction to Alain Badiou's philosophy,' in *Infinite Thought, Truth and the Return to Philosophy*, ed. and tr. Oliver Feltham and Justin Clemens (London: Continuum, 2003), pp. 13–15.

65. Deleuze, 'Immanence, a life', p. 31.

66. Michèle Le Doeuff, *Hypparchia's Choice, Hypparchia's Choice, An Essay Concerning Women and Philosophy*, tr. Trista Selous (Oxford: Blackwell, 1991), pp. 257–8. Originally published in French as *L'étude et le rouet* (Paris: Seuil, 1989). Le Doeuff appears to find this situation to be scandalous.

67. Deleuze and Guattari, *What is Philosophy?*, pp. 46–8 (47–9).

68. David Hume, *A Treatise of Human Nature* (Oxford: Oxford University Press, 1968), pp. 240–1.

69. Hume, *A Treatise of Human Nature*, pp. 232–51.

70. Michèle Le Doeuff, *The Sex of Knowing*, tr. Kathryn Hammer and Lorraine Code (New York and London: Routledge Press, 2003), p. 4, originally published as *Le Sexe du savoir* (Paris: Aubier, 1998). Le Doeuff focuses on how the intuitive came to be opposed to the discursive and attributed to women. See also Henri Bergson, *The Creative Mind*, tr. Mabelle L. Andison (New York: Philosophical Library, 1946), pp. 140–1. Bergson, *Oeuvres*, p. 1,356.

71. Le Doeuff, *The Sex of Knowing*, pp. 6–7; Le Doeuff cites G. W. F. Hegel, *Lectures on the History of Philosophy*, vol. 3, tr. E. S. Haldane (London: Routledge and Kegan Paul, 1955), p. 550.

72. Jean-Paul Sartre, *Being and Nothingness: An Essay in Phenomenological Ontology*, tr. Hazel Barnes (New York: Washington Square Press, 1971), pp. 139–40, originally published as *L'Être et Néant, Essai d'ontologie phénoménologique* (Paris: Gallimard, 1943), p. 133.

73. Sartre, *Being and Nothingness*, p. 142. I have retained the masculine pronoun since these descriptions are so uniquely those of Sartre (135).

74. Deleuze and Guattari, *What is Philosophy?*, pp. 47–8 (48–9).

75. Deleuze, *The Logic of Sense*, tr. Mark Lester with Charles Stivale, ed. Constantin V. Boundas (New York: Columbia University Press, 1990), p. 305, originally published as *Logique du sens* (Paris: Les Éditions de Minuit, 1969), pp. 354–5.

76. Deleuze, *The Logic of Sense*, p. 306 (355–6), emphasis added.

77. Deleuze, *The Logic of Sense*, p. 307 (356–7).

78. Sartre, *Being and Nothingness*, p. 532 (481–2).

79. Clarice Lespector, 'The buffalo', in *Family Ties*, tr. Giovanni Pontiero (Austin: University of Texas Press, 1972), pp. 147, 148.

80. Steven H. Strogatz and Ian Stewart, 'Coupled oscillators and biological synchronization', *Scientific American,* December 1993, pp. 102–9. 'A single oscillator traces out a simple path in phase space. When two or more oscillators are coupled, however, the range of possible behaviors becomes much more complex,' p. 10.

81. Lespector, 'The buffalo', pp. 154, 155.

82. Lespector, 'The buffalo', pp. 153, 152, 154.

83. Sartre, *Being and Nothingness*, pp. 475–6 (432). The paradox of transcendence.

84. See Deleuze, *The Logic of Sense*, p. 366, n. 12 (360, n. 11). Or, as Sartre expresses this, only by being-as-an-object can one assimilate the Other's freedom, yet one wants to be Other to oneself, one wants to be Other and wants oneself to be God, to use the Other's freedom as the basis of one's own acts.
85. Lespector, 'The buffalo', pp. 155, 156. The slowness of this encounter is of great interest.
86. Strogatz and Stewart, 'Coupled oscillators and biological synchronization', p. 107.
87. Strogatz and Stewart, 'Coupled oscillators and biological synchronization', p. 107.
88. Bergson, *Matter and Memory*, pp. 168–9; Bergson, *Oeuvres*, pp. 307–8. It is my hope to restore or, if necessary, to bring to Bergson a genuine sense of duration.
89. Bergson, *Time and Free Will*, pp. 29–2; Bergson, *Oeuvres*, pp. 22–49. It is a difference in nature or kind.
90. Maurice Merleau-Ponty, *The Visible and the Invisible*, tr. Alphonso Lingis (Evanston: Northwestern University Press, 1968), p. 143, originally published as *Le Visible et l'invisible* (Paris: Gallimard, 1964), p. 188.

2

'A Place of Love and Mystery'

Universality and unity

Some people are standing in the back of a sparsely furnished room. Others, in front, are sitting restlessly; a few are moving around, but the room is generally quiet. A woman, surrounded by men, steps up to a microphone. She whispers more than sings, breathing her words, running the lines together:

> God knows how I adore life
> When the wind turns on the shore lies another day
> I cannot ask for more
> And when the timebell blows my heart
> and I have scored a better day
> Well nobody made this war of mine
>
> And the moments that I enjoy
> A place of love and mystery
> I'll be there anytime
>
> Oh mysteries of love where war is no more
> I'll be there anytime.[1]

What sensibility releases this woman to avow publicly and directly 'God knows how I adore life?' It is a private, personal admission trembling through the words of the poet. Merely repeating these words in public, lacking the cover of music or alcohol, of a dimly lit club or a private space evokes discomfort among those who listen. The listeners squirm; they feel embarrassed that the woman is so exposed. They have a language for this. They view her ruefully as pathetic, and some leave the room in search of less visceral stimulation; something that will help them to understand something, to know something, to do something. She goes on; she does not stop at this initial disclosure even though it seems that to go further is to threaten her senses with complete disarray, to destroy her composure, leaving little, a pure flux, energy and material flows, nothing more. That would mean, minimally, that she would be subject to the exposure of her pathological existence, her intimations of the sensuous, her ontological, unconscious inclinations, her discrete affections, her absolute and unlimited nature, her diffusion, her distress.[2] But powerful forces are at work claiming her, ordering and organizing her sensibility and cognition in every respect. These forces emerge, not from her *own* sensibility, not from those flashes and streaks whose luminescence, intimate yet pervasive, culminate in her point of view, nor from those non-personal, unconscious mixtures without which no emotion, no cognition and no action would ever be assembled. They seem to come from elsewhere, from another space, a manifold with its own dimensions and structure. And they emerge in at least two distinct forms, one transcendent and one immanent.

The first force, as the power to organize not only thought but sensibility, to wrest it from the realm of *one's own,* and to thrust it onto a manifold wherein it may be determined by transcendental Ideas, is the form of thought unified by the 'I think,' when it harmonizes the faculties, thereby not only regulating but also reconciling their disparate powers. On this manifold, the manifold of goodwill, of desire, we might ask, if and when the 'I think' accompanies some 'representation,' does it change it? Moreover, does the 'I think' unify our consciousness, or is it the unity, the continuity that leads us to claim 'these representations are mine'?[3] And the second force, the second will deny harmony, anticipating enmity; not a revolution but a violent encounter, forcing all faculties to their limits. 'There is no *philia* which testifies to a desire, love, good nature or good will . . . There is no *amicability* . . . The dark precursor is sufficient to enable communication between difference as such, and to make the different communicate with difference.[4] Inquiry into the motives and aspirations of the first method will bring us to the question: 'What is love?' Inquiry into the motives and aspirations of the second, inspires another: 'What is hate?' Love and hate, what is most 'one's own' and also most 'Other' may, strangely enough, turn out to be the most discrete and situated aspects of our thought as well as the most universal.

Let us begin with this first 'outside,' the homogeneous manifold from which the dynamical ideas of relation appear and demand instantiation for the greater goal of unification. Formerly named 'categories of freedom,' a slogan that now resonates as a disturbing cliché, they were once thought to be the very elementary, fundamental or original, and practical, thus both universal *and* situated, immanent ideas, concepts derived from pure reason, regulating the 'free faculty of choice,' that is nevertheless called desire.[5] Unlike

categories of thought that must prove themselves outside of themselves, in representations of nature through the pure intuitions of
space and time, the categories of freedom dispense with the intuition
of space and time; they are purely productive, they *produce the
reality to which they refer*, yet they originate from the same source
as concepts which remain relegated to synthesizing representation,
to serving nature.[6] Purely intellectual concepts are functions; they
function as unifiers, bringing unity through the act of gathering
myriad representations (whether intuitions or concepts) under one
common representation; in this they function as judgments.
Moreover, the understanding asks for absolute unity; its concepts
ought to connect with one another according to one concept, one
idea that rules over all.[7] Moving continuously, in reverse, from the
contents of such judgments to their form, understanding uncovers
the idea organizing their unity. It infers from the form of judgments
that the transcendental table of the categories of understanding orig-
inates in the logical tables, in judgments of relation, quantity, quality
and modality. Making inferences in general logic is a straightfor-
ward process. Seeking the highest logical unity, reason reduces the
varied and manifold knowledge obtained through the understanding to the smallest possible number of principles which are universal conditions, and which remain transcendent in relation to
appearances, unable to be employed for cognition.[8]

   Unlike general logic, transcendental logic is faced with a manifold
of *a priori* sensibility, with representations of material existence made
possible by the unifying power of the spatial-temporal manifold, and
even these representations undergo further conversion. They must
undergo synthesis, they must be combined and connected in order to
be truly unified, in order to participate in that great continuum called
knowledge. Blindly, imagination does this using those same concepts
produced by the purely logical form of judgment.

> In this manner there arise precisely the same number of pure concepts of
> the understanding which apply *a priori* to objects of intuition in general,
> as, in the preceding table, there have been found to be logical functions in
> all possible judgments. For these functions specify the understanding com-
> pletely, and yield an exhaustive inventory of its powers. These concepts we
> shall, with Aristotle, call categories, for our primary purpose is the same
> as his, although widely diverging from it in manner of execution.[9]

Thus, along with Aristotle, whose purposes are declared to be the
same as Kant's, we will call these concepts categories.

Categories for organizing experience are derived from judgments that unify representations and so add to knowledge but something more is sought, something tending toward *universality*. Categories apply to all objects of possible experience. What conditions categories to do this? What 'gives birth' to concepts?[10] What makes possible, not merely knowledge from rules, but knowledge from principles, the apprehension of the particular in the universal through concepts? What makes this possible, the answer comes, is that every syllogism is a mode of deducing knowledge from a principle.[11] Where previously, in the realms of understanding, we moved from the contents of judgments to their form, we now breathe in even more rarified air. We take the form of judgments to be their content, that is, we take up the mere syllogism, the mechanism for deducing knowledge from principles, beginning with the singular conclusion, 'Kant is mortal,' and proceed, in *reverse*, step by step, to the first premiss in pursuit of the concept that contains the condition that makes it possible to use this predicate 'mortal' so confidently in this or any syllogism. The condition of 'mortal' is 'man,' as in 'All *men* are mortal.' 'Having first thought it in the major premiss in its whole extension under a given condition, [t]he complete quantity of the extension in relation to such a condition is called *universality*.'[12] And now, we stand before the unity of the universal from which the unity of a sublime totality shimmers before us. Applied to sensible experience, universality represents the sensible totality of conditions for any given condition, but this is not yet *absolutely* universal. By means of the continuity of logic, a continuity that takes us from any condition to the totality of conditions, a leap is made, a leap off and out of the conditioned continuum to the premiss that '*it is the unconditioned alone that makes possible the totality of conditions.*'[13] Here is unity, even if it requires a leap of logic, a leap of faith. Still, transcendental Ideas, the unconditioned for the totality of conditions, do not fall from the sky. Everything rests on the relations expressed in syllogisms.[14] Only the categories of relation are derived from or correspond to actual syllogisms, thus only the categories of relation are transmutable into transcendental Ideas. The category of substance is derived from categorical syllogisms, causality from hypothetical syllogisms, and community from disjunctive syllogisms. Categorical syllogisms represent the relation of the predicate to a subject or substance; hypothetical syllogisms represent the relation of a ground to its consequence (causality), and disjunctive syllogisms represent the relation of opposition between members of some division, the sphere of one excluding the sphere of another. Yet, taken as a whole, they form a community.[15] *Universalized*, each category leaps up to the unconditioned for a totality of conditions: self for substance, world for causality, god for community.

Still, one must be quite careful. It would be foolish and illegitimate to apply transcendental Ideas to objects of possible experience or to the laws of nature. Their reach is elsewhere. What, after all, do we mean by self, world, god? How is it that certain Ideas correspond to the connective, the hypothetical, the disjunctive? Categorical syllogisms, 'All men are mortal,' represent the relations of a concept or idea to a subject. Hypothetical syllogisms, 'If the earth turns, then the sun will rise and set,' are causal, manifesting the relation of a concept or an idea to the manifold of objects in the world of appearance, the synthesis of a causal series. Finally, there is the disjunctive relation, the disjunctive synthesis of parts in a system in relation to objects of thought, 'Either the universe has a beginning or it does not.' This is the relation of a concept or idea to all things in general. Transcendental Ideas are concerned only with *the unconditioned synthetic unity of all conditions in general*. Thus, the categorical syllogism taken back to the unconditioned finds the absolute unity of the thinking subject, insofar as it conditions the possibility of all claims that any subject is related to any predicate. Without the unity of a subject, no sensible intuitions and no synthesis of intuitions in a concept are thinkable. The unity of a thinking subject provides an Idea for the transcendental doctrine of the soul; the consciousness that accompanies all concepts. The hypothetical reveals the absolute unity of the series of conditions of appearance and provides the Idea for a transcendental science of the world. Lacking a concept of the unity of the world, it is impossible to think causality at all, since if we are seeking to establish the order of time between cause and effect, what follows something else must do so in conformity with a universal rule without which cause and effect are meaningless. For its part, the disjunctive synthesis literally locates the absolute unity of the condition of *all* objects of thought in general and provides the Idea for a transcendental knowledge of god. God is the pure *a priori* manifold of space, out of which things are determined to coexist in one time through the mutual determination of their position so as to constitute a whole. 'Either here or there,' each appearance stands outside of every other, each appearance is separate from every other, but together they form a whole.[16]

It is well known that the transcendental Ideas correspond to no objects of experience. Derived only from syllogisms, transcendental

Ideas give rise to illusion if we ascribe objective reality to them. Unlike the illusions of logic, transcendental illusions persist, even once revealed. 'We therefore take the subjective necessity of a connection of our concepts, which is to the advantage of the understanding, for an objective necessity in the determination of things in themselves.'[17] Nonetheless, springing from the very nature of reason, these sophistications of pure reason, from which even the wisest among us are unable to free themselves, each transcendental Idea gives rise to a necessary and unavoidable illusion, an illusion which, however, may be rendered harmless, and more, an illusion which may be employed in a positive manner. Human reason's *natural tendency is to transgress the limits of experience.* 'We are entitled to suppose that transcendental Ideas have their own good, proper, and therefore *immanent* use.'[18] Confined to their good, proper and immanent use, the Ideas of reason unify the manifold of concepts, *creating nothing*, but ordering everything, combining the greatest possible *unity* with the greatest possible *extension*. The illusion would be to imagine that these ideas have a source outside of reason and also, outside the empirical field; this would be, Kant cautions, like looking at objects reflected in a mirror and believing that they exist on the other side. But what exactly is it that these ideas are a reflection of? Lacking knowledge of any objects corresponding to these ideas, they are said to be 'problematic.' Particulars appear to be derived from the Ideas; in fact, all the particulars we can cite appear to be derived from the universality of the rule, but 'how are we to know all the possible consequences which, as actually following from the adopted principle *prove* its universality?'[19] The employment of pure reason is regulative but this is no small matter. It seeks unity through an *approximate* rule of universality; all its possible consequences can never be known, but everywhere we think the approximate universal rule, everywhere we think *unity*.

Under this regime, the poet, disclosing her sensibilities, her pure flux, her energy and material flows, her pathological existence, her intimations of the sensuous, her ontological, unconscious inclinations, her discrete affections, her absolute and unlimited nature, her diffusion, her distress, *should* submit all these 'powers,' to unification.

> Sensation, consciousness, imagination, memory, wit, power of discrimination, pleasure, desire, etc . . . Now there is a logical maxim which requires that we should reduce, so far as may be possible, this seeming diversity, by comparing these with one another and detecting their hidden identity.[20]

All this occurs in the name of the logical principle of reason which presupposes the transcendental law; it pursues what is diverse and dispersed, attenuating incongruities, achieving identity, reducing each and every dissimilar or diffuse sensibility, one by one, to some *fundamental power*, some axiomatic of sameness. We have no choice. Failure to assume the systematic unity of nature as objectively valid and necessary is tantamount to the declaration that there is no reason at all, that the world is not a manifold, that there is no continuum, no consonance, only a confusion of powers in nature, a heterogeneity and incoherence in nature and in understanding, disorder in the universe and discord in the soul. Without the axiomatic of a fundamental power, there can be no coherent use of the understanding, no order among concepts, no organization of empirical intuitions, nothing but the disintegration of mind and the decline of nature.[21]

Truly speculative – that is, theoretical – philosophers are unquestionably hostile to heterogeneity; yet although empirical thinkers endanger unity and extinguish the hope of universal principles, they will, of necessity, fail. For the nature of the manifold decrees division, that is, commencing with a genus, it can only be divided into species and subspecies and sub-subspecies. Nevertheless, any species or subspecies or sub-subspecies, remains a concept containing what is common to different things and so can never be completely determined. The *individual can never be attained*, and any and all discrete sensibilities are, by definition, irrational, an actual infinity of differences is incoherent. Were it not for the transcendental law of specification, there would be no *lower* concepts usable for seeking division to begin with. Instead, by means of this law, we are led to suspect the existence of lower and lower divisions, even when the senses are completely unable to disclose any such divisions to us. We proceed, in this way, always by division, always from what is most universal to what can only be subsumed under it. The law specifies a homogeneous manifold of genera, division into the variety of species, and finally, the affinity of all concepts, the systematic connection of high and low. There exists a universal horizon and its complete division, every species mediated by the smaller degrees of difference from any other. So profoundly are we determined by the unity of transcendental law, that all other approaches are doomed in advance; never can there be points which possess no extent, never can there be individuals, never can there be entities or events separated from one another by an empty, intervening space.[22]

Thus, we are encouraged to employ and to celebrate the transcendental principles as necessary Ideas of reason, which do not extend our knowledge, but which regulate it. First, connecting all appearances, actions and receptivity of the mind *as if* the mind were a simple substance persisting in its personal identity, persisting *as if* it were immortal. Then, connecting all inner and outer natural appearances *as if* there were an endless, limitless series of appearances with no beginning or end, even while regarding this series *as if* there were an intelligible ground outside all experience, a ground which is nothing less than freedom, the unconditioned outside the series of conditions. And finally, viewing all possible experience *as if* it formed a sensibly conditioned unity but also, *as if* the sensible world has a single, highest, self-sufficient ground, a self-subsistent, creative reason guiding our empirically employed reason, securing the greatest possible extension of the manifold.[23] So let us not fall into illusion, let us not be subject to the confusion and chaos of an undetermined intelligence.

Yet we can do more. We can do more than gaze into the mirrored reflection of the transcendental Ideas of immortality, freedom and god. We can discover their *reality*, not in intelligence, but in pure practical reason, concerned wholly with the determination of the will, with volition, with want, wish, need, or desire. If there really is freedom, if there is a god, even in the minimal sense of an *a priori* manifold, if the soul has a future life, the question is, what ought we to do? As transcendental Ideas, free will, god, and soul are meaningless, purely logical constructs. How can they be made meaningful? How can the purely animal will, sensuous and impulsive, pathological and perverse, how can such a will free itself from its affects, its inclinations, its weakness, its depravity, its unworthiness?[24] Where are we to look for the solution to this problem? Look in the mirror. Looking in the mirror, we see what we cannot otherwise see, not our own reflection, but that of the Ideal. In this sense the transcendental Ideas were always already the unconscious. Visible only through their mirrored reflection, but functioning always, to regulate the understanding and to provide a rule for what are called free acts of the will. Ideas, the concepts of reason, have no object that can be met with in any experience; they are heuristic fictions, thought-entities. When we do think these Ideas, we think something whose propositions are indemonstrable, blind, haphazard, even incomprehensible. Using such Ideas to explain any natural existence is tantamount to explaining something 'which in terms of known empirical principles we do not understand sufficiently, by something we do not understand at all.'[25]

The discovery of the Ideas of freedom, god, soul, world is tantamount to the discovery of the unconscious. Laws of nature tell us only what does happen. Laws of freedom, *reflecting on us*, tell us what ought to happen, what we ought to do. They are, moreover, intimately connected with happiness. What ought to happen? There ought to be happiness. Ideally, unconsciously, '*something is . . . because something ought to happen . . . something is . . . because something happens.*[26] Already, we are at the point where there is something rather than nothing. Some happiness happens because it is conditioned by the supreme cause, the sublime; happiness happens rather than nothing because it ought. And happiness is the satisfaction of desires, extensively, intensively, protensively; happiness with respect to the manifold, the intuition of all appearances in space and time; happiness with respect to degree, the influence on sense of an object perceived in an instant, sensation; and happiness with respect to duration, the necessary connection of perceptions, but only if we are worthy, only if the axiomatic of our thought is that of an intelligible being, free of empirical influence.[27] In other words, we know we are causal phenomena in nature, part of the dynamical whole, but we *think* we are free, that our actions are intelligent, that we do not follow blind impulse, that we follow a rule given to us without our knowing it.[28]

If we must be worthy to be happy, then the entire task of philosophy is radically reoriented. The task is not to become mired in speculation, speculative problems transcend human powers; the task is to analyze and define the situations in which we find ourselves and then to interpret in moral terms the meaning and value of the universe and human life.[29] Categories of freedom provide an axiomatic for the acts of any intelligible being. These acts do not refer to sensible experience nor to sensibility in any respect. The laws governing these acts *produce* the reality to which they refer; they produce an intention of the will removed from human experience, the more pure the better, but always unconsciously. In actuality, the categories of freedom may be said to be no more transcendental than they are empirical. Their operation is regulative but unconscious. Not a personal unconscious, dependent on the vagaries of empirical conditions, but a *universal* unconscious. We have seen glimmers of this already in the claim that sensation, consciousness, imagination, memory, wit, power of discrimination, pleasure, desire, all diversity should be reduced, based on comparison and the detection of some identity. This is a logical requirement.[30] We said that in the name of the logical principle of reason which presupposes the transcendental law, the diverse and dispersed, the incongruous are made to conform to some *fundamental power*, some *axiomatic* of sameness. It bears repeating that failure to assume the systematic unity of nature as objectively valid and necessary is tantamount to the declaration that there is no reason at all, that the world is not a manifold or a continuum, that there is no consonance but only a confusion of powers in nature, a heterogeneity and incoherence in nature and in understanding, disorder in the universe and discord in the soul. For Kant, this axiomatic is the systematic unity of nature as objectively valid and necessary. But when genus and species, recognition and identity are cast into oblivion, can this *axiomatic,* which we have identified as *continuity*, can it still compress and make all of nature conform to its rules? When the transcendental Ideas are no longer viewed as unconscious conditions for the possibility of experience but are taken as its unconscious point of genesis generating acts on the basis of continuity, what new *axiomatic* has taken the place of the old? What seems to have taken the place of continuity that unifies through knowledge is the promise of a disjointed/disjoined but superior, transcendent *exercise* of the faculties. Already, for Kant, what matters here is not what the faculties *know* but what they *do*, and what they do under the axiomatic of disjointed continuity is grasp 'that' in the world which concerns them and bring 'it' into the world without the benefit of common sense or good sense.[31]

> Because the Kantian critique remains dominated by common sense or the dogmatic image, Kant still defines the truth of a problem in terms of the possibility of its finding a solution: this time it is a question of a transcendental form of possibility, in accordance with a legitimate use of the faculties as this is determined in each case by this or that organization of common sense (to which the problem corresponds).[32]

We saw that the employment of pure reason is regulative; it seeks unity through an *approximate* rule of universality; its unity, we noted, is *purely hypothetical* until and unless it encounters the transcendental employment of understanding – the unconscious power of the one. We saw also the necessity of this, that the failure to assume the systematic unity of nature as objectively valid and necessary is tantamount to the declaration that there is no reason at all, that the world is not a manifold, that there is no continuum, no consonance, only a confusion of powers in nature, a heterogeneity and incoherence in nature and in understanding, disorder in the universe and discord in the soul. Now what, we might ask ourselves, has changed? Let us not be fooled by embedded assumptions. First of all, we *encounter* a series of images, long since relegated to the margins.[33] What are these images? Are they images of love, images of hate? It seems that in place of an imposed goodwill and a harmony that ensures thought to those who are capable of embracing the critical enterprise, philosophy is once again filled with violence, the kind of violence Socrates sought to tame in the *Republic*, through the humiliation of the sophist Thrasymachus who demands, among other things, to be paid for his work.[34] Out of the violence of the encounter with Thrasymachus, Socrates recalls the Idea of justice, an Idea not able to be remembered on the empirical level but immemorial, transcendentally. Forced by the encounter, the Idea, which can only be thought, is grasped. Yet, influenced by empirical, moral motives, Plato misses the opportunity to cast aside common sense and thereby clouds thought, introducing opacity where there could or should be nothing but translucence. Faced with the claim that something is both just and unjust, Plato insists on the law of non-contradiction, on the contrariety of the claim that justice is unjust and injustice is just. Each quality is limited by empirical recognition (no opposition in a sensible object), transcendental memory (similarity in reminiscence), identity in a concept (contraries must always be separated), and analogy to the Good (the Good is to thought as the sun is to sight).[35] For Socrates, the sensible discordant encounter with Thrasymachus, with contrariety, must be harmonized, but by a process which quells the discord through the imposition of the law of non-contradiction. Contrariety disrupts common sense and compels even the Socratic soul to probe, to problematize, 'arousing thought in itself.'[36] Having been *forced* into thought, Socrates recalls the transcendental Idea (thought aroused), the pure past that has never been present. Yet, coaxing Thrasymachus to become gentle, to cease being angry, Socrates proceeds as before, as if nothing hateful has occurred and so denies contradiction. He validates the transcendental Idea as an empirical, past-present, thereby filling pure thought with physical existence, clouding its translucence. The effect of this logic is to produce a concept determined by identity. As Justice is nothing but just, so the being of all sensibles is limited to real identity in a concept. This, in turn, is grounded in the analogy between thought, Truth and the Good which fixes the soul on truth and reality, turning it away from what is mixed with darkness. 'An extraordinary beauty, this Good. You surely do not mean this to be pleasure! Hush!'[37] Hush!, so that discord may be harmonized, so that contrariety may be resolved.

What Plato wants seems no different than what is wanted still. What is wanted, what is sought now, in philosophy, is an image of thought unsullied by the opacity of physical existence, that would be an image set free from recognition, similarity, identity, analogy. So we return to the scene of conflict and will its return without the bad faith of common sense. In this return, thought is once again *forced* by an encounter, not with sensibility but with the *being of the sensible*, its sign, *forced* by an *original violence*, whose *claws of necessity* arouse an otherwise *involuntary thought*, all the more powerful for being *illegitimate*. 'Thought is trespass and violence, the enemy.'[38] The passion to think is once again compelled by a disturbance that gives way to enmity, but this time in a manner that keeps open the discord among the faculties. First there is the clash with the unrecognizable sign, the being of the sensible that defies common sense and good sense, which, as the 'coexistence of contraries, the coexistence of more and less in an unlimited qualitative becoming,' can never be sensible but always, given as a sign.[39] Then there is the violated 'soul,' the fractured *I* that is *forced* to pose a problem and to forget, in the trauma of the violence, anything that can be recalled, anything seen, heard, imagined or thought, in order to sense and to recall that which has never been empirical, but only can be transcendental with respect to both sensibility and memory, what is essentially nonsense and forgetfulness. Thus, in the midst of this original violence, the faculties themselves are *forced* to their limits, *forced* into discordant harmony, the open-ended disorder of the faculties, so that each may pursue its 'own' 'essential' projects. So to each its own.[40] Sensibility is forced to 'sense,' to give meaning to that which is the imperceptible, but imperceptible insofar as it can *never be sensible* because it is not empirical. Memory is forced to a remembrance that is also forgetting, thought is forced to thinking that is also stupidity, imagination is forced to imagine and forced to what is impossible to imagine, language is forced to speech and to silence, and so on for innumerable yet undiscovered or yet-to-be generated faculties. This is a process that is no longer a matter of determining conditions, but of genesis, provided however, that one gives up the attraction of tracing the transcendental from the outlines of the empirical, and that each faculty is compelled to go to the triple limit of the 'final power,' the triple limit being what forces a faculty into being by means of what it is forced to grasp, what it is uniquely able to grasp, and what is empirically ungraspable.[41]

The transcendental past, the past that was never present is this new Idea, the solution to the problem posed in the encounter with the being of the sensible. Not surprisingly, we find that precisely such an encounter yields a tradition, albeit a compact one, in which the Kantian program is modified. For example:

> It must be conceded to Kant that 'the I Think *must be able* to accompany all our representations.' But need we then conclude that an *I in fact* inhabits all our states of consciousness and actually effects the supreme synthesis of our experience? This inference would appear to distort the Kantian view. The Critical problem being one of validity, Kant says nothing concerning the actual existence of the *I Think*. On the contrary, he seems to have seen perfectly well that there are moments of consciousness without the I, for he says '*must be able* to accompany.'[42]

The problem, we are advised, is the dangerous tendency, which insists on making the conditions of the possibility of experience into a reality, leading to the inappropriate question of what a transcendental consciousness would be, and what it would be, unquestionably, is an unconscious that constitutes our empirical consciousness.[43] The question, for Sartre, is whether the transcendental *I Think* unifies representations or if it is not the case that representations are unified so that it is possible to make note of an *I Think*. Seen only behind us in their mirrored reflection, Kant's transcendental Ideas, although not actual and not knowable, serve as unconscious conditions. Sartre would reverse the formula, privileging the *fact* of consciousness, a translucent consciousness that unifies itself, privileging this over the constitutive powers of a transcendental unconscious. Speculative consciousness must give way to practical reason. What matters is what a consciousness can *do*. Let us recall what was said above. Categories of freedom provide an axiomatic of continuity for the acts of any *intelligible* being. Yet, these acts do not refer to sensible experience nor to established theoretical understanding in any respect. These acts *produce* the reality to which they refer; they produce an intention of the will removed from human experience, the purer the better. It is a simple matter of pointing out that Kant never actually *deduced* empirical consciousness from a constituting hyperconsciousness. It is a simple matter of noticing that Kant derives the transcendental Ideas from the category of relation which is non-metric, dynamic not mathematic. The word 'regulatory' must not pass through our lips.

Reason, however, is not simply to be discarded, something Sartre tends to overlook as he struggles to keep consciousness clear, to eliminate any opacity clouding it. Freed from their conditioning function, transcendental Ideas may take on new dimensions. In an extension of this new tradition, we are again advised about how to read these texts.

> Kant never ceased to remind us that Ideas are essentially 'problematic'. Conversely, problems are Ideas . . . if, according to Kant, reason does pose false problems and therefore does itself give rise to illusion, this is because in the first place it is the faculty of posing problems in general. In its natural state such a faculty lacks the means to distinguish what is true or false, what is founded or not, in any problem it poses. The aim of the critical operation is precisely to provide this means since the science of metaphysics has to deal not with the objects of reason . . . but only with itself and the problems which arise entirely from within itself.[44]

The 'legitimate' function of Ideas is regulative, but regulative – when faculties are forced to their limits – *means* problematic. Lacking Ideas, understanding would remain imprisoned by *partial, empirical, enquiries* into this or that object, never allowing reason to pose problems whose solutions lie along the axiom of continuity. Ideas are already both transcendent and immanent. They are problems posed: 'How can partial, empirical enquiries be systematically unified?' thus immanent, but also solutions: 'What object outside the bounds of experience can be represented as undetermined (not known or given) and as providing systematic unification?' thus transcendent.[45] Once again, we know we are part of the dynamical whole, but we *think* we are free, that our actions are intelligent, that we do not follow blind impulse, that we follow a rule given to us without our knowing it.

This radicalized reading avers that Kant fulfills the promise of the purely immanent field, the field of the cogito, the absolute *I* which is translucent, pure consciousness of its empty self, pure immanence. 'The Kantian *I Think* is a condition of possibility. [However] it is indeed from the *Cogito* that an 'Egology' must take its point of departure.'[46] But then Kant allows the objects of undetermined Ideas to be determined by analogy with objects of experience, even while each Idea circulates the ideal of complete and infinite determination that 'ensures a specification of the concepts of the understanding, by means of which the latter comprise more and more differences on the basis of a properly infinite field of continuity'.[47] Given that the *I Think*, the unity of consciousness, accompanies every representation, *I Think* is the correlate of the object in general.[48] Thus transcendental Ideas are necessarily *repetitions* of the three aspects of the *cogito*. '*I am* as an indeterminate existence, *time* as the form under which this existence is determinable, and the *I think* as a determination. Ideas are exactly the thoughts of the Cogito, the differentials of thought.'[49]

Ideas promise a vast Egology, but the *I* that thinks is not the *ego* that experiences time and is determined in time. 'Each time we apprehend our thought . . . we apprehend an *I* which is the *I* of the apprehended thought, and which is given, in addition, as *transcending* this thought and all other possible thoughts.'[50] The *I Think* is forever split from the *I am*. The former is undetermined, the latter determined under the form of time, the passive and receptive ego, receptive of the activity of the *I* which is an Other. Nevertheless, as the condition of unity, it is within the *I Think* that a field of immanence is attributed to a Subject. Moreover, each Idea (self, world, god) retains all of its partial objects, the 'thises' and 'thats' of empirical inquiry, gathering them into its immanent problematic unity. For Kant, the Idea of self/subject remains referred to an object of sense, but communication between this and the other Ideas is cut off. The failure here, on Kant's part, is the empirical act of separating what can be distinguished, dividing the great plane of immanence into self, world and god, each of which are now wholly external to the others.[51] In themselves, Ideas should remain undetermined; they are not to recall either empirical sensibility or empirical memory. Yet, Ideas become determinable in relation to objects of experience and bear the ideal of determination for concepts of the understanding.

Kant's failure is his empiricism. Kant remains bound to empirical sensibility and empirical memory. This forces him to connect the inside, the spatial manifold, with the outside, the concepts of the understanding, by means of the schematism, a mechanism of unification, both cumbersome and awkward. Schemata are *a priori* determinations of time in accordance with rules. 'What the schematism of understanding effects by means of the transcendental synthesis of imagination is simply the unity of all the manifold of intuition in inner sense.'[52] A desirable goal for generating the manifold, but inappropriately achieved insofar as the route is external, a purely external harmony of intuitions and concepts. Thus, although Kant promises that transcendental Ideas are, in fact, productive, he misses the opportunity to posit immanent, serial connections between the undetermined, the determinable and the determination. He misses the opportunity for the encounter with Ideas as problems whose immanent genesis is a solution and falls back on Ideas as conditions for the possibility of knowledge and experience. Yet, it seems that conflict is always being realized, floating up to the surface, the miasma of bodies, and tumbling down from the heights, the condensation of Reminiscence. What can possibly bring about a refusal of harmony, unity, common sense, amity, goodwill, desire? Forms of recognition, themselves provocations, as is everything it seems, are also effects of the violent encounter, the differential in thought, contrariety. What will give rise to the generation of the pure, non-empirical, discordant, differentiable manifold, a structure that will abolish inside and outside, love and hate, unity and disunity, bringing everything to the same level, to the same surface? As it turns out, such a manifold is not that difficult to achieve. Recall the previous discovery that transcendental Ideas are necessarily *repetitions* of the three aspects of the *cogito*, that of the *I am* as an indeterminate existence, that of *time* as the form under which this existence is determinable, and that of the *I think* as a determination. But given this, what does this imply? What are the implications of the claim, not only that Ideas are exactly the thoughts of the *cogito*, but also that they are the differentials of thought? It is the *I Think* that accompanies all my representations, that harmonizes the faculties, sets them in motion and allows them to *recognize* an object as the same, to synthesize recognition in a concept.

Now, let us attempt to be perfectly clear about this. Synthesis, defined as the act of putting different representations together and grasping in one act of knowledge what is manifold in them, will turn out to be a mode of thought begging to be discarded, but at this point, it seems to be the only option.[53] All representations, as modifications of the mind, belong to inner sense; all our knowledge is subject to time, the formal condition of inner sense. The devil is in the principles governing ordering and connecting. The sequences of impressions are first run through and held together (synthesis of *apprehension*); they are held together such that the *I* that thinks can apprehend them one after the other (synthesis of *reproduction* in imagination); that they are apprehended requires not only consciousness of the identity of the self, but also consciousness of the necessary unity of the synthesis of appearances according to concepts that make it possible to think the identity of the object (synthesis of *recognition* in a concept). So-called inner sense or empirical apperception, merely empirical, always changing, always in flux, with no fixed and abiding self is there at the basis of all synthesis. It might be argued that it is our empirical helplessness that drives the syntheses and even gives them their form merely in opposition to the empirical.[54] Are we caught between the dogmatism of apprehension-reproduction-recognition, a series no more transcendental than psychological, and the 'blind play of representations, less even than a dream'?[55] Harmony of the faculties and identity in the object produce recognition such that nothing unexpected could ever appear and no problems could be posited, especially not in the form of Ideas.[56]

Universality and the sensible

Let us return for a moment to the poet, trapped, it would appear, by her pathological existence, her intimations of the sensuous, her ontological, unconscious inclinations, her discrete affections, her absolute and unlimited nature, her expansion and contraction, diffusion and distress. Her continued existence in this mode might imply a failure or inability to make sense of the structures that constrain her existence, in which case, her words do not yet even qualify as expression. They are mere nonsense, garbled bodily functions. Or, it might imply that not all events and not all structures of events have been accounted for, that there are still others. Perhaps, what is missing in her account is an Idea of freedom, existence as neither an *automaton materiale* nor an *automaton spirituale,* both of which would keep her enslaved to the connective synthesis, the causal chain in either the material or the psychological world.[57] Given her failure to evoke the unity of consciousness, the harmony of the faculties, and instead, to express herself from an ever-changing perspective, without a fixed time and space, without a fixed and abiding self, neither the laws of common sense nor the rules of good sense are called upon to order and organize her thought. Insofar as this is so, she is clearly outside the rule of reason, the logical maxim that defines the necessity of reducing diversity, the multiple, discrete instances of sensation, consciousness, imagination, memory, wit, discrimination, diffusion, distress. The unity of reason is *purely hypothetical* until and unless it encounters the transcendental employment of understanding – the unconscious power of the one from which, we are assured, we can never escape. Or perhaps what is missing in her account is any sign of a violent encounter with the sensible that forces her faculties to the limits of what they can do. That is, the profusion of part objects in her proximity have not connected themselves, she is not yet chosen by the world, by the connective synthesis, a process that produces 'man' within nature and nature within 'man.' Not yet a thinking automaton, for whom any words would be the effect of a machine and not of an agent, she is not ready to be torn apart, *disjoined*, and scattered to the wind, awaiting rebirth.[58] And if some power *were* to hold her in its grasp, until the next more powerful force comes along, this would raise the specter of the excluded middle. Indeed, '*nobody,*' she claims 'made this war of mine.'

Thus, the poet's pathology. Can she never escape what we will call the law of the manifold but which could equally well be called the law of the unconscious? 'This logical law of the *continuum specierum (formarum logicaarum)* presupposes, however, a transcendental law (*continui in natura*) . . . [giving] rise to all that is systematic in our knowledge of nature.'[59] Even if it *is* the case that the *I Think* need not accompany all our representations, the logical law of the unconscious power of the one remains – emerging with the full force of its drives – its eros and thanatos, its split subject. Yet, if we continue to insist on the coexistence of structures, one that allows both the setting aside of common sense *and* the non-encounter, the non-violent creation of an indeterminate perspective within a logic that evades the injunction against the excluded middle, then perhaps there is still the chance to think in terms of planes of consistency, though not necessarily other worlds. Pathologically excluded by their own nature from the continuum of inferences stretching back toward and leaping into the sublime, there are the discrete moments with which we began these wanderings: moments of place, moments of love, moments of mystery, moments of the timebell, moments of the heart, moments of a better day, discrete moments no more condensed by the genetic continuum than by the unconditioned. There are moments of diffusion, moments of distress, of expansion and contraction, likely incommensurate with the trajectories of desire, of life, not able to be subject to the rule of free will.

Can we continue to claim that such events persist, remarkable, continuously altered and altering; can we claim they exist, endure and influence other events? Even if this were granted for the moment, for the sake of argument, there are ways of refuting this. Let us not forget the powerful forces at work claiming the poet, ordering and organizing her sensibility and cognition in every respect. At least two such forces have professed to be capable of making claims on her: the first, empirical yet transcendental, tied to common sense and good sense, to the conditions of the possibility of experience or knowledge; continuity on a discontinuous manifold; the second, immanent yet transcendent and non-empirical, of which we have had intimations, no longer conditions of the possibility of experience but acts of the effective genesis of events; discontinuity on a continuous manifold. If through some relaxation of the faculties, some discord of their otherwise harmonious processes, the poet escapes the law of the manifold, the transcendent law, there is still its immanent manifestation. Immanent productions might prove to be the most powerful forces of all, capturing material and energy flows, turning bright light into a fog of gray, tempering astonishment into clever invention, disabling diffusion with affirmation, devitalizing distress with negation, pacifying pleasure and pain. Given the manifold of desire and the imperative of disjunction, the imperative that all affects and percepts will be connected, forming substances, then disjoined, torn apart, then conjoined again forming a disjointed, differentiated world, in this world, along with pain,

> pleasure is continually disappointed, reduced, deflated, in favor of strong, noble values: Truth, Death, Progress, Struggle, Joy, etc. Its victorious rival is Desire: we are always being told about Desire, never about Pleasure. Desire has an epistemic dignity. Pleasure does not . . . Our society . . . can produce only epistemologies of the law (and of its contestation), never of its absence or better still: of its nullity.[60]

Unification, order and ordering are at stake here; the ordering and organization not only of thought but also sensibility, wresting it from the realm of 'one's own,' from what consists of pleasure or pain, expansion or contraction, an ever-changing perspective, and returning it to the *continuum specierum* as well as the *continui in natura*.

Can we now think about our poet as someone who abolishes within herself all barriers, all classes, all exclusions? If not by breaking apart the harmonious synthesis of the faculties and being herself broken apart by the continuous movement in which each already disjointed faculty, driven to its limits, communicates the violence of the sensible encounter to the next, thereby generating the free form of difference, awakening the different within that difference, then how? 'By a simple discard of that old specter: logical contradiction,' thus someone who

> mixes every language, even those said to be incompatible; who silently accepts every charge of illogicality, of incongruity; who remains passive in the face of Socratic irony (leading the interlocutor to the supreme disgrace: self-contradiction) and legal terrorism (how much penal evidence is based on a psychology of consistency!).[61]

Such a person, a poet, a woman, would be the mockery of society. But if this poet's place of love and mystery, her deliberate diffusion, her discriminate distress, can be non-isotropic, unpredictable and irregular, but also undistributed, can we account for this? Perhaps it is too late. Dialectics links successive positivities, suffocating anarchy. Irony proceeds from sureity, possession of truth. And violence is a supreme value, well coded, not a matter for knowledge, predicated only on what a pure consciousness can do.[62] Yet, pleasure and pain, diffusion and distress suspend or congeal recognized values – neutering them when to neuter is defined as to castrate, emasculate, fix, geld, spay, or sterilize; no wonder the claim is made that to neuter is the most perverse form of the demonic. Diffusion – distress, expansion – contraction: they are *separatrices* between attractors, a slow-down, no faster than the speed of light. Diffusion – distress, expansion – contraction: minimally, they mark the leap or fall into catastrophe, into the tear; maximally, on a different scale, they are the effects of rays of light, photons unendingly accommodating one another, altering every past, invariably in motion, yet almost always unnoticed, unthought, unfelt, without value, non-isotropic, a vertical din, where each hand skips over the next, a shimmering standpoint. Diffusion – distress, expansion – contraction, carried by the grain of the throat, do not aim for clarity, for translucent thought, but for the theater of sensitivities, pulsional incidents, abrasions, language lined with flesh, the patina of consonants, voluptuous vowels, articulations of the body, the tongue, the ears, eyes, skin and nose, oscillations of light. They are the close-up, where the event breaks apart into a multitude of discrete elements, breath, gutturals, fleshiness, granular and vibrant 'it granulates, it crackles, it caresses, it grates, it cuts, it comes,' such pleasure, such pain, that is diffusion, that is distress.[63] By definition then, each shimmering perspective does not replicate its own past. Each is atopic. In this structure, harmony as well as conflict are meaningless, resulting in neither the intentionality of consciousness nor the meaning of the event. A lightening strike, the past that alters and is altered by the light of events it comes into contact with, mediately and immediately, surely must be able to engage its own 'ideas' beyond 'doxa' (opinion) but also beyond 'paradoxa' (dispute), and also (and this we will examine shortly) beyond fixed social functions and structural functioning insofar as every event allows for the otherwise excluded middle, enjoying both the consistency of an event, but also its collapse and fall as what is today neither true nor false, *may yet* be true tomorrow or false tomorrow, depending on what newly emerging past influences it and intersects with it. Diffusion and distress, expansion and contraction, pleasure and pain may never be joined to the synthesis of the faculties nor to their violence and discord, neither their cause nor their effect. If so, then they are not conditioned by intuition, understanding and reason; they are not reverberations of the original violent encounter with sensibility; they are not faculties driven to the limits of their powers, veering toward the sublime manifold, a pure spatial continuum, they are neither nature nor 'man' but something else.

The dark precursor

Yet, the continuous manifold, that axiomatic expressing sense, generating events, presses on. Its 'neutrality' permits sense to be distributed as the expressed subsisting in propositions and as the event occurring in states of bodies. Surprisingly, however, sometimes, in circumstances not clearly defined, perhaps undefinable in terms of translucence and genesis, sometimes production collapses or the smooth surface of continuity is rent open by explosive forces or by something so negligible as a snag. Then, it is rumored, bodies fall back into their depths, words lose their sense and become nothing but bodily affections, pure sounds. How can this happen? If the univocity of Being inhabits a surface if all heights and depths have been brought to the surface for the sake of ontological intelligibility, how can anything slide off the surface, fall through the topological limit of the skin or fall beneath the neutrality of sense?[64] The word 'metaphysical surface' tells us very little about the boundary between corporeal depth and the distribution of language or expression. The observation that there is a physics of surfaces as the effect of deep mixtures may be 'true.' However, whether or not this or any physics is capable of endlessly assembling the variations and pulsations of the *entire* universe, enveloping them inside mobile limits, remains to be seen. Moreover, what are the implications of the claim that the physics of surfaces is an *effect of deep mixtures*? If such mixtures are actual (real in space and time), and their surface effects are virtual (real but not actual), then do bodies fall back into their depths or are they always already there, expressed on the surface only by means of sense?

The history of philosophy is overrun by themes of heights, depths, surfaces, lateral movements, directionality, symmetry, asymmetry, movement high to low, low to high, levels, layers, interiority and exteriority. This is not accidental. We find ourselves unable to think without such characterizations. We do not know if there is anything to say without these themes, or if they are, at least some of them, absolutely necessary to philosophy. In fact, they are more than themes. They are essential ontological questions. Ontologically, we take our orientation from them, regardless of what we might wish to proclaim regarding the primacy of phenomena. But every idea, every structure and every event has some limit. It is precisely such limits that are of interest here. Ontologically then, the question is, is it possible to recognize these limits, yet to maintain an ontology in which Being is univocal, in which being is said of each and every thing in the same way? Consequently, no hierarchy, no privileged beings.[65] Beginning with the differential continuum, the surface, the transcendental field, the frontier between corporeal depth and language or expression. What are the limits of the surface? On it, something is continuously produced, and produced as a continuum, a process of production, an endless process producing, recording and distributing. Recall the limits of Kant's first critique. We said that speculative pure reason gives way to practical reason, for what matters is what a consciousness can *do*. Thus categories of freedom, which provide an axiomatic for the *acts* of any *intelligible* being, which do not refer to sensible experience nor to theoretical understanding, are now crucial. They *produce* the reality to which they refer; for Kant they produce an intention of the will but one that is removed from human experience, the more pure the better. When a consciousness is unclouded and translucent . . . anything can happen. In the sensible encounter, the faculties are stirred up; they are conflicted and agitated. This, it has been argued, is what puts thought in motion, what frees it from the empirical and from categories, from both resemblance and recognition. Sartre has provided the clue for how to proceed, having argued that the unity given by the *I Think* need not accompany all our representations. The pure transcendent consciousness, no longer burdened with the task of unification, need never be confused with the *I am*. The purely animal will, sensuous and impulsive, pathological and perverse, sets thought in motion only in order to free itself from its affects, its inclinations, its weakness, its depravity, its unworthiness.[66]

Kant has advised us that we can overcome this empirical weakness by looking into the mirror. Looking in the mirror, we see what we cannot otherwise see, not our own reflection, but that of the Ideal, the unconscious that conditions our thought. Visible only through their mirrored reflection, but functioning always, to regulate the understanding and to provide a rule for what are called free acts of the will, Ideas, the concepts of reason, have no object that can be met with in any experience; they are heuristic fictions, thought-entities. When we do think these Ideas, we think something whose propositions are indemonstrable, blind, haphazard, incomprehensible. The discovery of the Ideas of freedom – god, soul, world – is tantamount to the discovery of the unconscious. Laws of nature tell us only what does happen. Laws of freedom *reflect on us*, tell us what ought to happen. The Idea subsumes its object in the form of a single continuity. 'However, while it is true that continuousness must be related to Ideas and to their problematic use, this is on condition that it be no longer defined by characteristics borrowed from the sensible or even geometric intuitions . . . Continuousness truly belongs to the realm of Ideas only to the extent that an ideal cause of continuity is determined.'[67] Neither fixed quantities of intuition, nor variable quantitites in the form of concepts of the understanding operate here. Intuitions are particulars; concepts of the understanding are generalities; both arc cancelled. 'We have passed from one genus to another, as if to the other side of the mirror.'[68]

Forced to its limits, each faculty is disrupted; the unity provided by its transcendental exercise fragments. Without the unity of the *I Think*, each 'representation,' is *not mine*, and the faculty of intuition, rather than identifying, forces sensibility in the apperception of space and time through what is imperceptible, what *it* cannot recognize, that is, the co-existence of contraries. In its confusion it must call upon the faculty of concepts and the faculty of Ideas to pose a problem, to make sense of what is utter nonsense. Thus perplexed, driven by nonsense, the transcendental Idea is aroused, but we have no knowledge of it. Rather, lacking concepts, the imperceptible, the sign brings forth the power of transcendental Memory. Lacking the unity of an *I Think*, lacking any sensible – which is to say, empirical – recognition in a concept, the final faculty comes forth grasping whatever in the world concerns it and brings it into being. What is it that the faculties can do? What faculties can do is a matter of *practical power*, of will, of desire. The power of an *I Think* is an illusion; the power of will freed of the *I Think* is a power that freely produces the world – without subjects, without objects. Only the power of the virtual, the power of abstract production, will itself, desire itself, is real. As ontological forces, the faculties are productive, they produce the reality to which they give sense. Thus, the transcendental Ideas, connection, conjunction, disjunction, derived from the logical categories of *relation* are the modes of production. They connect the part-objects to desiring-machines; they carry out the dis-organization or dis-tribution, and consumation-actualization of the flayed manifold of free will, freed of linear causality. The divine manifold of disorganization and distribution is here to order and organize, to produce both thought and the world, to spit out entities that look like subjects or objects or worlds but are merely effects. God, after all, has already been defined as the pure *a priori* manifold of space, out of which things are determined to coexist in one time through the mutual determination of their position so as to constitute a whole. 'Either here or there,' Kant confirms, each appearance stands *outside* of every other. So if we no longer define the transcendental Idea by characteristics borrowed from sensible or geometric intuitions, then the continuity of the manifold is not given as the pure form of intuition. The continuity of the manifold is given only as the transcendental Idea, the ideal production, the ideal distribution of the disjunctive synthesis in which each *simulacrum* is distributed *without relation to any other*, upon which the ideal free wills are actualized.

It is a sublime Idea, dynamical and distributive, arising not as the ideal of harmony, but as the genetic power of violence, 'the *dark precursor*, enabling communication between difference as such, making the different communicate with difference: the dark precursor is not a friend.'[69] The genetic principle is violence and violence is axiomatic. Not *philo-sophia,* liking wisdom, inclined to wisdom, but *miso-sophia*, hating wisdom, that is to say, embracing disharmony. 'Nature, to be precise, is power. In the name of this power things exist *one by one* without any possibility of their being gathered together *all at once.*'[70] The power of nature is not the Kantian Idea of world; world, like subject, is an effect of the power of nature which is the Idea expressed through disjunctive synthesis. The power of nature is the divine power to break apart anything that has been connected, transforming every 'and . . . and . . . and' into 'or . . . or . . . or.' The remainder is the world, the residuum is the subject, an effect of the intensive states through which it passes. It is the con-junction of fragments, bands of intensity, potentials, thresholds, and gradients; harrowing, emotionally overwhelming, living and consuming every intensity, every affect and percept, living every concept.[71] The great danger here would be slowness. Even the speed of light is slow when speed is everything; speed is nature/god; it is divine energy. Otherwise, the simple connections become unified, part-objects harmonize, habits form, relations appear where previously there were only continuous connections. If nature/god is slow, it falls behind in its divine task, which is to disconnect what has been connected, to keep separate, to tear apart what otherwise might be related. For if sensibility is connected to understanding and understanding is connected to reason, it is a simple matter to conclude that if there is sensibility, then there must also be reason. Then reason will trace its path through the empirical. Then the *I Think* will accompany all of our representations, then we will represent to ourselves a world. But this world would be an illusion and insofar as we live this illusion, its *necessary* and inevitable products are schizo or paranoic or catatonic states, inescapably the effects of the divine manifold's differential distribution, the *axiomatic*, its *axioun*, what is thought to be worthy, what has value.[72] Following from this axiomatic, any being completely cut off from synthesis manifesting a zero degree of desire would fall into catatonia; but to both affirm and deny, to be taken up and connected, then to have those connections torn apart is to live the heroic, human life, the life of Prometheus, torn apart, *disjoined*, every moment of every day, reconnected, *conjoined* by morning, inheritor of a tortured, harrowing world.[73] Nothing in these processes is personal, yet all are real. Given the divine axiomatic, the dark precursor, the violent, disjunctive synthesis, the transcendental Idea that distributes each *simulacra* without relation to any other, 'Our belief in gods rests upon *simulacra* which seem to dance, to change their gestures, and to shout at us promising eternal punishment – in short, to represent the infinite.'[74] What can this portend if not that the transcendental Idea of the world has altered? We are no longer protected from the ravages of the mathematical and dynamical sublime.

So it appears that given the disharmony, the violence that unhinges each faculty, even those not yet discovered, none of these operations will be what it once was. What will be connected? What will be conjoined? And disjunction, will it synthesize either/ors or affirm them all, independently of one another? If thought is truly not to trace a line through the empirical, then everything rises to the surface and the transcendental Idea of the pure *a priori* manifold out of which all things are determined to coexist organizes them all. Denied the satisfaction of repetition, both the understanding and sensibility pose new problems, again and again and again. Just as sensibility fails with respect to recognition, the faculty of cognition fails with respect to representational identity. Pushed to its limits, it must think new concepts; it is the continuous creation of concepts, an agonizing consumption of intensities.[75] What matters is not what an individual *consciousness* can do, but what *does*, what *gives*, what provokes thought and what is thought in a continuous process driven by the dark precursor, the violent axiomatic in which every connection is violently disjoined, then conjoined, oscillating wildly. Clearly, a parallel has been established between the divine productive manifold of desiring-production and forms of social production. But can we claim more? Can we say that the dark precursor inclines us in the direction of Hesiod's somber myth of creation?

> Some say that Darkness was first, and from Darkness sprang Chaos. From a union between Darkness and Chaos sprang Night, Day, Erebus, and the Air.
>
> From a union between Night and Erebus sprang Doom, Old Age, Death, Murder, Continence, Sleep, Dreams, Discord, Misery, Vexation, Nemesis, Joy, Friendship, Pity, the Three Fates, and the Three Hesperides.
>
> From a union between Air and Day sprang Mother Earth, Sky, and Sea.
>
> From a union between Air and Mother Earth sprang Terror, Craft, Anger, Strife, Lies, Oaths, Vengeance, Intemperance, Altercation, Treaty, Oblivion, Fear, Pride, Battle; also Oceanus, Metis, and the other Titans, Tartarus, and the three Erinnyes, or Furies.
>
> From a union between Earth and Tartarus sprang the Giants.[76]

Every union is undone by its own discordant productions; for every connection, a disjunctive synthesis emerges to separate each event, both from its sense and from other events, destroying codes, pushing ahead of itself the detritus of life, actualizing it as pure value, the value of savagery, tyranny or capital.

Are discord and violence one with the real? Consider the social production of capital, with its own dark precursor, the axiomatic that breaks apart every connection in order to capitalize it, to value it in terms of money and nothing but money. Is this violence the inevitable and necessary outcome of divine disjunction? Certainly, if this is the case, then the synthesis of schizos and of an axiomatic of abstract quantities (money) that keeps moving further and further in the direction of the deterritorialization of the socius, destroying all connections, unleashing free will, producing isolated bodies and nonsignifying sense, then that too is real, all of it.[77] Perhaps this is why 'no political program will be elaborated within the framework of schizoanalysis,' the *miso-philosophe* does not mix 'himself' up in politics but commits to a mechanical view of the real, doing away with fear of the gods, who do not exist, as well as fear of punishment in the afterlife, which is a dream, practising cheerfulness, moderation, temperance and simplicity, in order to live as pleasantly as possible, without illusion, in a world whose continuous production of expression (prospects, functives, percepts, affects, concepts) makes it interesting enough to live in, but whose violent axiomatic makes it ultimately, a world from which one willingly departs.[78]

Mysteries of love

For the poet, this would mean that, what I have suggested assembles an ever-changing perspective, the rays of light, luminescent emanations of stars, planets, clouds, mountains, forests, seas, plants, animals, humans, vast cities, solitary sites, objects, images, sounds, tastes, odors, caresses – all – all would be illusion. Instead of shimmering light, she would be the effect of dispersed and dispersing intensities, partial, fragmented and fragmenting First, the connective syntheses in which what is most her own, her discrete delusions, not yet understood in their spatio-temporalization, will be judged to be partial and no more than partial. Each of these delusions will be connected to something else, something contiguous that interrupts it or draws it off, carrying her self away from herself into new connections. These connections are unanticipated but deemed necessary in order to articulate desire, not her desire, not desire coming through her or from her, not the desire that makes her, but the only kind of desire left to her, desire itself, an immanent binary-linear sphere of possible differentiations. So her little delusion-producing machine is forced to follow the law of connection, the law of desiring-machines. She *feels* something and so must *produce* something; that is the *law*. How is it possible to have such a feeling? The answer to this question might reconnect her to questions about what is 'one's own,' to diffusions in the connections producing this feeling as well as the connections it is determined to pursue under the rule of the dark precursor.[79] For Kant, connective synthesis was defined in terms of the relation of the predicate to a subject or substance. But in the sensible encounter, in the clash with an unrecognizable sign, the being of the sensible defies common sense and good sense, so there will be no subjects and no objects. Subject and object have come undone in the encounter with the coexistence of contraries, the coexistence of more and less in an unlimited qualitative becoming that can be defined as free will or as desire. The transcendental use of categories, that is, their use as Ideas of reason gives reality to the supersensible Ideas of god (the *a priori* manifold) freedom (the unconditioned series), and soul (the cracked *I*). This is not a question of quashing desire; precisely the opposite. It is precisely the encounter with the unrecognizable sign, the chaos of nonsense that signals the univocity of desire, that desire is everywhere and everything, that desire and the unlimited qualitative becoming are one and the same. The manifestations of desire are the effects of distribution since it is distribution that ultimately constitutes the empirical subject whether it is a human being, a work of art, or a social policy.[80] Already for Kant, in the matter of free will, the ground of choice is not empirical. It is an unconditioned practical law, in the face of which every subject is passive.

The distribution of desire is the task of the disjunctive syntheses, set in motion by the (in)sensible encounter to determine the plane, to distribute its events. Disjunctive synthesis might be considered to be the act of god who plunges down from the heights and immediately sets about generating its objects by splitting apart every primitive organization that has sprung up in its absence. The divine power of disjunctive synthesis arrives. The dynamical category of relation breaks up the monotonous binary linearity of the law of connection. The synthesis forestalls what might be considered the false antinomy between the poet's unconscious spatio-temporalization, which is to say, her impulsive and spontaneous eruption into an otherwise undisturbed linear causality, between her otherwise blind sensuous impulses and the forces which might give her a rule she must follow, a purely intellectual determination. In this sense, pleasure can only be the result of the determination of the will by reason and what we will to do can be seen as a *feeling*. Indeed, there is a feeling, a feeling of constraint, of passive restraint that the poet is made to embrace insofar as it is said to produce the same effect as pleasure. No longer blind and slavish, no longer varying and growing, no longer a burden, no longer discontent and out of control, the pleasures of passive restraint will not plague her with any sensuous burden, a burden which would not be commensurate with the pure practical determination of desire, nor with its pure practical creation.[81] In compensation, to resolve the antinomy, she is offered death. She is offered the dark precursor. Of course, death is inevitable but sometimes, there is an appearance of choice with respect to its form. That is not the 'death' being offered here. Whether she wills it or not, whether she thinks it or not, she will be torn apart, she will be Promethean, which is to say, schizo, and if not schizo, then catatonic, neurotic, paranoid . . . always overtaken by the forces through which 'she' passes; affects, percepts, concepts, prospects and functives; she consumes them all and they consummate themselves through her, through her materiality. In this regime, she can only hope for interesting, amusing or remarkable forces, forces that are decoded and deterritorialized; it is always a matter of what a force can do. Thus, the necessity of moving quickly, quickly before these affects, these percepts, these concepts, prospects and functives, these flows are overtaken by the capitalist socius, by the inevitable quasi-causality of the continuous manifold decreeing barbarism, feudalism or capitalism, always some full body ready to appropriate productive forces. Yet, if something else is still possible, if her effective slow-down, her path through wild intersecting separatrices, can release her from the endless mobility of the continuous manifold, and if it is possible to exist on the basis of another scale, a minute and uncertain scale, then something else may be able to be thought and lived. Then she might emerge and re-emerge inside a zone of indetermination. Attracted to or compelled by intimations, as instantaneous as they are unpredictable; radiating from showers of brilliance; diverted and influenced by other brightly glowing rays of light emerging from the past to form and inform her; a swath that is most intimate, most her own, creating a spatio-temporalization shaped as both an intensely private realm, touching the heart, and an extensive, worldly realm open to anyone who is sensible of the wind when it turns on the shore, or anyone who wanders onto the scene where the woman recites these words, wounding herself in an interval in which love is inseparable from mystery and mystery inseparable from one's own.

Notes

1. Beth Gibbons, 'Mysteries,' from Beth Gibbons and Rustin Man, 'Out of Season' (New York: Systemtactic, 2003).
2. See Immanuel Kant, *Critique of Practical Reason*, tr. Lewis White Beck (New York: Liberal Arts Press, 1956), pp. 74–82, where Kant characterizes our nature as sensuous beings. See also Henri Bergson, *Matter and Memory*, pp. 168–72, Bergson, *Oeuvres*, pp. 307–11, for Bergson's exposition of the ontological unconscious.
3. Jean-Paul Sartre, *The Transcendence of the Ego*, tr. Forrest Williams and Robert Kirkpatrick (New York: Farrar, Straus, Giroux, 1957), p. 34, originally published in French as 'La Transcendance de L'Ego: Esquisse d'une description phénoménologique', in *Recherches Philosophiques*, VI (1936–7).
4. Deleuze, *Difference and Repetition*, p. 145 (189). The dark precursor is the action of forcing faculties to their limits precisely through their disharmony.
5. Kant, *Critique of Practical Reason*, p. 68. The categories of freedom do not need intuitions and so *immediately* become cognitions.
6. Kant, *Critique of Practical Reason*, p. 68. 'The autonomy of the will is the sole principle of all moral laws and of the duties conforming to them . . . The sole principle of morality consists in independence from all

material of the law (i.e. a desired object) and in the accompanying determination of choice by the mere form of giving universal law' (p. 33).

7. Kant, *Critique of Pure Reason*, A67–8.
8. Kant, *Critique of Pure Reason*, A305–10, B362–7. Perhaps we may
infer that the goal of the logical employment of reason is then unity and
not knowledge.
9. Kant, *Critique of Pure Reason*, A79–80.
10. Kant, *Critique of Pure Reason*, A299, B355. 'Following the analogy of
the concepts of understanding, we may expect that the logical concept
will provide a key to the transcendental' (A299, B356).
11. Kant, *Critique of Pure Reason*, A300, B357.
12. Kant, *Critique of Pure Reason*, A321–3. 'A pure concept of reason can
in general be explained by the concept of the unconditioned, conceived
as containing a ground of the syntheses of the conditioned' (A322, B379).
13. Kant, *Critique of Pure Reason*, A79–80, B104–5; emphasis added.
14. 'The relation, therefore, which the major premises, as the rule, represents between what is known and its condition is the ground of the different kinds of syllogism', Kant, *Critique of Pure Reason*, A304, B360.
15. Kant, *Critique of Pure Reason*, A73–4, B98–9. Kant seems to take the
eminent role of syllogisms almost as a given, as if this had been a fundamental axiom from the start.
16. Kant, *Critique of Pure Reason*, A333–6; B390–3 and A176–219;
B218–66. Deleuze refers to these Kantian syntheses in *The Logic of
Sense*, pp. 294–5 (242–3).
17. Kant, *Critique of Pure Reason*, A297; B353. Subjectively necessary,
given the demands of the categories of relation prescribing the alternatives of sense or non-sense.
18. Kant, *Critique of Pure Reason*, A643; B671. Perhaps this may be called
the axiom of housekeeping.
19. Kant, *Critique of Pure Reason*, A647; B675. Norman Kemp Smith
argues that Kant is inconsistent here, first claiming objective reality for
unity after claiming that such principles are merely hypothetical. It may
be that Kant is simply progressing logically from what is hypothetical
to what he argues we must assume in order for reason to be coherent;
Norman Kemp Smith, *A Commentary to Kant's 'Critique of Pure
Reason'* (New York: Humanities Press, 1962), pp. 547–50.
20. Kant, *Critique of Pure Reason*, A649; B677. All this occurs in the name
of a logical axiom, but what principle does this axiom serve?
21. Kant, *Critique of Pure Reason*, A649–52; B677–80. See also Kemp
Smith (p. 551) who notes that by combining homogeneity and specification, Kant obtains continuity.
22. Kant, *Critique of Pure Reason*, A657–60; B685–8. With this is eliminated the possibility of discrete space and time, intrinsic to quantum and
also discontinuity.

23. Kant, *Critique of Pure Reason*, A672, A685; B700, B713. What is at stake here is intelligibility.
24. Kant, *Critique of Pure Reason*, A800–4; B828–32. This would be, I think, cognitive unworthiness and, only secondarily, moral unworthiness.
25. Kant, *Critique of Pure Reason*, A771–3; B799–801. We do not know these rules, but their efficacity is unquestionable.
26. Kant, *Critique of Pure Reason*, A806; B834; emphases added.
27. Kant, *Critique of Pure Reason*, A162–82; B202–24. Literally then, all sensibility ought to be conditioned by this axiomatic.
28. Kant, *Critique of Pure Reason*, A800–4; B828–32. So the problem becomes, how to become conscious of this rule.
29. Lewis White Beck, *A Commentary to Kant's 'Critique of Pure Reason'* (Chicago: University of Chicago Press, 1966), p. 571.
30. See above, page 00(56); Kant, *Critique of Pure Reason*, A649; B677.
31. Deleuze, *Difference and Repetition*, p. 143, (186–7).
32. Deleuze, *Difference and Repetition*, p. 161 (209–10) For the 'genetic' view, see also p. 162 (210).
33. See Michèle Le Doeuff, *Philosophical Imaginary*, tr. Colin Gordon (Stanford: Stanford University Press, 1989) where Le Doeuff argues that there is no pure rationality, that anything argued in philosophy is embedded in a web of images. In other words, the a-rational determines the configuration of concepts and intellectual strategies. See Le Doeuff, *The Sex of Knowing*, p. 224, n. 49.
34. 'While we were speaking Thrasymachus often started to interrupt, but he was restrained by those who were sitting by him, for they wanted to hear the argument to the end. But when we paused after these last words of mine he could no longer keep quiet. He gathered himself together like a wild beast about to spring, and he came at us as if to tear us to pieces', Plato, *Republic*, tr. G. M. A. Grube, rev. C. D. C. Reeve in *Plato, Complete Works* (Indianapolis: Hackett Publishing, 1997), 336b.
35. 'The sun is not sight, but is it not the cause of it, and also seen by it? – Yes. Say, then, I said, that it is the sun which I call the offspring of the Good begot as analogous to itself. What the Good itself is in the world of thought in relation to the intelligence and things known, the sun is in the visible world, in relation to sight and things seen', Plato, *Republic*, 508b–d.
36. Plato, *Republic*, 524e. Without contrariety and contradiction, would Platonic thought have developed?
37. Plato, *Republic*, 509a. See Deleuze, *Difference and Repetition*, pp. 139–42 (182–5).
38. Deleuze, *Difference and Repetition*, pp. 139–40 (182). In spite of Deleuze's critique of Kant, that there is still too much empiricism; although for Deleuze too, the sensible encounter is decisive, only the sensible gives rise to contradiction and non-sense.

39. Deleuze, *Difference and Repetition*, p. 141 (183–4). It is the same clash as that decried by Plato, but this time without the resolution in harmony.

40. Deleuze, *Difference and Repetition*, pp. 140–1 (183–4). Without this forcing, Deleuze believes that we remain ignorant or minimally habituated.

41. Deleuze, *Difference and Repetition*, pp. 143–4 (186–7). For Deleuze, faculties that are not forced to their limits are condemned to habituation. This transcendental past has been interpreted as a version of Bergson's ontological memory, but how one understands this is entirely a matter of the structure within which it is placed. Here, the structure requires the elimination of temporalization, making time a parameter of space.

42. Sartre, *The Transcendence of the Ego*, p. 32.

43. Sartre, *The Transcendence of the Ego*, pp. 33–40. Such a pure consciousness has no need of realization and ceases to be pure if realized.

44. Deleuze, *Difference and Repetition*, p. 168 (218). Deleuze cites Kant, *Critique of Pure Reason*, Introduction, p. 57.

45. Deleuze, *Difference and Repetition*, pp. 168–9, (218–20).

46. Sartre, *The Transcendence of the Ego*, pp. 36–42, 43.

47. Deleuze, *Difference and Repetition*, p. 169 (219–20).

48. Gilles Deleuze, *Kant's Critical Philosophy, The Doctrine of the Faculties*, tr. Hugh Tomlinson and Barbara Habberjam (Minneapolis: University of Minnesota Press, 1984), pp. 15–16, originally published as *La Philosophie critique de Kant* (Paris: Presses Universitaires de France, 1963), pp. 24–5.

49. Deleuze, *Difference and Repetition*, p. 169 (220).

50. Sartre, *The Transcendence of the Ego*, p. 43.

51. See Hume, *A Treatise of Human Nature*, 'Simple perceptions or impressions and ideas are such as admit of no distinction nor separation. The complex are the contrary to these, and may be distinguished into parts', p. 2. See also Deleuze, *Difference and Repetition*, pp. 169, 170 (219, 220–1).

52. Kant, *Critique of Pure Reason*, Transcendental Deduction (B): A145, B185.

53. Kant, *Critique of Pure Reason*, A77, B103.

54. Kant, *Critique of Pure Reason*, Transcendental Deduction: A98–111.

55. Kant, *Critique of Pure Reason*, A112.

56. Deleuze refers to this as good sense and common sense which together yield recognition, *Difference and Repetition*, pp. 133–4 (174–5). He also argues that, transcendental claims aside, Kant derives the synthesis in a purely psychologistic, empirical manner. This would imply that the universal is far from assured in the case of recognition (p. 135 (176–7)).

57. Kant, *Critique of Practical Reason*, pp. 100–1.

58. Gilles Deleuze and Félix Guatari, *Anti-Oedipus*, tr. Robert Hurley, Mark Seem, and Helen R. Lane (Minneapolis: University of Minnesota Press, 1987), pp. 2, 3, originally published as *Anti-Oedipe* (Paris: Les Éditions de Minuit, 1972), pp. 7, 8. For Kant, connection produces a substance by relating concepts, while conjunction produces a world by relating propositions.
59. Kant, *The Critique of Pure Reason*, A660; B688.
60. Roland Barthes, *The Pleasure of the Text*, tr. Richard Miller (New York: Farrar, Straus and Giroux, 1975), pp. 57–8, originally published in French as *Le Plaisir du texte* (Paris: Éditions du Seuil, 1973), pp. 91–2.
61. Barthes, *The Pleasure of the Text*, p. 3 (9–10). See also Deleuze, *Difference and Repetition*, pp. 144–5 (188–9).
62. Barthes, *The Pleasure of the Text*, pp. 36–7, 44 (60, 71).
63. Adapted from Barthes, *The Pleasure of the Text*, pp. 12, 65–7 (22–3, 103–05). Barthes, of course, only concerns himself with the *pleasure* of the text. I extend this to pain beyond the text to the world. This anticipates, I believe, Barthes' own move in *Camera Lucida*. Moreover, rather than limit the discussion to the concepts of pleasure and pain, already so circumscribed and coded in every philosophical text, I will sometimes use the terms diffusion and distress, expansion and contraction.
64. Deleuze, *The Logic of Sense*, p. 125 (150–1). For sense in relation to bodies and to language, see my *Gilles Deleuze and the Ruin of Representation*, pp. 214–25. On the 'neutrality' of sense, see Alain Badiou, *Deleuze: The Clamor of Being*, p. 34. For the relation between bodily sounds and language, see my 'Writers are dogs, on the limits of perception for thought', in *Crossings*, No. 4 (Fall 2001).
65. I have discussed univocity in *Gilles Deleuze and the Ruin of Representation*, pp. 22–8 and 138–9.
66. See above. Kant, *Critique of Pure Reason*, A800–4; B828–32.
67. Deleuze, *Difference and Repetition*, p. 171 (222–3). Thus, Ideas cannot be known by any empirical means. The Idea of the continuous manifold is a pure universal and we pass from one genus to another *as if to the other side of the mirror.*
68. Deleuze, *Difference and Repetition*, p. 171 (222–3). Thus, the universal can consist neither of particulars nor generalities. What is left?
69. Deleuze, *Difference and Repetition*, p. 145 (189). Thus, the dismissal or overturning of the Platonic friendship in philosophy, a friendship calling for harmony and unity. See Deleuze and Guattari, *What is Philosophy?*, pp. 2–6 (8–11).
70. Deleuze, *The Logic of Sense*, 'The simulacrum and ancient philosophy', pp. 266–7 (307–9). Nor can things be united in any combination adequate to Nature which would then express them all at once.
71. Deleuze and Guattari, *Anti-Oedipus, Capitalism and Schizophrenia*, pp. 19, 20 (26). Deleuze and Guattari attribute the idea of consumption

of intensities to Antonin Artaud. On this point, I demur. See Antonin
Artaud, 'Le pèse-nerfs', in *Oeuvres complètes* (Paris: Gallimard, 1956),
vol. 1, p. 112.

72. See 'axiology' and 'axiom' in *Webster's New Universal Unabridged
Dictionary* (New York: Simon and Schuster, 1979).

73. Eugene Holland, *Deleuze and Guattari's Anti-Oedipus* (London:
Routledge Press, 1999), p. 35. Holland describes catatonia as no syntheses of any kind, paranoia as repelling connective syntheses, and
schizophrenia as affirming both connective and disjunctive synthesis
and therefore the only synthesis that actually produces a subject.
Perhaps it is more accurate to say that schizophrenia is an affirmation
of disjunction and conjunction, the latter being a fragmented, tortured
world, not a connected and coded world.

74. Deleuze, *The Logic of Sense*, 'The simulacrum and ancient philosophy',
p. 277 (321).

75. Deleuze, *Difference and Repetition*, pp. 140–5 (182–9).

76. Hesiod, *Theogony*, 211–12, cited in Robert Graves, *The Greek Myths:
1* (New York: Penguin Books, 1980), pp. 33–4. Erebus, in addition to
being the brother of Night, is the name for the dark passage under the
Earth, between Earth and Hades.

77. Deleuze and Guattari are quite cagey about this. In *Anti-Oedipus* they
state that the parallel between desiring production and social production
is merely phenomenological, that they are not drawing conclusions about
the nature and relationship of the two, and that they are not providing
any sort of *a priori* answer to the question of whether the two are *separate and distinct productions* (p. 10 (16)). Capitalism is clearly identified
as violent in its decoding and deterritorialization (breaking apart all connections) and doing this from within, destroying the coded socius in order
to make it a body without organs (p. 33 (41)). However, it is desire that
produces, real desire or 'the real in itself,' and social processes are among
its productions, thus social and desiring production are the same production, although under two different regimes (pp. 379, 380 (455, 456)).

78. Deleuze and Guattari, *Anti-Oedipus*, p. 380 (456). See also *What
is Philosophy?* for an account of these forms of expression. The pre-
scriptions regarding how to live are the practices espoused by Epicurus.

79. Deleuze and Guattari, *Anti-Oedipus*, pp. 2–7 (7–13); Eugene Holland's
precise and contextualized account of *Anti-Oedipus* points out that the
organ machine is invested with Freudian notions of drive, investment,
cathexis and polymorphous perversity such that it should be defined as
'any partial-object which gives or gets a charge or flow of energy
through a connection', Eugene W. Holland, *Deleuze and Guattari's
Anti-Oedipus*, p. 26.

80. See Kant, *Critique of Practical Reason*, pp. 20–1 and 29–30, where
Kant states that reason is concerned especially with the faculty of desire,

with determining this will according to rules (hypothetical and categorical imperatives) but only insofar as the ground of choice is *not empirical* (thus not in pleasure or pain) but only according to an *unconditional practical law* in relation to which every single subject is passive.

81. Kant, *Critique of Practical Reason*, pp. 118–23.

3

'Love and Hatred'

Love and masochism

The previous chapter began by posing a question. What sensibility releases the poet to speak, publicly and directly, to admit her vulnerability, to say, 'God knows how I adore life'? What connects her to the realm of the sensible, to what she calls 'mysteries of love'? Is her departure from the spheres of good sense and common sense an affirmation of the nonsense that is their foundation? Or, does she resolve her separateness, does she slow her cognitive or active response to perception by opening herself to her own pleasure and pain, her discrete diffusion and distress, her multiple networks of influences, thereby departing from the only scale on which autonomy is possible? Is she spinning into another structure of relations, a structure that is finite yet lingers, that is almost transparent to its past and the past of the world; a structure that precipitates a distinct point of view, an absolutely new spatio-temporalization, not merely a continuous, smooth transition? Philosophers may have some difficulties accepting this. Hume has shown us that impressions and ideas of relations (resemblance, contiguity, causality) organize the mind, but that they constitute an autonomous logic; they are the manner in which the mind passes from one term to another. In this they provide the mind with constancy or universality; the association of ideas allows the mind to go beyond any contingently given experience and to connect it to an other contingently given experience, whether or not this is warranted. For Hume, the Ideas of self, world, and god are the effects of these distinct impressions; they are the illusions, connected by imagination.[1]

That the system of cognition is ruled by illusion and belief scarcely matters, since reason's principle purpose is not the production of knowledge but, as Hume reminds us, to serve the passions. But here too, human nature appears unworthy. Love and hatred are characterized, along with passions like grief and joy, pride and humility, as two among the violent passions. These passions appear to us to be violent because they arise directly from or in relation to pleasure and pain. Insofar as the etiology of such pleasures and pains may be illusory and steeped in misunderstanding, we might wish to be particularly attentive to the difference between the *quality* of pleasure and pain operating on the body as opposed to the *subject* on which it is placed. Contrary to expectations, it does not seem to be another person or object that causes passion.[2] The *object* of love or hatred *is* another thinking person, a person with sensations, reflections and actions of which, it seems, we cannot be conscious. Love and hatred themselves, it is argued, originate with *our own* sensation, insofar as they are inextricably linked to pleasure and pain, and pleasure and pain are *one's own*. Simply stated, the bodily sensation of love is whatever is agreeable, perhaps extremely agreeable, and the bodily sensation of hatred is whatever is not. So the claim that, on a bodily or affective level, pleasure causes love and pain causes hatred accounts for the relative violence of these passions; they are directly caused by the impressions which we feel with the greatest force.[3] What this implies is that unlike principles of association which allow the imagination to connect anything with anything and so easily fall into illusion, passions, especially violent passions like love and hate, restrict the mind. Love and hate, the violent passions, are thought to be directed to the objects closest to us, assuming that whatever is closest would produce the strongest sensation in us; so those objects, whose own sensibilities may well remain opaque to one's own, nonetheless gain privilege.

If this is so, if love and hate are felt but felt only in relation to the proximity of some constant cause, then why are love and hate not contingently apportioned by imagination like any other impression? Ideas include nothing more than what is contained in sensory impressions insofar as relations are external and heterogeneous to their terms. Association establishes relations that are purely external to the terms it relates, even though, in doing so, association exceeds the givens of experience.[4] But love and hate, and the passions in general, do not. It is difficult to accept the claim that love and hate arise as relations external to the terms they relate because if they did, then it might happen that anyone could love or hate and be loved or hated by anyone else. All that would be required is physical proximity. Clearly this is not the case. Love and hate seem to be something other than proximity effects, for love and hate appear to involve something like what are called internal relations, some connection whose terms are not contingently external with respect to one another, some sensible affection that is not opaque but nearly transparent. Of course, if

Hume is right that one loves what is closest to oneself, then passions *are* mere proximity effects and nothing more. But is this so? Is this what the poet calls 'mysteries of love'? If love and hate are external relations, an effect of proximity, then would it be possible for anyone to stop loving someone they once loved, or to stop hating once they hate while remaining in proximity? Would we not love or hate, not only our partners, parents and children, but also co-workers, employers, employees, neighbors, cashiers, bus drivers, waiters, teachers, anyone with whom we have external but proximate relations? How then can we maintain the idea that love and hate and other violent passions are external? Are we not encouraged by these questions to seek out other solutions, other structures?

Hume commits himself to the position that whoever is connected to us receives our love in proportion to that connection *without enquiring into his other qualities*. But what is the nature of this connection? Is it nothing more than contiguity in space and time, simple immediacy? Searching for some explanation, a sensible interval emerges. It seems that we human beings search continually for amusement and distraction in order to forget ourselves and to excite our spirits. The mind is insufficient; it is not enough and cannot be its own entertainment, and so it seeks foreign objects, objects of whose sensibilities it is declared unable to be conscious. Yet, when such an object appears, the 'mind' awakes as if from a dream, blood flows in with a new tide, the heart is elevated, the whole person acquires some vigor which he or she cannot command in solitary and calm moments. Company, this sensible interval asserts, presents the liveliest of all objects, a rational and thinking being like ourselves. Such a being manages to find a way to *communicate to us* all the actions of her/his mind including the *inmost* sentiments and affections, and miraculously lets us see in the very instant of their production all the emotions caused by any object. All lively ideas are agreeable, all the more those of a lively and entertaining person. This excitement of the spirits, this elevation of the heart, this vigor causes mere ideas to become a passion, to become love, for it gives a strong and sensible *agitation* to the mind.[5] Love and hate do not seem then to be merely external relations of proximity, fascination with the image. Something else incites love; a timebell rings the heart, a wind turns and turns on the shore, a transparent sensibility excites and exhilarates, and all of it is unable to be commanded, unable to be compelled into solitary and calm moments. Perhaps, rather than proximity, contiguity and habit, it is a vulnerable sensibility that opens one to love. And of all the senses, it is the ontological unconscious that is the most intimate and immediate, one's own constantly changing sensibility, the myriad, subtle influences that modulate and modify, shaping our receptivity, illuminating our cognition, inciting our actions. Smell, hearing, sight, even touch are all effects of this sensibility, but coarser, adapted, expectant and therefore perceiving what is expected. Physiologists have defined sensibility in chemical and physical terms, and differentiated it from perception which tends to be addressed in psychological terms. Thus perception is connected to the way in which information gathered and processed by the senses is interpreted, while sensibility is usually identified as sensation and is defined as the process of detecting a stimulus – or some aspect of one – in the environment.[6] Called *sensitivity*, it is described as the capacity of an afferent neuron to detect a physical or chemical change in its endings and to transmit this information to the nervous centers, usually via a chain of neurons. Sensation is then defined as the emergence of such sensitivities into consciousness. It is significant that sensation is not limited to the habitual five senses as pain, for example, has been shown to be felt from almost any locus in the body, with a few notable exceptions. Physical pain may also be distinguished from pain that is the affective quality of distress – counterpart to the usually pleasant sensation of pleasure. Moreover, pleasure and pain are not the only sensations arising from the body; in principle any afferent pathway is a potential source of sensation. And although it is possible to share with others the pleasantness or unpleasantness of a cause, there is no guarantee that pleasure or pain, diffusion or distress, will likewise be shared.[7] So it is a vulnerable sensibility that emerges new and in the moment with every perception. Perhaps this is why we love, perhaps this is why one says 'I love you.' Of course, for the philosophers, the emergence of new sensitivities may not be what matters. What matters is usually the question of how to extend emotion beyond those objects taken to be closest to oneself, to extend love and hatred beyond privileged objects to society at large, to culture, while preserving them as violently, as vividly as when they were directed to merely proximate persons. What matters is how do we pass from a limited sympathy to an extended generosity, how do we create institutions that persuade or force the passions to go beyond their partialities and to form moral, judicial, political sentiments such as the idea of justice?[8] The project of translating love into justice clings tenaciously to philosophy.

It is no secret that from Plato to the present, philosophers have worked tirelessly to detach love from the mystery of 'one's own' and that on this basis, philosophical discussions of the ideas of love have incited a certain degree of uneasiness and panic, leading to unhappiness and policing by philosophers. Love, especially sexual love, is frequently understood to be an emotion that disrupts or limits the individual's commitment to the active, public sphere, returning humans to the deplorable domain of what is wholly 'one's own'. And 'one's own,' without hesitation, is overwhelmingly characterized in negative tones as passive, personal, promiscuous, private, so disordered and indiscriminate that it condemns its intimates to nothingness. Plato often cautions against private pleasures and pains, arguing that the realm of the senses is the realm of one's own, that it is not only a threat to the well-being of the city but also to the individual's intellectual soul. Others must also be protected against this threat, so the philosopher imagines a city in which all women live a purely public life as wives in common to all men and no woman is the property of any single man although women remain the property of the city.[9] Men and women live communally and eat communally. No one has private property, nothing is 'one's own.' Yet it seems that the citizens, especially the women, ask for more. Thus there is a constant threat, the threat that a powerful obstacle to the attainment of harmony will surface. The threat lies in the suggestion that what cannot be taken away and held in common is intimacy, the 'inborn necessity to have intercourse with one another.'[10] Glaucon attempts to advance this idea to Socrates, arguing that the necessity of sexual intimacy is not mathematical but erotic and must, inevitably, be considerably more forceful in persuading and compelling the mass of the people. A mathematical or rigorously dialectical formulation of love would appeal, minimally, to right opinion, to public discussion or debate, and finally to the quest for universal truths, but sexual intimacy would seem to be thoroughly embedded in the passive, personal and promiscuous realm of appetites and attraction, a mysterious arena, immune to the law of non-contradiction. Unmoved, unconvinced of this immunity, Socrates permits himself to operate with the assumption that promiscuity is inextricably linked to *proximity*, and that what *he* desires proximately is available. What he *desires* is to prohibit promiscuity as impious and indiscriminate. So he desires to make marriage as sacred as possible, cautioning that sacred means discriminate, and implying that whatever discriminates is beneficial, that whatever separates citizens is advantageous, never to one's own, but to the city. Thus public life supplants one's own promiscuous inclinations, meaning one's proximity relations, and only after child-bearing years will inhabitants be granted an interval in which to engage in their own pleasures and pains. Only then will they be released from public duties to their own dissolution and distress, able to fall in love indiscriminately, to finally ask for nothing more.[11]

Still, it is questionable that inhabitants will finally be sanctioned to enjoy 'their own' inclinations, inclinations that are less and less likely because only *common* feelings bind the city together. Isolated and private feelings dissolve the city's unity, harmony and intelligibility. Moreover, it appears that feelings, in particular, are defined as completely private phenomena, unrelated to the network of sensible influences coming from others and from the world. Defined as private, the very idea of *common feelings* becomes impossible if not absurd, for passions, as purely private, are thought to restrict particularly the range of mind and to fix *privileged* ideas and objects, and are therefore prohibited. Words like 'mine' and 'not mine' or 'another's' are distinctly problematic. This is because, in the realm of right opinion, they are needed, they are necessary to establish logical distinctions, to affirm non-contradiction, but their implications, when they seep into the intimate realm of one's own sensibility, are disturbing. Private sensibilities, pleasure and pain, diffusion and distress, would be permitted only if they were able to be distributed so that whatever happens to any citizen, good or bad, could be shared with all who dwell within the city's gates. Yet, since passions are defined as purely private, all citizens are fettered, restrained from contemplating private misfortunes or tragedies, frustrated from any attempt at activities whose pleasure promiscuously (indiscriminately) veers away from the good of the harmonious city and its souls. They are, and must be, emotionally bankrupt, they must perceive, think and act, nothing more. The separation of men and women, and of men and women from their own children, is only the start. The prohibition on privileged ideas and objects extends to houses or land or any type of possessions, since one 'man' calling anything his own, not merely property but also wives and children, ideas and sentiments, instantiates private pleasures, private pains and private perspectives both material and immaterial.[12] Individuals may own nothing, nothing but what cannot be removed in the final instance, one's own sensibility and the influence of a multiplicity of events in the world on one's own sensibility, an influence that is taken to be so chaotic as to reduce perception to nothingness and the mind to sophistry. In the effort to still this influence, everything else will be held in common, sparing citizens the dissension and remorse that comes with possession, especially

violence and anger as they arise from personal disputes over ownership, and jealousy provoked by erotic and intellectual passions. For
these reasons, prohibiting one's own promotes a stable and moderate
life and is the path to happiness.[13]

Even in modern and contemporary philosophy, love and hate, if it
they are discussed at all – and most often they are not – are evaluated
and classified largely in disconcertingly Platonic terms as active and
passive, public and private, terms that over and over lead to an
impasse. Michèle Le Doeuff cites the essays on marriage that John
Stuart Mill and Harriet Taylor wrote for one another, 'each text a gift
of love designated for just one person and not for the printing press,'
although only Taylor addresses Mill directly as 'you' while Mill refers
to no one in particular.[14] Purportedly in love with a feminist, Mill, in
1832, cannot yet fully imagine emancipation for women. Although he
anticipates that laws governing love between men and women must be
made by both, yet it remains the male's right to synthesize the two.
This, as Le Doeuff points out, is consistent with his position elsewhere,
that women are intuitive while men are theoretical. Since intuition is
aligned merely with the perception of facts, it appears that in theoriz-
ing, men do not possess the facts they might need. Their theories seem
to function independently of facts, yet the man in love with a woman
remains irrevocably responsible for the theoretical exposition of his
lover's intuitions, no less, as we will see, than for the theoretical exposition of her consciousness.[15] This is a peculiar situation since, as Le
Doeuff also points out, in the history of philosophy intuition was once
assumed to be an important and valid mode of knowledge in its own
right. Intuition was thought to function in cooperation with other
kinds of thought and even to be the best possible form of knowledge,
that which either sets thought in motion or completes it.[16] Yet, by the
time Hegel wrote the *Phenomenology*, intuition had been replaced by
conceptual labor and intuition itself was discredited, characterized as
immediate knowledge, perception or mere sensibility *without* knowledge, that which does not know itself – like plants which consist of
beautiful thoughts but no knowledge – it is that which is wholly one's
own. And since Hegel is explicit that women correspond to plants, is
it so difficult to conclude that women uniquely make use of intuition,
a now discredited way of knowing?[17] Thus we move from love to
women, to intuition, to one's own.

More recently, we are shocked to find Simone de Beauvoir characterizing love as 'the woman's whole existence' chosen by most
women, even if they can chose independence.[18] In love, the woman

100

gives up all hope of transcendence and subordinates herself to the other, to the point of masochism. For his part, the man may exhibit jealousy, but only insofar as he possesses a will to exclusive possession of the woman as an object. Nonetheless, Beauvoir holds out for the prospect of 'genuine love,' in which 'neither would be mutilated . . . For the one and the other, love would be a revelation of self by the gift of self and enrichment of the world.'[19] She theorizes that love may have a transformative effect for men who affirm themselves and find themselves altered by the experience of love. 'Woman' is the means by which 'man' gains knowledge, knowledge of himself and of the world around him, but this will never be the case for woman, Beauvoir maintains, until woman is fully independent, economically and existentially, moving toward her own ends, transcending herself.[20] Although it is anecdotal, it may be significant that Beauvoir lived most of her life in public, writing her books in cafes, living in hotels, meeting with friends and lovers in restaurants.[21] Her novels are full of thinly disguised versions of women and men who were her friends, lovers and admirers as well as enemies and jealous rivals. For her, active, public life seems to have subsumed any possible private and passive life, and she is thoroughly dismissive of receptivity and the entire sphere of one's own.

Surprisingly, Sartre attenuates the private-public dichotomy when he refers to love in its most ideal form as 'an organic ensemble of *projects toward my own possibilities*,' a construct which appears to rend open the previously impermeable boundary between the passive, personal and promiscuous, the place of love and the so-called public world, shared and harmonious or shared and tumultuous.[22] Much depends on the framework within which projects toward one's own possibilities are posited. It might be the case that such a love, with its emphasis on transcendence in the direction of one's own possibilities, is simply another version of self-love. 'Falling' in love might turn out to be a situation akin to the concern of the ancient Greeks, for whom, it has been argued, wild eros creating havoc was not problematic; rather, they were troubled by self-love. Human beings, 'launching into love,' in and from their 'self-investment or self-preoccupation,' are 'fixed on their own egos and full of grandiose fantasies about themselves and their power over others; or they are fixed on their own superegos and full of fantasies about how grandly they suffer and must bear the suffering of the world; or they are fixed on their own bodies in the manner of hypochondriacs.'[23] In this case, the beloved is an 'Echo' who repeats the acts and words of the self-absorbed lover.

The lover produces a new version of her/himself who loves as she/he loves and on her/his terms.[24] Or, equally likely, transcendence in the direction of one's own possibilities might be another means by which an individual is transmitted from nothingness and non-being, a seemingly obscure, private and passive realm, into the lighted but still dim world of an objectified in-itself, and finally into the glow of the public, active world of choice. This kind of love would again take the form of a transit, a passage, an escape from the realm of the sensible and the indiscrimination of promiscuity, the messy fluidity of sexual contingency and intellectual sophistry where influences are multiple, connected only by the mystery of love.

In spite of appearances, the attempt to probe the connection between love and one's own is not a matter of arguing over interpretations of Plato, Taylor and Mill, Hegel, Beauvoir, Sartre or any other philosopher. It is much more a question of the spinning, spatializing and temporalizing relations between points of view, information in motion, traveling, state to state, relational, but not deterministic. Can we ever know, on this day and in this time, from where, out of what discrete but combinatorial influences we intuit and conceptualize love? What is its relation to 'one's own'? What sensibilities are spinning into these concepts and what emerges out of this relational network of confluences? What concepts, what teaching, what lives combine, are taken up, spun, tossed, reeling, always on the move, at speeds slow enough to be absorbed and intuited yet fast enough not to be perceived and understood? In this foraging about, any beginning may seem to be arbitrary, yet the beginning need not be unmotivated; it is a complicated perspective, absorbing and emitting rays of light near and far, making possible the intuition of one's own influences. If we absorb and intuit, we are also effusions, every one of us, richly textured combinations of circumstances, incidents, ideas, so many images, so many states spinning toward us, toward one's own panorama, then radiating away from ourselves, a spectacle linked to all the others. And inevitably, given that we are not alone, some past states, some combinations oscillate among multiple perspectives, linking them together.

Given that we are not alone, *we are ourselves a crowd*, influenced by other crowds who are themselves linked to others and others again, other crowds and other states. We have seen that good sense and common sense tend toward consistency and uniformity, but is this not a struggle? Do we not pay for this with our lives, by which I mean, more than old age, do we not die from the struggle for consistency?

Can we expect more from the plane of immanence where we are first assembled, then brutally torn apart, tossed in every possible direction, then reorganized so as to be torn apart again? On this plane, there is no struggle, but also no spatialization, no temporalization; dilution and distress, beauty and ugliness, transparency and light are nowhere. There, everything is grey, grey, grey. Moreover, on those planes, we wander alone, love and hate do not avail themselves of us. We have noted (in Chapter 1) how the *a priori* possibility of the Other is the stage upon which real characters or variable subjects are actualized as expressions of that field and do not exist outside of that field. On this scale, when an Other appears in the midst of the possible world they express, any 'I,' as the expression of a different possible world, must be first be annihilated; the hope for intimate relations fades into shadows and mist. Yet, none of these structures comprises unalterable truths; they merely inform us of the limits of imagination, understanding and reason. Contemporary epistemologies and ontologies, both those in service to social and political power and those opposed to any system of domination, those advocating the disassembling of all codes, remain committed to structures enacting visibility and unconcealment, turning away from interiority, the unperceivable, the ungraspable, seeking also the elimination of heights and depths.[25] Rather than targeting specific groups who may be empowered to disclose, disseminate or divulge, the unperceived and unknown themselves are now pulled from hiding. If every event is brought to the surface, there to be connected, disjoined and split apart, and ultimately reconnected to something new, then intensive force is differentiable from so-called terrorist activity only in its bloody and deadly details. Both are indiscriminate in their violence, no matter how cautious. One cannot simply destroy the codes of others without also destroying one's own and vice versa.

If it is the case, however, that new faculties can arise and take shape, then perhaps we will be fortunate and some new senses will emerge and engage us in the form of faculties for which our sensory organs – although not necessarily our sensibilities – are currently too coarse. Such faculties, elusive and subtle, might arise out of the realm of the sensible on another scale; they might provide us with the opportunity to depart from the continuum of violence, the game of eluding death, the infinity of affects, percepts, concepts, prospects and functives, where faculties are broken apart and forced to their infinitesimal limits. Of course this is not easy. The absorption, emission and intuition of states, of overlapping influences structured in relational networks, makes them the focus of hesitation, the slow-down that allows for the emergence of some glimmering light, and this obliges us to have more than new ideas. Ostensibly new ideas are often nothing more than disguised and deflected variations of existing structures or orders. Thus rather than commencing with unique but fully-formed ideas, sensibility and intuition might be attended to – hesitation might be the necessary condition of alternative structures – partial, disordered and originally indiscriminate modes of sensibility might yield new ideas or even ideas inconceivable in the existing structures. If the absorption and emission of sensibles yielding pleasure and pain, love and hate, effects of diffusion and distress, of one's own, could begin far from ideal projects – it might be initiated by the most subtle data, that which is transparent, ephemeral, the data of light, of glittering, relational networks passing from state to state. Dimension-independent relational structures might send out their shoots, from a still illuminated past into a radiant present, influencing, informing, spinning out along innumerable networks, engaging and emanating, sending both the information we have absorbed and that which we radiate though our interactions. It may be that once these ideas were conceived of as belonging to an epistemology of impressions, impressions of sensations and reflections on those sensations. The limit of this structure of external, proximate differentials lies in the manner in which it circumscribes encounters, restricting them to singular events that resemble, connect, are conjoined to or disjoined from one another: subject – object, male – female, here – there, mother – child, mouth – breast; connections that are no less mechanical than that of plug – socket or mortar – stone.[26] But the myriad rays of light, illuminating and influencing events, when they are not completely imperceptible, tend to exert their influence unnoticed, even in the midst of our participation in them. Given that such relational networks are vast but not infinite and always subject to alteration from out of the past, we can see how easily we might be misled about our ownmost sensibilities and faculties, our own stories and histories. Mostly we feel joy and happiness when we are expected to, and we feel sorrow and sadness when it is required of us. Illuminating an interruption or an interval in which we can slow down or refrain from these demands is exhausting and troublesome; fragile states require separation and cushioning.

Imagine then a student, still a young woman, but one who became a philosopher, who expressed skepticism when her professor effused over the edifying sacrifices of women intellectuals.[27] Advised, by the same professor, not to tax herself with Kant who is difficult and whose morality is not a matter of edifying sacrifices but requires heroic gestures of thought, the philosopher finds, for reasons which are unjustifiable, that the prohibition remains startlingly effective. Why, we wonder, given her general audacity, her lack of respect for the professor and his interdiction, why in all her years since leaving that teacher and that school has she still not read this text? The philosopher is concerned with the strength of the prohibition, the educators who clearly judged that girls behaving badly is a disruptive and disturbing norm, but a norm nevertheless covering an enormous range of behavior from not sitting straight, to speaking in slang, to making noise, to engaging in wanton sex.[28] The promiscuity of all these acts was to be guarded against; the female students were to be prevented from engaging in such dissipative acts and were given no positive replacements for their deprivations. The shocking discovery that the philosopher finds in Rousseau's *Emile* that 'girls must be restricted early' in their language, manners and bodies, in their sexuality, in their sensibility, still does not convince her that the prohibition, the interdiction is powerful enough to keep her in her place.[29] And she is right. For it appears that she has been bounded by something else, by the general admonition against one's own, by the admonition to engage in no behavior that is not able to be construed directly and immediately as taking place for the public good. Yet, reading these lines, this fearless and unstinting account, there is perhaps another question that might be asked, the same question that was asked about the poet. What sensibility releases one who is a philosopher to avow, openly and publicly, 'I have never read the *Critique of Pure Reason*'? How private, how personal is this admission, trembling through the words of the philosopher.

This sensibility, intimate, passionate, is also a transcendence. This would not be transcendence through affirmation, choice, knowledge or action, but a transcendence through what has been called, 'uncertainty.' When some elusive sensibility, some pleasure or pain, some diffusion or distress influences a person and is absorbed and acceded to in a moment of hesitation, an interruption between perception and action, something entirely new may arise, a new relation mixing diffusion, distress, hope and fear. Granted the strength of philosophical prohibitions in the realm of the passions, the realm of passivity, the private and singularly personal, such acknowledgment, if it is possible at all, would have to take place in some obscure interval, in some normally unacknowledged hesitation between our receptivity, the

combinatorial relations, connecting us to a multiplicity of perspectives and states in our world, and our fascinated but characteristic
responses to those intrusions and the intuitions they might give rise
to. Yet, such hesitation is precisely what our perception and understanding, our continuous connections, our affects, percepts, concepts,
prospects and functives, our reasoned but circumscribed modes of
sensation, perception and thought block. So the idea of love and its
relation to one's own may entice us with conceivable new theoretical
combinations but are we able to immerse ourselves in these influences
and images when we absorb them, and ourselves emit other newly
combined influences and images? What we absorb is always multiple,
inextricable from the causal networks giving rise to it; what we emit
is always multiple, each state being made up of a host of influences.
We should not be surprised that even the most volatile, explosive ideas
involve a sensibility that we may call 'one's own.' If combinatorial networks make us, they also make our ideas, images, perceptions, states,
effects of the mingling of the multiplicity of pasts, pasts constructing
new spaces and new times as they mingle and mix. If this is what life is,
if this is what thinking is, then the incapacity to think and live in this
way will certainly throw us back into the orthodox and classical realm
of mechanized repetition or quasi-deterministic planes of immanence.
If we do not intuit or otherwise grasp the influences and images, we
may nevertheless act on them, but we act blindly and unfeeling, failing
to absorb the complicated geneses, the effects of contingent but motivated associations, the role they play in our intuitions and in our pursuits. Thus if within the context of transcendence, the ideal transit
toward one's own possibilities, 'love' seems to be impossible outside
of the relation to an Other only in the most 'primitive' dimensions,
those of direct connection with the Other as affective-sensory being,
and not in the transcendence-constituting realm oriented by absorption, emission and intuition, then it is clear that we have barely begun
to evoke and engage with these sensibilities.

If the Other as an affective-sensory being is passive and promiscuous, erogenous and disordered, emerging always out of chance combinations and transparent influences, then the Other is indiscriminate,
not a being at all in the sense that she/he is not yet either an in-itself
or a for-itself. In a certain sense, she/he is not even a body. She/he
is not organized and integrated; lacking identity; she/he is an interactive circulation of states, absorbing and emitting information on
relational networks that spatialize and temporalize as they spin into
multiple perspectives, then spin away again, into the world. This is

evidenced in the concept that for an ordered and organized subject, a free transcendence, impassioned and affective connection with the Other as a free and independent being, and not as a sensory-affective, spatializing-temporalizing perspective, leads to conflict. This is not because love is nothing more than the raw demand for physical possession. Such possession would amount to little more than ownership, a mechanical arrangement easily obtained by those with power, wealth or the capacity to induce or command proximity by whatever means available, psychical, chemical or intellectual. Neither is love an act of perfect freedom. To be loved because one's qualities conform to a list of ideal merits, or simply because the Other has run out of options, amounts to no love at all. What is called love, if it is true love, must be pure, volatile, exhilarating. But this pure love is posited as the curtailment of freedom precisely insofar as when in love, the lover seems to accept a limit on her/his transcendence, on her/his access to the world and to all the objects, persons and acts possible in that world. Infinity and the infinitesimal are no longer thinkable. Loving in this pure way, the lover risks returning her/himself to the status of a possession. In seeking to be the whole world for the Other, the lover may become a thing standing in for all the things in the world, which is to say an object.[30] Although this object may be chosen, indulged, cherished and adored, nonetheless, within the confines of this structure, the wish to attract the Other, to fascinate the Other, to hold the Other in one's orbit in order to become a beloved and desired object, virtually eliminates all existing and new relations with the world. The lover rotates round and round the same point of attraction, profoundly limiting her/his trajectory and exposure to the infinity of percepts, affects, concepts (prospects and functives being less likely to come into play here). Likewise the acts of the avowedly fascinating being must somehow be confined, not to that private and personal but still promiscuous world, a network of relations, but to the world constituted in the slender trajectory between the lover and the beloved.

If the disordered and indiscriminate nature of a relational affective-sensory, spatializing-temporalizing being must be transformed into a unilateral relation between lovers, these trajectories, with their attractors and repellers, are quasi-deterministic histories, connected, torn apart and conjoined in accordance with the supervenience of the public demand for harmony and intelligibility. Love must be justified, so rumors fly. 'Tell us, what do you see in her?' or 'Don't you think he is just looking for security?' or 'Do you think she really loves him?' Love's place in the public realm must take precedence over the disorderly interfaces between lovers and, more pointedly and to its detriment, over the indiscriminate realm of the sensible, the luminous realm of absorption and emissions. Some justification is called for and so one is posited. Perhaps the lover first attempts a circuit in which the beloved becomes the foundation of all meaning and value and the entire public realm is to be judged on that basis alone. But this, in turn, calls for an appeal to a higher order, an ideal of love that legitimates and universalizes the affective bonds. Intellectually this remains a solipsism, not even of two, but merely of one to infinity; not worldly meaning and value, provisional, contingent and capable of vacillation, but infinite meaning and value, evoked by an active process, a becoming, still passively embodied and lived, but as if determined by a higher power, by the very ideal of love. The asymmetry of such a relation is provisional, for the positions and roles of lover and beloved can always be reversed and love, so defined, can also turn into hate. What the ideal implies, however, is that for the one who is loved, all of her/his own possibilities are being fulfilled. Facticity, contingency, love of the world, all evaporate. Imagine the associations, the relations between your own sensibilities and those of other persons, other states and points of view in the world. Speculate on the intersecting influences between yourself and the words you write, the language in which you think, the window out of which you gaze, the rooms through which you make your way, the wind, the sky, the sea, the hill or mountains, the bird gazing from outside through the window, the little ant that makes its way across the sill, the storm that rushes wild into the night. For an ideal of love, all these sensibilities risk becoming irritating reminders of the uncertain universe, the world in which networks of states influence and are influenced by other networks of states giving rise to spatialization and temporalization, selves and others, things and worlds, always in combinations, always relational.[31] In this coupling, love could only imply transcendence if it were to remain open to the vast array of combinations of events and sensibilities in the world, regardless of how partial or ineffectual, how arbitrary and disconnected, only if it were to openly and continuously act and chose to act in the world on the basis of what is given and what it gives. But such activity would not be the ideal love, since ideal love must be a purely active force, doubly transcendent in relation to the primitive dimensions of the sensory-affective realm.

In the end, love is said to have the appearance of an illusion, to be 'a game of mirrors,' a symmetry, an eternal dissatisfaction and deception in which, at best, the partners trade places endlessly, now active, now passive, now subject, now object, now this, now that.[32] Thus discouraged and despairing, the disappointed lovers may make the final plunge into public immanence which is also personal immanence, denying all civic roles, ceasing to act at all, and gravitating toward unanticipated but predictable actualities, masochistic relations. Objectified though still intelligent, the beloved becomes a cherished object, a work of art, fetishized and forlorn:

O rêveuse, pour que je plonge
Au pur délice sans chemin,
Sache, par un subtil mensonge,
Garder mon aile dan ta main.

. . .

Vertige! Voici que frissonne
L'espace comme un grand baiser
Qui, fou de naître pour personne,
Ne peut jaillir ni s'apaiser.

Oh dreamer, that I may dive
in pure pathless delight, understand
how subtly to connive
to keep my wing in your hand.

. . .

Vertigo! How space quakes
like a great kiss, wild
to be born for no one's sake
but can neither spring forth nor be stilled.[33]

Placing himself in the hand of the Other, the lover collapses into the in-itself, total determination from without, complete estrangement and rupture. He becomes an intensive, strongly affected object, 'another fan.' Or, more formidable in her object status, she becomes an assemblage of intensive affects, a sculpted being whose natural habitat is a frozen garden, visible in the harsh light of winter evenings. She produces an inescapable effect on her admirer; he disappears into the dream world, overcome by vertigo, swooning in the face of the Other's powerful intensities, her power to attract or repel. Of course, while the beloved may find pleasure in her/his transformation into a work of art, there is also prostration, the submissive gesture. And conceptually, even in the thrill of transforming love into an idealized work of art and the lover into a subservient creature, this lover remains the masochist of Severin's manuscript, 'Confessions of a Supersensualist,' who pens humiliating lines: 'To love and to be loved,

109

what joy! And yet how this splendor pales in comparison to the blissful torment of worshipping a woman who treats one as a plaything, of being the slave of a beautiful tyrant who tramples one underfoot!'[34]

This idealized, symbolic passivity, replete with irony, is far removed from the pain and perversity of psychoanalyst Wilhelm Reich's masochistic patient, a small child, severely beaten by a vicious father for soiling himself and thereafter given contradictory signals from each parent about the value and role of sensuality.[35] Terrified by his beatings, Reich's patient feared actual castration and so fails to express himself in the idealizing images of the Sartrean masochist for whom the affirmation of intensities and events is always an option and oppression does not exist. For Sartre's and Severin's masochist, the desired woman is a species of ironist, one who simultaneously acts yet remains totally passive, who posits herself in her sexuality and annihilates what she posits in a single gesture. She is not merely a liar. The liar at least participates in the transcendent, cynically affirming a transcendent truth yet negating it in transcendent language, while denying to the world that she/he lies.[36] The desired woman, worse than a liar, is a Platonic sophist who affirms neither what is nor what is not, whose act is only apparently aimed at the truth when in fact it belongs to contradiction, whose irrationality arises from her failure to reflect the standard established in memory by the Idea , and who lacks both knowledge and right opinion; the Idea thus escapes her.[37] So in the Paris of the 1940s or the Athens of 370 BCE, when women fail to meet the expectations of their husbands, dates or physicians for amorous adventures, it is a failure to attain the ideal, a failure to affirm intensities and infinities, a failure to move at infinite speeds, even at the cost of self-destruction.[38] Let us not forget that the female lovers Plato admires are those who edifyingly sacrifice their lives to save the lives of their lovers.

The effect on projective would-be lovers is to force them into a masochistic stance, to make them play the role of the beloved when in fact they would each prefer to be the lover, to put into play the totality of the immanent affective field as a stage on which to perform, as a set of quasi-deterministic axioms, a space-time manifold. In this way, the lover *hopes* to make love exist through others and for others. Objectively the lover is sincere and respectful; objectively, the 'woman' knows the 'man's' intentions toward her; objectively, she knows she will have to 'decide,' (although what is never clearly stated) and also, objectively, it is certain that she ignores the man's urgency.[39] As Le Doeuff has commented, the man's consciousness, which is to say, the transcendental Idea, the plane of immanence, knows better than the woman what she is feeling, thinking, knowing. She forces the man into the situation of playing the masochist because she does not acquiesce to what the man wants, because she exists as a function of his desire, an attractor who disappoints his interest and so fails to be carried away by the ideal.[40] Make no mistake, the dramatic gestures intrinsic to the woman's role must not escape our attention. She is said to be profoundly aware of the desire she inspires; she poses like a statue, stimulating adoration, yet she demands the satisfaction of being addressed in her full freedom. When the amorous man takes her hand, she neither acknowledges this nor pulls her hand away. Instead, she stays her gestures, arresting the moment, taking advantage of the dramatic interruption to increase the element of suspense to the greatest level possible, turning her companion into a victim of her suspension which aims to secure a slow-down to the point of no activity, no animation at all, a paralysis of Platonic reminiscence, transposing the moment into pure fantasy. She begins to speak about herself with great animation, her face flushed, her eyes full of light, her consciousness a display of the greatest possible freedom reaching to accomplish the highest ideal she can aspire to – the separation of her sensuous nature from her intellect, her flesh from her soul. In short, she is icy, she is cruel, she disavows her sensuous nature in order to attain a supremely impersonal sentimentality, the climax of splendor and perfection.[41] But it is an ironic gesture, a sophistic ploy, because she can never escape her flesh, which now is identified with her perspective, just as her perspective is identified with an isolated immanence.

Contemplating her body as if from above, from a higher dimension, the woman reflects on her own flesh as on a passive object whose possibilities have entirely escaped it. The effect of her assumption of the view from above is to reduce the amorous male to existence as mere in-itself, while she divides her own existence between facticity and transcendence, whereas as we noted in the previous chapter, the expectation is that she would privilege the *fact* of consciousness, a translucent consciousness that unifies itself, insofar as what matters is what a consciousness can *do*. The acts of an *intelligible* being *produce* the reality to which they refer. Stubbornly, the icy woman persists. And why? Because, as *Venus in Furs* avows, 'Most men are so common, so lacking in verve and poetry' that she does not think that she could love one above one month.[42] Modern men, she complains, rely on reason alone and so fail utterly to appreciate love as pure bliss and bliss as promiscuity. Having made nature into an enemy, their sensuality is vulgar; they remake the Greek gods into forces of evil and condemn sensuality with threats of damnation. As a purely frivolous woman, she takes love seriously, admiring the sensuality of the pre-Socratic and pre-Christian Greeks, that of pleasure without pain, which is to say, love without masochism.[43] For modern men, love and women are hostile forces to be defended against, in spite of the pleasure they intimate; and they are to be indicted for the pain they incite – they are women behaving badly. This is why the amorous male appears to be subject to the dominating powers of the idealized woman, but in fact it is the so-called masochistic victim who dictates that the woman is merely the first step on the ladder of Diotima. After all, it is Sartre who accuses his Venus of bad faith, who condemns her as a coquette for the sin of contradiction and sophism, for alternately denying both her body and her intellect, for contemplating her sensuous being from above as a passive object whose possibilities escape it even while she functions as an attractor.[44]

Love and one's own

Displacement operates everywhere. For philosophers, noble lies are at least a behavior of transcendence, a normal phenomena of *mit-sein* presupposing one's own existence, that of the Other and that of one's self for the Other. It is a project which carries one away with it, whereas the sophist's gestures imply an immersion in the private sphere of one's own and in the personal that is promiscuous, which is to say, *indiscriminate.* In this light, it is literally ironic that Plato posits the prohibition on 'one's own' as his own desire since this seems to break 'his own' rule against asserting that anything, even an idea, is 'mine' or 'one's own.' If the rule against 'one's own' is not arbitrarily applied but is in some sense common, Plato must show in what sense this rule is common and in what sense it is not merely his own desire. This means that with reference to the immanent necessity of men and women to have intercourse with one another, including that of men with men and women with women, he must not merely calculate how to persuade or compel the mass of people to obey the rulers and to leave aside their own pleasures and pains, he must also address the intimate aspect of this necessity. He does this in the *Symposium* where the lover who loves the beautiful or the good appears to desire 'That they become his own' since possessing the good or the beautiful makes one happy.[45] Yet Diotima is made to caution Socrates. She is made to argue that no one takes joy in what is his own, but only in what is good, that love is wanting to possess the good forever.[46] This is to be achieved by a singular means, that means is to give birth in beauty, in body or in soul. It is birth because it goes on forever and love desires possession of the good forever.[47] But the possession of what goes on forever cannot be a personal possession, it cannot be one's own. Nothing that is 'one's own' goes on forever; not only the body – hair, flesh, bones and blood – but the soul too – manners, customs, opinions, desires, pleasures, pains, fears. None of this remains – it can never be eternal. To possess something that goes on forever, mortals must turn to the sphere of what is immortal and ideal, what is never one's own. This sphere is made accessible through love.

> A lover who goes about this matter correctly must begin in his youth to devote himself to beautiful bodies. First, if the leader leads aright, he should love one body and beget beautiful ideas there; then he should realize that the beauty of any one body is brother to the beauty of any other and that if he is to pursue beauty of form he'd be very foolish not to think that the beauty of all bodies is one and the same. When he grasps this, he must become a lover of all beautiful bodies and he must think that this wild gaping after just one body is a small thing and despise it.[48]

Having been turned away from the love of one body, the lover is freed from the threat of seeking to make that body 'his' own. Rather than attending to his own love and the body of the beloved, the lover turns to souls, seeking to give birth to ideas. Unfailingly, the beauty of bodies is relegated to *a thing of no importance*. The lover gazes, not at the body of the beloved, but at the world that is always understood to be beyond, its activities and laws, customs and knowledge, transcendent in relation to all perspectives, there to give birth to 'glorious and beautiful ideas and theories' love now not an intimacy but something public, love of wisdom. This is the final love of what 'neither comes to be nor passes away, neither waxes nor wanes' and so can never be made one's own.[49] This love is a movement upward. Loving correctly, one is lead to the final and highest mystery of Love, that love of the absolute, pure, unmixed, and unpolluted by mere human flesh, the great nonsense of human mortality, that love of divine beauty, that ultimate and final love which turns away from the intimacy of the beloved in search of unpolluted beauty.

In all this, Glaucon's suggestion that intimacy might be a vital relation between human beings appears less and less likely. Not just sex, an externally related event, a proximity event, easily arranged, easily controlled, but intimacy. This would be a relation that is both self-organized and that alleviates the tendency toward disorder *and* violence; toward homogeneity and bifurcating equilibria; toward entropy *and* infinite speeds, each of which precludes intimacy. Love appears to be easily forgone, victim of an act of transcendence which moves differentially and indifferently from one body to another facilitating intellectual growth through the practice of making comparisons and encouraging the search for unpolluted beauty. In fact, Plato is little worried about promiscuous love and the love of one's own because he knows that the soul's transcendent trajectory is inevitable; it is written on the soul whose tri-partite form of appetites, opinion and intelligibility guarantee that the individual will be driven beyond love for his or her own body and beyond the desire to make the beloved body of the other one's own. Even degeneracy is not love of one's own insofar as no aspect of the soul, not even its appetitive nature, leads the soul first to its own body and then to the loving adoration of the body of another. To be degenerate, to be a glutton or a sexual adventurer, is not to love one's own body nor the body of the other. The great mysteries of love are not love at all. Women and men love themselves and others so little that they must be tempted into giving birth by the promise of beauty, the promise of honors or the promise of wisdom, the highest mysteries. Love of appetite, opinion or wisdom is not love but the inevitable transcendent trajectory of one's own soul, a scale of self-interest and fascination with one's plane breathtaking by comparison with the Greek Narcissus, who, proud in his own beauty, plunged the dagger into his own breast, fatally wounding himself since he could not possess himself. Love would demand that it is possible to have something that is 'one's own,' that there is a truly intimate necessity, but none ever appears in Western philosophy. Drowned in appetites, goaded by honors, or transformed by wisdom, there can be for us no love.

So perhaps we should not be surprised that Plato makes Diotima the source of these ideas and Sartre makes the woman into a sophist. For the Greeks and for Sartre, women are less able to resist pleasures and they enjoy sex too much. Moreover, they are slow, they lack the free-floating desire that would allow them to move from one object to the next, making comparisons based on beauty, nobility and intellectual performance. Although the pre-Socratic Greeks identified active and passive, dominant and submissive sexual roles with males and females respectively, Plato eliminates receptivity entirely, replacing it wholly with the project of the beloved's intellectual growth, initiating the trajectory from appetites to right opinions to knowledge.[50] This is why both Plato's and Sartre's lovers urge the beloved to 'be like me' and 'do what I do,' so that when 'I' take 'your' hand, 'you' should also take 'mine.' All events must be symmetrical. The spatio-temporalization of a particular point of view is eliminated in favor of either a mythic ideal past or what is the same, the ideal present of transcendence. In either case, spatio-temporalization has been reduced to a parameter of the framework, the so-called real past crossed out. The beloved object should take up the demand that she/he is an attractor on the Other's trajectory and respond mimetically, making the Other into an attractor on her/his trajectory. Imitation or symmetry are always the key to knowledge. Thus, if there is to be love, women and some men must become *'amateurs,'* imitators of their idol's or mentor's Ideas/ideals, rather than persons who emerge out of their own spatializing and temporalizing relations, their absorption, emission and intuition of overlapping states in the world, states whose numerous and evolving perspectives give rise to intimacy, to love and hate, to dissolution and distress, to myriad newly forming sensibilities, and to what is completely new.[51] No need here for mentors and mentees since each and every one is always a crowd, never alone, never a single one, multiple but not infinite.

Love and the world

Though their numbers may be few, some philosophers have attempted to think about sensibility, often through a study of the passions. Among these, there is a significant agreement that passions arise as sensation or at least in conjunction with sensation, whether this is expressed as an original impression (David Hume) or as an original affectivity (Henri Bergson and Jean-Paul Sartre) or, as William James has (famously) claimed, bodily feelings are prerequisite to any emotion.[52] As Sartre characteristically argues, although all hatred is hatred *of* someone, and therefore already a *constituted* affectivity, that is, consciousness of the world, such intentionality can and must be distinguished from affective qualities.[53] Even while recognizing the extent to which consciousness *exists* its body, that is, takes over or has an effect on the body, Sartre also acknowledges that this way of speaking *neglects* the body, passes it by in silence in spite of the fact that affectively, consciousness is nothing except body, and beyond the body; the rest is literally 'nothingness and silence.'[54] Yet, in our total fascination with our own transcendent trajectory, what we pass over in silence is the intimacy of affective life, the life of pure affective sensibilities surpassed by our projects from which point of view *they* (affective sensibilities) are nothing at all. This life might be characterized as 'mood' or as 'non-thetic,' or closer to Hume, as the purely agreeable or disagreeable of physical pleasure and pain, or, as I have called it, 'intimacy,' 'diffusion,' 'distress.' In any case, it is said to be mostly expressed in the flesh of the intentional consciousness of desire, a desire that Sartre designates as 'trouble,' the troubled water of consciousness. Although we might expect such a designation for the disagreeable sensations of pain, it seems a bit curious that the pleasurable affective quality associated with love is lived as troubled water as well. Still, we have also seen that categories of freedom, insofar as they provide an axiomatic for the *acts* of any *intelligible* being, do not refer to sensible experience nor to theoretical understanding. They *produce* the reality to which they refer; an intention of the will removed from human experience, a pulsion, propelled, hurtling away without a past to hinder or handicap its movement, absorbing little so as to remain unclouded and unperturbed. Thus, it might be interesting to examine so-called love and hate more closely, as passion and emotion, to determine if and under what circumstances affective qualities are lived as troubled water.[55]

If love and hatred are caused by or associated with the influence of pleasure and pain on/in the body, they are perhaps most readily connected to sex whether it is characterized in terms of the satisfaction of desire or its so-called sublimation. Apprehending the other's lived, affective sexuality, that sexuality is *suffered* as a passion is suffered, so it is encountered as something absorbed and experienced as something felt; a feeling often given the name 'desire.' Satisfaction need not be the object of desire, rather, existing sexually for an other as a particular person and not merely as a sexual object provides desire with its own intentional consciousness distinct from the less complex but usually accompanying affective intentionality whereby one seeks directly to be satisfied. Feelings referred to by the name desire arise in relation to apparently direct affective connections; the eye of the beholder glances toward the curve of the thigh, the graceful neck, the muscled shoulder; a hand grazes the body. But the glance or the caress are not isolated events, thus they most often are affirmed by the total form in situation. The beautiful neck, the gracious curve are beautiful or gracious in terms of the revelation of the other's body, a perspective and existence which evolves from a multiplicity of combinatorial relations, overlapping, partially merging, self-organizing, yielding *that* body, every point of view a crowd. 'Desire is nothing but one of the great forms which can be assumed by the revelation of the other's body,' where this *revelation* implies an entirely original state, so much so that each revelation of the other's body arrives at something completely new, an emergent and newly created state.[56] It is a state in which *the observer participates*; each one of us who feels this 'great form' does so as the effect of combinatorial arrangements, elements of causal sets in which we are always implicated. In surrendering to this great form, this passion for the other that comes to us from the world, from the light of the stars, we first subject ourselves to the temporal relations of a multiplicity of occurrences in the world, occurrences behaving as light itself, absorbing and emitting influences, altering and reflecting one another, refracting and dispersing information. These events reflect *on us*, leaving their trails, their memory images, although we do not perceive nor do we thematize such impressions. Then narrowly, we localize the array of emanations in the pleasure and pain of our own body, and in the moment between absorbing the evolving brillant images that spin toward us through the other – falling into place from a multiplicity of others – and our response to this, we are engulfed by this passion, intoxicated within this desire. In sensing ourselves subjected by the spatio-temporal arrival of events emanating through the body of the other, we feel our own body as well, our absorptions and emanations, our light and our transparency, our own skin and muscles, our own heart beat and breath, we feel them as states or images or passions engaged by the world, in danger in the world, lived as some strange, pure feeling, consciousness making itself the body which it already exists. Between the spatio-temporalization of luminescent events emanating as the body of the other and our return to agency, there is passion, the great form created by the revelation of the other's body, invading more and more of one's own existence, unstoppably. But, without the spatio-temporalization of past events, the discrete change, the arrival of new combinations of spatialization and temporalization; without the hesitation in which our own conscious idealizations and active projects are slowed, no intuition is possible, and without the felt apperception of the other's body as the pleasure or pain of one's own, no desire, no love, no hate, that is to say, no emission of light, no beauty, no dissolution and distress, would light the way.

Such an awareness may be distinguished from a *purely cognitive* awareness. 'For the For-itself to choose itself as desire is not to produce a desire while remaining indifferent and unchanged,' for to do so would be to veer dangerously in the direction of Sadian sex which translates the agony in the bodies of the libertines' victims into the sexual vibrations of their torturers, a psychic pleasure, putting reason purely in service to pain.[57] Once we are engaged, desire wholly compromises us. Our projects, our acts, and even our intentions are slowed to the point of suspension as the spinning combinations of events en-lightens each perspective, opening sensibilities, mixing, melding, yielding an intuition. An obscure sentiment becomes a deep emotion by gradually permeating more and more of the past of one's present sensations and ideas, to the point where one is no longer perceiving the same objects in the same way. It is a difference, not of degree, but of kind. It is not a matter of more feeling, in the sense of a greater magnitude of feeling, but of a fully combinatorial relationality among heterogeneous and multiple sensibilites.[58] As every perspective emerges under the influence of the unperceived, unknown past that informs and invents us, as light rays diffract into spectra, the pleasure, the pain, the passions are absorbed, admitting sensations and ideas, coalescing in new perspectives as they alter those they pervade, widening the range of passion. Such passion, if we may still name it 'desire,' may begin with the slow emergence of the past, a past that absorbs events mixed with other events, a past that composes each one of us, and that we intuit, a past that alters in relation to a multiplicity of other pasts with which it intersects, a past that comes to light as an ever changing spatio-temporalization. Emerging, finally, as a point of view out of the labyrinth of spatializing – temporalizing states such passions color perceptions and memories, issuing images, like heat or light, infusing every state, opening them all to desire.[59] As Sartre admits, albeit confusedly, when desire overtakes you, overwhelms you and paralyzes you, you cannot mistake it for anything else. 'Can one imagine employing the same words to designate hunger?'[60]

Desire demands that we impede our projects, thwart our trajectories, in order to open into desire, to *be* compromised by the suspension of pure active agency and conscious idealization, in order to give way to sensible awakening, a revelation and intuition then, not only of the body of a particular other, but also of one's own body, made by means of the revelation of the world. The eyes, ears, mouth and skin have limited sensitivity; the chemical changes on the retina's light receptive cells last but a tenth of a second. But by waiting, can we not increase our exposure to photons in the manner of a photographic plate?[61] Can we not be compromised by our own sensibility so as to suspend or slow our response to perception? If this is possible, it is because desire is not the appropriation of the other's agency or capacity to be an agent, but the absorption of the other as flesh, as light, as translucent, thus barely visible, as an emergent past, as a multiplicity of emergent pasts, altering in relation to one another. Thus we never *perceive* either ourselves or the other as flesh. Perception belongs to activity and agency, to our projects and plans in the world. Flesh as a purely sensible state is present, but as a spatial and temporal upsurge from the past into and of the present. Compromised by passion, by the transparency of sensibility rather than the opaqueness of consciousness, our feelings, imaginings and actions may displace and distress as much as they urge us forward into action. Their strange or alien character should not shock us since they arise not simply from our own so-called personality and projects but from our insertion in the sensible and luminous life of the world, the personality and projects of all states that may combine with our own. Given not only the glance that connects the eye to the neck or shoulder or thigh, the hand that reaches out to form the shape of the curve, the grain of the voice that reaches the ear, the electrification of the skin when touched, the light that fills space, dissolving boundaries, the transparent luminosity of the sensibility of dispersion or distress, given all these combinations of states, it is through the absorption of the past, its intuition in the present and emission into the world that desire is made real. This is not the look or feel of objectification or the darkened opacity of troubled consciousness – it is the glance of pleasure, the touch of sensuousness, the radiance of light, the interaction of states, the immersion of each one in the other, bringing the other's flesh to life both for the other and for oneself. Seeing and touching, hearing and tasting, scents and sensibilities all converge; as even the look is felt and not simply seen. For if the eye bears magical powers, how much more magical is it as it intertwines with all sensibilities, both those perceived and those unperceived? 'The body is made flesh in order to touch the other's body with its own passivity; that is, by caressing itself with the other's body rather than by caressing her . . . placing one's own body against the other's body . . . to place against'.[62]

Through this upsurge of one's own body and that of the other in the present, the two enact an utterly impossible scenario. They exist within a shifting, interacting network of relations, a multi-faceted milieu, an incandescent atmosphere of sensibilities, innumerably incarnated, simultaneously affectively sensible and desiring through and in relation to those plentiful and profuse events which bring each into a direct yet multiply mediate, felt relation to the other insofar as they are all of the world. Not possession of an object but mutual absorption and emission of states, transparent to sensibility but exciting and disturbing the otherwise clear waters of an empty intentional consciousness. For its part consciousness will always be disturbed when affective sensibility imparts its pleasures and pains in the sensory-motor system of the body which consciousness exists. Why? Is it that in desiring a particular person we, more radically, subject ourselves to the spatio-temporalizing emanations of the sensible qualities of a host of states emerging into the world? The concepts that we invoke to account for the motion of these vast relational networks describe a structure that proceeds as the discrete spatio-temporalization, our so-called point of view. These concepts can radically modify our ideas about love and hate. *Sensibility*, as we imagine it here, involves very small distances and times that do not exhibit the familiar patterns of perception or consciousness. We perceive objects or events, but sensible, discrete states 'become the transcendent ensemble which reveals my incarnation to me.'[63] Insofar as their alterations reach *our* sensibility, igniting pleasure as well as pain, dissolution and distress, they too are absorbed, and sometimes felt as immediately sensible; they are not perceived; they are not the objects of consciousness. The situation is such that despite the apparent solidity of the world around us, everything is made up of such sensibilities.[64] The dry air wounds, the wind pierces, but the warm sun opens the senses like flowers and the fragrance of plants infiltrates the pores, once again opening the heart. This desire *comes from the world*; it overtakes us and compromises us within the world and insofar as sensibilities, influenced and affected in this way, produce pleasure, produce pain, dissolving us, distressing us, they give rise to desire for the world too. Desire for the world, a vulnerability that makes possible an interval in which we slow our projects and agency, intuit images left by the myriad sensibilities, and for the first time, we begin to love. We love, not just the other, but first the world and then – both self and other.

Yet most of the time consciousness remains fascinated by its attractors, its repellers, its breathtaking, speeding trajectories. Moving too quickly to intuit its own sensibilities, they are totally opaque to it – they fill it like troubled waters. Immersed in its illusions, it is enthralled by the acts it takes for its own. Thus, we purveyors of consciousness begin to perceive and then to plan. What, we demand to know, can be the *meaning* of this desire that opens the incarnated being to love? Consciousness chooses itself as desire but may do so in a number of different ways. One may simply believe in love, believe oneself to be in love and believe the other to be in love with oneself. Giving into one's own impulses is the most immediate meaning-giving but requires trust, that is, a decision to believe and to conduct oneself according to this belief. Believe in love and love becomes the meaning of one's own acts and the acts of others. Living in this meaning is living in love; it is living in the midst of non-thetic consciousness, absorbing, intuiting, emitting the world. But *consciousness* does not have such an intuition. Consciousness is both believing and aware that it is believing. It *knows* something. Pushed along its trajectory, torn apart, disjoined then conjoined at infinite speeds, its belief vanishes into the shadows. What is left is knowledge of its former mode of existence, its intuitions, its translucency, its living illuminations coming from the stars, from the heart of the Other and the still beating hearts of a multitude of Others. Thus, belief and with it love are lost forever to infinite speeds. The luminous rays radiating as spatio-temporalizations illuminate the darkness but never fall upon the lovers. Caught in the acceleration, the intensification of becoming, they move so quickly that they break apart, disintegrate and never feel themselves shining in the brilliant light of love.[65] From here, from this nowhere and nothing, all belief looks like non-belief and all faith looks like bad faith. So we should not be surprised either if we discover that here too all meaning looks like nonsense, since all beliefs are disarmed in advance, so is all meaning.

Thus in asking, 'what does this love mean?' we are either asking about the nature of becoming, the n-dimensional trajectory, the affects, percepts, concepts, prospects and functives, conjoined, only to be ruthlessly severed, torn from their past, or we are in bad faith. In seeking the meaning, we swiftly cease to let ourselves be made, flesh and spirit, body and breath, made by the spatio-temporalizing networks of events spinning toward us from the world then outward toward the flesh and spirit, body and breath of a particular person. In this, we cease to exist as flesh – and we begin to look. First one and then the other looks. This is not the illuminated glance of the eye to the body intertwined with the touch of the caress, the taste, smell and sound of the past of the world; this is the look of consciousness, the look of *freedom*, the death of desire. In this look our 'being-in-the-midst-of-the-world' is rapidly transformed into a death throe, abandoning our always renewed life. For when we look at the other in this way, each has to defend him or herself from the other's freedom and each seeks to transcend the other's freedom so as to make it collapse. And if the other escapes, it is a deadly escape into a transcendent relation with respect to all the objects in the world and with respect to a particular person. From now on, we can only 'grasp' the other as a body, a psychic object, a facticity, and 'although all the acts of this body can be interpreted in terms of freedom, I have completely lost the key to this interpretation.'[66] Such is the price of meaning, the pursuit of the ideal.

Perhaps it is this same pursuit to which Roland Barthes passionately commits himself and his readers in *A Lover's Discourse*. Opening the first pages, the reader is startled to find herself in the midst, not of a discourse between two lovers at all, but instead, isolated, enduring an *extreme solitude* within a discursive site, along a trajectory assailed by a seeming infinity of fragments, fragments whose connections arise from an established code or which in their very connection constitute a new code. Affects, percepts, concepts, prospects, relentless, discontinuously continuous are ordered and organized, systematized, habituated, then once again, violently torn apart, in a ritual of becoming that lacerates and mutilates once coherent events and worlds, leaving the lover tattered and worn, awaiting the next recoding, the next amorous encounter. This is the site where the reader finds 'someone' 'speaking within himself, *amorously*,' but apparently also '*confronting* the other,' the presumed 'object of love' who speaks not a word in return, who seemingly has no voice, so speaks not at all. Instead, the speaker 'discourses,' articulating in fragments what 'he' has read, heard, and ostensibly felt or been made to feel through a romantic reassociation of ideas, a recoding that takes place all around him, leaving him forsaken, ignored, disparaged, until at a certain point, he connects the dots, he affirms his trajectory.[67] The one who speaks muses and amuses *himself* by staging an utterance, unfolding the *meaning* of the figures in his amorous vocabulary. Such utterances are the figure in action, an athletic oratory, but one, nevertheless, 'stuffed into a role, like a statue,' from which the lover may exclaim, 'ah, so that was me!'[68] The site is reserved for the lover who fills it, attending or not to the figures and fragments bearing down on him, distributing themselves horizontally. There can be 'no transcendence, no deliverance, no novel,' so you may look for meaning, give it meaning or search for the '*aside* which accompanies this story (and this history) *without ever knowing it*,' since the figures of love cannot be organized or hierarchized in relation to a particular end.[69] Meaning is not in the story, but in the trajectory, the aside, in the affirmation of the transcendental lover who speaks and says:

S'abîmer/ to be engulfed. 1. Either woe or well-being, sometimes I have a craving *to be engulfed* . . . 2. The crisis of engulfment can come from a wound, but also from a fusion; we die together from loving each other: an open death, by dilution into the ether, a closed death of the shared grave . . . 3. Therefore, on those occasions when I am engulfed, it is because there is no longer any place for me anywhere. The image of the other – to which I was glued, on which I lived – no longer exists; sometimes this is a (futile) catastrophe which seems to remove the image forever, sometimes it is an excessive happiness which enables me to unite with the image; in any case severed or united, diffused or discrete, I am nowhere *gathered together*; opposite neither you nor me, nor death, nor anything else *to talk to*.[70]

Reading these initial observations uttered by a speaker who clamors to be engulfed by love, it begins to be apparent that the lover's discourse is not a reflection on a relation between lovers as much as it is a displacement of the relation to the beloved into a staged discourse, an image-repertoire as Barthes calls it, one which circumscribes and pre-determines the presumed events of love and so gives them meaning. That is to say, the discourse Barthes articulates is not the expression of new relationship which has been created between lovers and the world nor even between lovers and language. It is a trajectory on which the old codes are always being torn apart. The nodes and blanks, outbursts and declarations are ordered and organized, figured now into a half-coded, half-projective discourse to which the lover and love itself succumb. For Barthes has already decided that if, in love, the habitual relation to language is lost, so that a set of pre-existing codes no longer operates to inform and orient the feeling as well as the relation between lovers, then the speaker inevitably undergoes the most profound alienation; suddenly he has no one and nothing to talk to. This situation must above all be avoided. The relation of the speaker to his love-discourse must be structured by what the lover says, by what he is made to say, by what passes through his mind and is marked. There is, then, a site held in reserve, a system waiting for its coding to emerge from the discourse as it assails the speaker, converges on 'him,' connecting 'his' fragments although always able to sunder them. Without this the lover no longer knows how to situate what Barthes imagines must be a chaos of feelings and would be engulfed by them, leading to a dead end. Barthes' amorous subject moves at so great a speed, that he escapes the intuition of his own sensibilities, that dissolution and distress, transparency and illumination coming to him from interacting combinations of events in the world. Such an intuition could allow him to constitute an entirely new relation to the world, to the other, and to his own creative and sensible processes. Still, he moves, he moves as if pursued by Eyrines. He is not sensible of the diffusion and distress, the coloring of pleasure and pain localized in the body, at once creating and recreating both body and world, and so he does not pause in the interval between sensibility and speech. As such, his desire comes not from the relation to the world and to the particular other, an other who is herself/himself made by a multiplicity, a crowd, and made anew in every spatio-temporalization of the world.[71]

In the lover's discourse, the speaker is driven by his 'arguments,' his 'instruments of distancing' his sentences that form and break apart, leaving their mutilated ruins behind, a terrified and suspended sensibility. Putting his *faith* in the image-repertoire, insensible with respect to the glimmering illuminations of the stars, the lover embarks on a wild ride, one that offers the consolation that within the discursive chain, the connections and disconnects, the codes and decoding, the figures that 'stir, collide, subside, return, vanish, with no more order than the flight of mosquitoes' lies the 'encyclopedia of affective culture,' a discourse defined by absence and anxiety, errantry and exile, silence and scenes.[72] Perhaps it is not unexpected then, that attention to the actual figures of the discourse of Barthes' lover returns us, to the reminiscences that Denis de Rougemont reserves for the mythological Tristan and Iseult whom, he argues, love not one another, but love only their passion, thereby defining and attaining a truly transcendent love. By his own admission, the figures Barthes defers to are, to a great extent, the figures of passionate love and hate, according to which only the sufferings of love lead to self-understanding. They are figures generated by courtly decoding, a movement that simultaneously reconnects what it tears apart, but so swiftly as to remain practically invisible, a reconnection for which connection = death.

> Tristan and Iseult do not love one another. They say they don't and everything goes to prove it. *What they love is love and being in love.* They behave as if aware that whatever obstructs love must ensure and consolidate it in the heart of each and intensify it infinitely in the moment they reach the absolute obstacle, which is death. Tristan loves the awareness that he is loving far more than he loves Iseult the Fair. And Iseult does nothing to hold Tristan. All she needs is her passionate dream. Their need of one another is in order to be aflame, and they do not need one another as they are. What they need is not one another's presence but one another's absence. *Thus the partings of the lovers are dictated by their passion itself,*

and by the love they bestow on their passion rather than on its satisfaction or on its living object.[73]

Tristan and Iseult, whose passion does not emanate and explode from the rays of its mediate and immediate events, unmistakably come to be marked by newly forming codes of courtly love. Their affair is figured by external adversity which Tristan, the knight, easily overcomes, but once the external obstacles are defeated, the obstructions they meet are those which they themselves devise, a device that now may be called bad faith. 'Bad faith seeks by means of "not-being-what-one-is" to escape from the in-itself which I am not in the mode of being what one is not.'[74] Bad faith is the original sin. Escaping it supposes 'a self-recovery of being which was previously corrupted,' a being that originally is what it is not and is not what it is. Their partings and separations, Tristan's marriage, Iseult's return to King Mark are the effects of their attraction to that singular force called passion. Such a passion is not an emanation of their love for one another; it is merely an incitement to increase their consciousness of passion.[75] As Hegel has made clear, in the Western tradition, consciousness and self-consciousness demand of a 'man' that he test himself in a life and death struggle, and the struggle of passion serves this purpose well. 'What we pursue is what promises to uplift and excite us, so that in spite of ourselves we shall be transported into the "real life" spoken of by poets. But this "real life" is an impossible one,' impossible because the life and death struggle demands a passion whose only truly satisfying outcome is produced by the pain of obstruction, suffering and death.[76]

Such a passion is, as Sartre appears to contend, exactly what all relations to the other mediated by a consciousness in search of meaning end up as – a love from the standpoint of self and not from the standpoint of the other, such that the beloved comes to be hated as much as loved. This would be because shame reveals to me that I 'myself' am at the end of the other's look, that I am the object of that look, that I have forgone or foreclosed the only meaning that counts, that which does not deny or delay the disintegration of self and world.[77] Yet the attempt to love and be loved invokes a triple destructibility that culminates in masochism. First, insofar as to love is ostensibly little more than the wish that the other will love more or first, love is a contest whose goal of making the other wish to be loved thereby weakens her/his subject status, that is, her/his status as not being what she/he is. This parrying merely serves to reveal the extent to which love is a deception, an unattainable ideal, a game of infinite mirroring in a world in which thought has long since passed through to the other side. But it is a deadly game, for having passed through the mirror and finding ourselves on the other side, it is evident that the more one is loved, the more one loses her/his being. Secondly, there is the danger that the other will always come to her/his senses and so inflict object status on the lover, the beautiful, masochistic object, halting or slowing their trajectory, a powerful attractor. Thirdly, love is, in any case, ultimately impossible since, for consciousness, it can only survive when the infinity of virtual connections within the continuous manifold are reduced to those of two persons, in order to avoid the shame or pride that love engenders when others or when the world witnesses it.[78] Little wonder that in this version of love, conflict is the original meaning of being-for-others since the aim of each is to enslave the other in the life and death struggle that holds for lovers as well as for friends and enemies.[79] This desperate situation may be laid at the feet of the conception, often assumed in Western philosophy, that to love must mean to be united, that love would be a continuous affirmation of all affects, percepts and concepts, never to be ripped apart. But when all relations to the other are mediated through conflict, uniting with the other, as Sartre affirms, can only mean death, as the other continually transcends all attempts to make the other's freedom recognize one's own.[80]

Failing to differentiate between the sensible spatializing and temporalizing emanations of events in one's world that engender love, and something that is quite different from love, the identification with the other, the lover is eventually driven by her/his consciousness of passion to masochism. This time, the lover attempts not to absorb the other while nobly protecting her/his otherness, but instead, seeking to be absorbed by the other's subjectivity, she/he becomes an *object* of desire, radically in-itself, an object for whom transcendence is wholly denied. Given that this kind of love is posited, not intuited, it can only be posited from the standpoint of self and not from the standpoint of the other. In the end, even masochism is doomed. As much as the self attempts to throw itself into the vertigo of self-as-object, it cannot. It fails utterly to be 'fascinated' by its own alienation because it cannot apprehend itself in this condition. Even situating oneself as an object is an act of transcendence. The masochist's capacity to demand to be whipped, scorned or humiliated is subject to her/his capacity to be transformed by more affects, percepts and concepts. As such, it indicates a release from the particular attractor in whose orbit she/he has circulated, fascinated, and a return to the infinite speeds and differentials of a continuous trajectory.[81] The only possibly successful expression of love, on this account, appears to be Tristanian self-annihilation since every other attempt to 'unite,' to identify with the other, results in the eventual affirmation of a subject, a dead-end literally. Even if contemporary lovers of passion do not always go to their deaths, there are always the ever-present substitutes of indifference, hatred and sadism, modes of being that confirm the pervasive tendency, in the Western world, to conceptualize love as an impossibility if not an altogether logical contradiction.[82]

Indifference, in fact, appears as a relief from the stress and pressures of any attempted meaningful identification with the other. Rather than aspiring to unite with the other, an endeavor sure to be met with miserable failure, one may simply accept that on a certain scale, one is completely alone in the world. Practically, this calls for avoiding others when necessary, but more importantly, simply imagining that *they* neither see nor have any knowledge of oneself, so that their demands on oneself as much as their efforts to aid or assist or to love are, cognitively, nothing more than interference in one's own transcendence, in one's projects. In short, in the attitude of indifference, others become 'functions,' not fully human, reduced as much as possible to the unplanned effects of one's own encounters. Immured by indifference, one may choose to be kind or to be cruel, it matters little, since all others are already reduced and thereby denied their freedom and subject status.[83] This too *is* the death of desire. If desire were to be, as Sartre claims, desire for the transcendent object, then it is completely contradictory, for only subjects transcend. No wonder the demoralized lover experiences anxiety and confusion, since if a subject makes the other into an object, even if only to dismiss that other, she/he no longer transcends and the subject cannot even conceive of what it wishes to appropriate. Veiling the other's being with their pure function merely obfuscates. For even from the ever-vigilant position of transcendence, indifference, the attempted reduction of the other, remains ineffective as a means of preventing the other from seeing or knowing oneself and so from interfering in one's projects. It cannot put an end to the interference – one *will be seen*, no matter how indifferent one remains, no one is alone on every scale. Our penetrability, our lack of imperviousness makes us susceptible to being influenced and to influencing others to and from numerous perspectives. Indifference merely throws one back upon oneself, upon the 'terrible necessity of being free' and upon the profound 'anxiety' of the truth that *one can never see without being seen,* just as one can never touch without feeling oneself touched.[84] Indifference is therefore, and in a fundamental manner, the utmost effort to deny intimacy, and if sustained, inevitably takes its practitioners, its victims, to the realms of what is called hatred, but is actually sadism. Sadism, the cold persistence of the pursuit of the other's facticity as a means of avoiding the deathly reciprocity of being-in-the-midst-of-the-world, that appears, inevitably, the moment pleasure is achieved and the questions about meaning, that is to say, bad faith, commence. Thus just as the romance legends claim, pleasure would be the death and failure of passion. Even what is called hatred, in this context, is diminished as an emotion, as it is less love gone wrong than a slightly more extreme version of sadism in which one wishes to destroy the objectified other to ensure the impossibility of her/his freedom.[85] In fact, it seems as if transcendence demands the dissipation of all violent passions, love *and* hate, in favor of the intensities of affect, percept and concept.

For the lover's discourse, even as the lover absorbs himself in his amorous discoveries, and possibly for all devotees who, like Tristan and Iseult, and like Sartre, explore love in the context of the Western world's courtly traditions, traditions enveloped by pure transcendence, the worthiness of ideal love is an insupportable or unbearable situation which 'can't go on.' The lover's discourse is a 'series of No Exits,' in which every scene threatens to take up 'the art of catastrophe' because there is no way to win, no way to get what one wants.[86] Perhaps the lover clings to this pathos because it is moving and theatrical; it allows her/him to dramatize the death of desire and to re-enact it for her/his own conscious idealizations. The tearing apart of codes by the rush of differentials *is* electrifying. Rougement suggests that this sort of enactment of love as deadly has come to dominate all experience of love in the Western tradition to the extent that the invocation of love as passion is caught up in the rejection of what have come to be largely middle-class moral codes which reflect social conformity. Yet the destruction of one code is carried out by means of another. That is, what comes in the place of the more secular marriage code continues to bear the vague imprint of religious symbolism. Most of this symbolism has long since lost any reference to its original purpose which was the complete and absolute condemnation of fleshly love as wholly sinful and as the work of the Prince of Darkness and the affirmation of purity, of transcendence, of the ideal.[87] Instead, lovers in the Tristanian tradition have become objects of admiration and envy, entangled in a disturbing but alluring web whose often public and passionate staging is inherently irreconcilable with love for one another insofar as it excludes intimacy and idealizes passion. With respect to marriage in particular but the so-called love relation in general, 'all young people breathe in from books and periodicals, from stage and screen, and from a thousand daily allusions, a romantic atmosphere in the haze of which passion seems to be the supreme test that one day or other awaits every true man or woman.'[88] It has been suggested that such a 'myth' arises as a *reminiscence* when it has become dangerous or otherwise impossible to express openly and directly something that is obvious regarding social or religious matters or when it becomes dangerous and impossible to express something obvious about affective relations. Plainly, that is the case here where the hidden affective link is between the passion generated by a particular kind of mythically derived love and utter and inescapable unhappiness leading to death.[89] But less clear is the intimacy of sensibilities, the beautiful relation to the world, to the many hearts and spirits, and to the flesh of the world, prelude to that profound intimacy with others.

Rougement's analysis is, of course, historically circumscribed. He determines that the Western marriage institution was founded on three types of 'compulsions.' First, the ritual of the purchase or abduction of the bride dating back to primitive peoples; secondly, the social compulsions of money, blood, family, and rank, which constituted marriage as a community or family practice; and thirdly, the religious compulsions of eternal vows which exclude any and all temperamental vagaries, alterations of character, and most importantly, changes of taste and external circumstances. However, to the extent that these traditional compulsions have lost their value and meaning, so the more recent compulsion to flaunt such conventions might also have become vain. The impulse to challenge and denounce traditions that no one any longer respects is increasingly without point or purpose. It does not require much research to ascertain that in Western nations, adultery is commonplace and fidelity in marriage is slightly ridiculous precisely because either choice appears so completely *conventional*.[90] We are eager to be torn apart, to undergo chance affects, percepts, and concepts rather than circling in the same old trajectory. Yet, if it were to be the case that every perspective is already a crowd, and that it influences other, yet to arise perspectives that are also a crowd, this would have to influence all of our ideas about religious and political institutions as well, for we are then no longer individuals, but crowd phenomena. Concerning the institution of marriage, what may have occurred is that, without our fully realizing it, the system of marriage and the system of passion are, in fact, no longer in tension and no longer conflict with one another. Their mere juxtaposition appears to be an archaic configuration, an empty form of expression whose form of content has disappeared without the least trace. Yet, as individuals and as a society, Western men and women cling to the code of passion as the only means of rebellion against the lingering feudal and Christian constraints of tradition. The moment for the creation of new values seems long overdue, but from where will they emerge? Will the lover whose desires have been gratified be able to turn his or her love from love of the meaning of passion to love of the 'beloved,' the active love of a being whose life is matchless and independent? Or, need the beloved remain juxtaposed between the moribund and defunct alternatives of socially prescribed marriage and commitment and the phantom life of the passionate stranger, fugitive, vanishing, inciting only pursuit? [91] Are we condemned to an existence in which 'there is no other world beyond passion except another passion, which [we] must pursue in another turmoil of appearances each time more fleeting.'[92] Tristan and Iseult had, at least, the benefit of a mystic passion, whereas contemporary men and women live in the midst of a category breakdown; the transcendental is no longer available in any form.

Recognizing this, Sartre appears to suggest that our relations with the other may fail to reach intersubjective levels altogether. When we love, the *meaning* of love is that we are no longer master of the situation; the meaning of love is that our conscious projections and idealizations will never be the true meaning of that love. The meaning of love is that the true meaning of love will be a transcendence that will always exceed the projects of consciousness. The meaning of love is that the other looks at the beloved as an object, conferring spatiality on the beloved who is conscious of her/himself as both spatializing and spatialized, a unified and organized whole that maintains its capacity to look, to act, to confer meaning. But love as intimacy has no meaning. This way of speaking , we concur, *neglects* the body, passes it by in silence in spite of the fact that affectively, consciousness is nothing except body, and beyond the body; the rest is literally 'nothingness and silence.' It is a spatialization and temporalization in which we are first open to the world in order to be open to one another, not a universal, ideal spatio-temporalization, but an intimate, fleshly duration in which the question of meaning loses value once and for all. In its place emerges something sensible, some shimmering light that is the emanation of freedom only insofar as it cannot be consigned to the dustbin of meaning.[93]

Notes

1. This is Gilles Deleuze's analysis of Hume in *Pure Immanence, Essays on A Life*, pp. 35–44, originally published in French in *La Philosophie: De Galiléé à Jean-Jacques Rousseau* (Paris: Les Éditions de Minuit, 1972). Deleuze sees the universality of relations as lying at the foundation of modern logic as developed by Bertrand Russell.
2. David Hume, *A Treatise of Human Nature* (Oxford: Clarendon Press, 1968) pp. 276, 330. Hume's theory is prescient with respect to Freud insofar as the latter also posits some internal sensations (drives) that seek objects in the external world.
3. Hume, *A Treatise of Human Nature*, pp. 329, 331, 332.
4. Deleuze, *Immanence, A Life*, pp. 37–8. This allows association to be an organizing principle for the mind.
5. Hume, *A Treatise of Human Nature*, pp. 352–3. What is not so clear is how one person can communicate to another the liveliness of their mind, since every idea and every mind must be separate.
6. Michel Cabanac, 'What is Sensation? *Gnoti se auton*', in *Biological Perspectives on Motivated Activities*, ed. Roderick Wong (Northwood, N. J: Ablex, 1995), p. 404.
7. See Cabanac, 'What is Sensation? *Gnoti se auton*'. Cabanac states that Merleau-Ponty's view, that it is not possible factually to distinguish sensation from perception, is an extreme effect of the Gestaltist view that sensation and perception are part of a global experience (p. 403).
8. Deleuze, *Immanence, A Life*, pp. 46–7. Deleuze himself seems to have had no answer to this question. I am suggesting that it is not the right question, that the right question engages us in a completely different structure.
9. Plato, *Republic*, 457d.
10. Plato, *Republic*, 458d. Implied but never developed is the notion that bodily fluids and body parts are passed between sexual partners to the point where it becomes difficult to distinguish their sources. DNA testing has managed to re-establish these boundaries, sometimes to women's benefit but sometimes not.
11. Plato, *Republic*, 461c. Separation and segregation are again the dominant structure here.
12. Plato, *Republic*, 466b. The identification of passion with one's own is not always made, but it seems as though ideas are held to be common to all while sensibility remains private.
13. Plato, *Republic*, 466b. Stability and moderation are, I believe, ontological values, prior to being ethical values.

14. Le Doeuff, *The Sex of Knowing*, p. 199. Le Doeuff is particularly fascinated by amorous relations between philosophical couples.
15. Le Doeuff, *The Sex of Knowing*, pp. 200–1. Le Doeuff will find the same tendencies at work in Mill's relation to Taylor and Sartre's relation to women in general.
16. Le Doeuff, *The Sex of Knowing*, p. 4. Intuition appears to play the former role (setting thought in motion) for Deleuze.
17. Le Doeuff, *The Sex of Knowing*, pp. 6–7.
18. Simone de Beauvoir, *The Second Sex*, tr. H. M. Parshley (New York: Knopf, 1953), 'The Woman in Love', pp. 642, 644. This view may be contrasted with the more comprehensive treatment of Beauvoir's ethics offered by Debra Bergoffen in her book, *The Philosophy of Simone de Beauvoir, Gendered Phenomenologies, Erotic Generosities* (Albany: SUNY Press, 1997).
19. De Beauvoir, *The Second Sex*, p. 667.
20. De Beauvoir, *The Second Sex*, p. 667–8. The necessity for women's economic independence is, in my view, indisputable. It is the problematics of transcendence that remains questionable in Beauvoir's position.
21. Elizabeth Wilson, *The Sphinx in the City* (Berkeley: University of California Press, 1991), p. 63. Wilson's colorful account makes it clear that in addition to Beauvoir, there were a significant number of educated and independent women of various nationalities living independent lives in Paris.
22. Sartre, *Being and Nothingness*, p. 477 (433).
23. Elizabeth Young-Bruehl, 'Where do we fall when we fall in love?', *Journal for the Psychoanalysis of Culture and Society*, vol. 8, no. 2 (Fall 2003), 280, 281. Young-Bruehl cites Anna Freud, 'On Adolescence', *The Writings of Anna Freud*, vol. 5 (New York: International Universities Press, 1974), pp. 136–66.
24. Young-Bruehl, 'Where do we fall when we fall in love?', p. 281.
25. Meyda Yeóenoólu, 'Veiled fantasies: cultural and sexual difference in the discourse of orientalism', in *Feminist Postcolonial Theory*, ed. Reina Lewis and Sara Mills (New York: Routledge Press, 2003), pp. 543–44. Yeóenoólu argues that Michel Foucault has popularized these ideas in academic circles, but they tend not to be applied to Western academics in general but only to the so-called empowered other. Who exactly is this other? See Michel Foucault, *Discipline and Punish, The Birth of the Prison*, tr. Alan Sheridan (New York: Vintage Books, 1979), pp. 200–2.
26. Gilles Deleuze, *Empiricism and Subjectivity, An Essay on Hume's Theory of Human Nature*, tr. Constantin Boundas (New York: Columbia University Press, 1994), ch. 2, originally published in French as *Empirisme et subjectivité: Essai sur la nature humaine selon Hume* (Paris: Presses Universitaires de France, 1953). The association of ideas – resemblance, contiguity, and causality – find themselves soon eliminated in

favor of connection, conjunction and disjunction which possibly evade causality, taking on the character of a much purer form of association.

27. Le Doeuff, *Hyparchia's Choice*, p. 144.
28. Le Doeuff, *Hyparchia's Choice*, p. 145. This is another example, for Le Doeuff, of the attempt to keep women in the *amateur* relation with respect to philosophy.
29. Jean-Jacques Rousseau, book V, p. 709, cited in Le Doeuff, p. 146. Rousseau's position is all the more shocking in light of his avowal elsewhere that women are no less intelligent than men but that insofar as public life corrupts, they should be kept out of it. See Jean-Jacques Rousseau, *Discourse on the Origin and Foundations of Inequality*, tr. Roger G. Masters and Judith R. Masters (New York: St Martin's Press, 1964).
30. Sartre, *Being and Nothingness*, pp. 478, 479 (434, 435).
31. Sartre, *Being and Nothingness*, pp. 482, 483 (437–438). Sartre's view of love as an impediment to one's own transcendence may be the core of his philosophy, if not also its basis.
32. Sartre, *Being and Nothingness*, pp. 490, 491 (444, 445). The symmetry of this relation is crucial here.
33. Stéphane Mallarmé, 'Autre éventail', tr. C. F. MacIntyre, *French Symbolist Poetry* (Berkeley: University of California Press, 1958), pp. 70–1.
34. Leopold von Sacher-Masoch, *Venus in Furs*, tr. from French by John McNeil (New York: George Brazillier, 1971), p. 129. This relation also retains its symmetry.
35. Wilhelm Reich, *Character Analysis*, tr. Theodore P. Wolfe (New York: Farrar, Straus and Cudahy, 1961), p. 221. Reich's hostility toward Freudian psychoanalysis seems to stem from Freud's disinclination to address the pain and trauma produced by the moral code and to focus instead on fantasy.
36. Sartre, *Being and Nothingness*, pp. 87–8 (86–7).
37. Plato, *Republic*, 602a. This would be the case whether it is the Platonic Idea or the differential Idea.
38. 370 BCE is the year in which Plato founded the Academy in Athens.
39. Sartre, *Being and Nothingness*, pp. 96–7 (94–5). The trajectory upon which these events occur seems to be that of the man for whom the woman is an attractor.
40. Le Doeuff, *Hyparchia's Choice*, pp. 62, 67. Cited in Louise Bassett, *Paradoxe Assurément: Michèle Le Doeuff's Philosophical Imaginary*, unpublished Ph.D. thesis, Australian National University, 2003, pp. 43–53.
41. Sartre, *Being and Nothingness*, pp. 96–8 (94–5). Gilles Deleuze, *Masochism, An Interpretation of Coldness and Cruelty*, tr. Jean McNeil (New York: Georges Brazillier, 1971), pp. 30, 31, 45, 46, 47, originally

published in French as *Présentation de Sacher-Masoch, Le Froid et le Cruel* (Paris: Les Éditions de Minuit, 1967).

42. Sacher-Masoch, *Venus in Furs*, tr. Jean McNeil, pp. 137, 139.

43. Sacher-Masoch, *Venus in Furs*, pp. 120, 121, 132. Unlike Sartre, Sacher-Masoch attempts to let the woman speak for herself.

44. Sartre, *Being and Nothingness*, pp. 98, 99 (96, 97).

45. Plato, *Symposium*, tr. Michael Joyce, in *Plato: The Collected Dialogues*, ed. Edith Hamilton and Huntington Cairns (Princeton: Princeton University Press, 1961), 204d–e.

46. Plato, *Symposium*, 206a. Thus a wise woman will caution against love, embracing the noble lie.

47. Plato, *Symposium*, 207a.

48. Plato, *Symposium*, 210 a–b.

49. Plato, *Symposium*, 211a.

50. David Halperin, 'Why is Diotima a woman?', in *One Hundred Years of Homosexuality and Other Essays on Greek Love*, ed. David Halperin (New York: Routledge Press, 1990), pp. 129, 132. Halperin suggests that this is reciprocity, I would argue that it is more likely imitation.

51. Michèle Le Doeuff, 'Women and Philosophy', in Toril Moi (ed.), *French Feminist Thought* (Oxford: Blackwell, 1987), pp. 181–209.

52. Henri Bergson, *Creative Evolution*, tr. N. M. Paul and W. S. Palmer (New York: Zone Books, 1988), ch. 1, in *Bergson, Oeuvres*, pp. 487–577; Sartre, *Being and Nothingness*, pp. 435–6 (395–6); William James, 'What is an Emotion?', *Mind* 9, pp. 188–205. This narrowly framed position has been the subject of an enormous amount of contention. See, for example, Peter Goldie, *The Emotions, A Philosophical Exploration* (Oxford: Clarendon Press, 2000), pp. 51–7.

53. Sartre, *Being and Nothingness*, p. 435 (395).

54. Sartre, *Being and Nothingness*, p. 434 (395). Sartre's account of affective life can be moving and profound, but remains subject to the constraints of transcendence.

55. Sartre, *Being and Nothingness*, p. 436, 503 (396, 455–6). Sartre echoes Kant in his concern that consciousness not become clouded.

56. Sartre, *Being and Nothingness*, p. 502 (455). Crucial here is the idea of revelation rather than fascination.

57. Sartre, *Being and Nothingness*, p. 502 (455). See Leo Bersani and Ulysse Dutoit, 'Merde alors', *October* 13 (1979), 23–35. Bersani and Dutoit recognize that, politically, sadism is a kind of fascism, allowing for the elimination of partners.

58. Henri Bergson, *Time and Free Will*, pp. 8–9; Bergson, *Oeuvres*, pp. 9–10. I am making every effort to adapt Bergson's single memory cone with multiple layers to the structure of multiple event cones in relational networks. See *Matter and Memory*, tr. N. M. Paul and W. S. Palmer (New York: Zone Books, 1988), p. 162; Bergson, *Oeuvres*, p. 293.

59. Bergson, *Time and Free Will*, p. 10; Bergson, *Oeuvres*, pp. 10–11. This description, parallels, I believe, Bergson's own.
60. Sartre, *Being and Nothingness*, p. 504 (457).
61. Tony Hey and Patrick Walters, *The New Quantum Universe* (Cambridge: Cambridge University Press, 2003), pp. 24–5. 'Light from the star causes chemical changes in the retinal cells of the eye . . . the cell reverts to its normal state after about one-tenth of a second . . . [this] limits the sensitivity of the eye for detecting faint objects . . . Photography can overcome this limitation of the eye by storing the changes in a permanent way on photographic emulsion . . . if we wait longer and increase exposure of the photographic plate, more photons will arrive.'
62. Jean-paul Sartre, *Being and Nothingness*, pp. 507–8 (460). Sartre's own structure seems to disallow him from accepting any but nihilating consequences from this encounter over which he nonetheless lingers.
63. Jean-Paul Sartre, *Being and Nothingness*, p. 509 (461). In this manner, transcendence takes on a new meaning. The creation of every perspective in causal sets evokes transcendence.
64. I am paraphrasing. 'The problem is that *everything* is quantum mechanical. Despite the apparent solidity of the world around us, everything is made up of atoms and electrons, the same atoms and electrons that are supposed to be peculiar, wave-particle, quantum objects', Hey and Walters, *The New Quantum Universe*, p. 173.
65. Sartre, *Being and Nothingness*, pp. 114, 115 (109–11). Since for Sartre, life without intentional consciousness is object-life and nothing more, he never looks at the meaning-structure of consciousness.
66. Sartre, *Being and Nothingness*, pp. 510, 511 (461, 462, 463). Without the key to interpretation, the acts of the (other's) body are sense-less.
67. Roland Barthes, *A Lover's Discourse, Fragments*, tr. Richard Howard (New York: Hill and Wang, 1978), pp. 2, 3, originally published in French as *Fragments d'un discours amoureux* (Paris: Éditions du Seuil, 1977), pp. 6, 7. The terms 'extreme solitude, ignored, displayed' are all used by Barthes in the prologne.
68. Barthes, *A Lover's Discourse, Fragments*, p. 4 (8). This implies that the lover, mistakenly or – what is the same – in bad faith, identifies 'himself' with where he has been.
69. Barthes, *A Lover's Discourse, Fragments*, pp. 7–8 (11–12). Thus the lover wishes to break codes apart, to seek 'his' love in a realm of freedom.
70. Barthes, *A Lover's Discourse, Fragments*, pp. 10, 11 (15, 16). The confirmation Barthes provides is that connection = death.
71. Barthes, *A Lover's Discourse, Fragments*, pp. 5, 6 (8, 9, 10). Throughout this paragraph, I have paraphrased using Barthes' terminology.
72. Roland Barthes, *A Lover's Discourse, Fragments*, pp. 5, 6, 7 (8, 9, 10). These terms are the names of various figures-fragments of the book.

73. Denis de Rougemont, *Love in the Western World*, tr. Montgomery Belgion (New Jersey: Princeton University Press, 1956), pp. 41–2, originally published in French as *L'Amour et l'Occident* (Paris: Plon, 1940).

74. Sartre, *Being and Nothingness*, p. 116 (111). There is nothing uniquely modern about the concept of bad faith.

75. Rougement, *Love in the Western World*, pp. 43, 44. One might claim that they want to know the meaning of their love.

76. Rougement, *Love in the Western World*, p. 51.

77. Sartre, *Being and Nothingness*, p. 350 (319).

78. Sartre, *Being and Nothingness*, p. 491 (445). Paradoxically, shame or humility depend on some connection, possibly even some code that can only be established through a relation that is not merely proximate, but affective, that is sympathy. 'A violent lover in like manner is very much displeas'd when you blame and condemn his love; tho' 'tis evident your opposition can have no influence but by the hold it takes of himself, and by his sympathy with you. If he despises you, or perceives you are in jest, whatever you say has no effect on him', Hume, *A Treatise of Human Nature*, p. 324.

79. Sartre, *Being and Nothingness*, p. 475 (431). In this way, Tristan and Iseult's indifference toward one another at least relieves them of hatred, sadism, masochism.

80. Sartre, *Being and Nothingness*, p. 511 (462–3).

81. Sartre, *Being and Nothingness*, pp. 491–3 (445–7). The inevitable failure of any human being to make themselves into an object is commensurate with the inevitability of bad faith. Yet, any transcendence is continuously attempting to make the Other into an object, thus to put them in the situation of being in bad faith. So, the question arises, who is responsible? Both? Neither?

82. Sartre, *Being and Nothingness*, pp. 494–534 (447–84).

83. Sartre, *Being and Nothingness*, pp. 495–6 (448–9). In practice, then, indifference appears to be the most powerful position any transcending subject may assume. There is no reason to believe that most subjects would not pursue it rather than risk suffering the effects of human conflict, namely bad faith. However, women, notably, in Sartre's analysis, are more likely than men to exist in bad faith – a failure on their part to practice indifference.

84. Sartre, *Being and Nothingness*, pp. 496, 497 (449, 450, 451). Of course, these are never simultaneous acts.

85. Jean-Paul Sartre, *Being and Nothingness*, pp. 510, 515, 532 (462, 466–7, 481–2).

86. Roland Barthes, *A Lover's Discourse*, pp. 140, 142, 143 (167, 169, 170). Yet, this so-called 'catastrophe' seems to involve no break, no leap, no transition to a new manifold, but rather a continuity, an extensity on which the previous affects, percepts, concepts are easily recycled.

87. Rougement, *Love in the Western World*, pp. 276, 277. This sort of millennialism may well continue to infect all philosophy. Bad faith appears commensurate with the rejection of fleshly sensibilities and the embrace of fleshly indifference.
88. Rougement, *Love in the Western World*, p. 277. It is a passion for indifference.
89. Rougement, *Love in the Western World*, p. 211.
90. Rougement, *Love in the Western World*, p. 279. Rougement endorses a modern version of Christianity. I do not follow him in this as a workable solution. Some would argue that current forms of church and state are codes that will be or must be undone, leaving the bare individual, effect of an infinity of affects, percepts and concepts, to wander alone.
91. Rougemont, *Love in the Western World*, pp. 286, 284. I have refashioned Rougement's argument to suit another one, one still merely suggested and not yet clearly stated.
92. Rougement, *Love in the Western World*, p. 285.
93. Sartre, *Being and Nothingness*, pp. 355–7 (323–5).

4

'Under Western Eyes'

Disjunctive justice

Once again, perhaps surprisingly, in the last chapter we found our-selves again influenced by the poet; the poet who absorbs and intuits, who is an ever-changing point of view, an effect of combinatorial net-works, light emanating from stars and planets, clouds and mountains, forests and seas, plants, animals, humans, vast cities, desolate plains, objects, images, sounds, tastes, odors, touch. She too emits shimmer-ing light. Let us begin by reminding ourselves that the words she uses, the language she speaks, the gestures she performs are the words and language, the gestures and performances of a crowd, a host of states combining, contributing, influencing one another and influencing her at every moment, at each arrival, when she speaks and gestures, emit-ting her own spatializing-temporalizing nexus. Thought on another scale, from a certain distance, she could still be conceived as little more than the effect of dispersed and dispersing intensities, partial, frag-mented and fragmenting. First, the connective syntheses in which what is most her own, her partial and discrete delusions would be connected to other partial and discrete elements that interrupt and carry her away from herself into new connections, unanticipated but apparently necessary. Necessary in order to articulate a desire that is not her desire, but desire itself, the immanent binary-linear sphere of possible differentiations. Her little delusion-producing machine would then follow the connective law of desiring-machines, which is, if she 'feels' something, she must 'produce' something, something that, neverthe-less, will be torn apart; that is the law of the dark precursor. In that scale, connective synthesis, defined in terms of the relation of the predicate to a subject or substance, this synthesis of connection comes undone in the violent encounter with an unrecognizable sign. Where contraries coexist, the being of the sensible defies common sense and good sense. Here, there will be no subjects and no objects, and we are left with the coexistence of more *and* less in an unlimited qualita-tive becoming that can be defined as free will or as desire. This is the structure that calls for the transcendental use of categories. Their use as Ideas of reason gives reality to the supersensible Ideas of god (the *a priori* manifold of unlimited qualitative becoming) freedom (the unconditioned series), and soul (the cracked *I*). Desire and unlimited qualitative becoming are one and the same but the manner in which they are distributed constitutes empirical subjects as human beings, works of art, or social policies. In other words, reason is concerned with the faculty of desire, with determining this will according to rules (hypothetical and categorical imperatives) but only insofar as the ground of choice is *not empirical* (thus not connected to pleasure or pain) but instead, wholly in accordance with an *unconditional practical law* in relation to which every single subject is passive.

The distribution of desire by means first, of the connection of fragments, and then as the production of the disjunctive synthesis is set in motion by the (in)sensible encounter with the transcendental Ideas that determine the plane and distribute its events. Disjunctive synthesis arises as the act of a god, a *deus ex machina* descending from the ontological heavens to create its objects by tearing apart every primitive organization that has sprung up in spite of its vigilance, and substituting an ongoing deterritorialization-reterritorialization. Now, everywhere, there will be consumption of existing goods, release from this, and then, new consumption directed toward newly stocked goods, whatever they may be.[1] Everywhere, there are so-called flows, effects of the sale of property, the circulation of money, new means of production, new products, new workers, unemployed workers, all contingently conjoined, intensifying, speeding up, all the while anticipating the dark precursor. The dynamical category of relation breaks up the monotonous binary linearity of the law of connection. For the poet, we claimed, this synthesis forestalls what might be considered a false antinomy between spatio-temporalization, the spontaneous eruption of her combinatorial networks, her special sensibilities, into an otherwise undisturbed linear causality, and the forces which strive to give her a rule, a purely intellectual determination. In the latter case, pleasure or pain, diffusion or distress, expansion or contraction are the result of the determination of the will by reason. What we will to do is a *feeling*, but given the rule, it is a feeling of constraint, of *passive restraint* that produces what we take to be pleasure, just as Plato's citizens of the *Republic* are said to achieve the highest levels of pleasure by following the rules dictated to and by their own souls. No longer blind and slavish, no longer varying and growing, no longer a burden, no longer discontent and out of control, the pleasures of passive restraint do not plague us with any sensibility or intimacy that would be incommensurate with the pure practical determination of desire and its pure practical creation.

Still, as we noted, on the scale of dynamical systems, the poet can be offered some compensation; to resolve her antinomy, she is offered death; it is the gift of the dark precursor. That is, on this scale, on this manifold, regardless of what she wills or thinks, she will be torn apart, she will be Promethean, a schizo, and if not, then catatonic, paranoid, or if a capitalist, neurotic; it is only a matter of which forces take hold of her. And yet, we hold out the possibility of other scales, of spatializations and temporalizations which are self-generating, bringing forth both the actor and her acts, displays of brilliance, diverted by a multiplicity of gleaming events, emerging from the past, a swath that takes form as what is most intimate, most her own, a place shaped as both an intensely private realm, touched by her heart, and an extensive, worldly realm open to anyone sensible to the scene where the woman enacts these words, wounding herself in an interval in which love is inseparable from mystery and mystery inseparable from one's own.

Nevertheless, some possible confusions might first be cleared up. In particular, the lack of clarity regarding outmoded uses of the concept of perspective. The realm of productive distribution, the continuous manifold, is not that of the Renaissance objective observer. This confusion and mingling of two systems, so different in their productions has been something of a diversion, a side-trip that distracts us, leads us astray. Productive distribution, the continuous manifold has remained hidden, nearly invisible, while intensive criticism has been leveled against a much less dangerous target, perspective. The perspectival observer of the work of art is said to be detached, maintaining visual distance from what is viewed so as to attempt to be in no way implicated in what is observed. The viewer maintains her point of view insofar as the perspectival artist uses techniques that guarantee the rationalization of representation, the rendering of what is perspectivally correct. This way of seeing the world constitutes the world as spatially and temporally hierarchized, 'a space organized in relation to a point of view through which order is imposed on the random variety of [homogeneous spaces].'[2] The question of whether the fixed point lies within or without the field in question is a matter for specialists. What remains is the idea of a 'privileged point,' a vanishing horizon, a symmetrically composed mechanical field, the illusion of three dimensions. Roughly, the advantage of such means are that any observer, using the same techniques, will achieve exactly the same results as any other observer insofar as the view here is intellectual and only partially perceptual. All observers are, as fixed points, ideally the same, and all observations are rationalized representations, thus they too must be the same. This view of the observer as the place holder of a privileged point does construct a privileged subject, a dominant viewer with no present time and place contemplating a proportional and hierarchical world. Such a view does imply specific and possibly on-going social, political and economic structures as well. Nevertheless, it is a view whose geometry remains fundamentally two-dimensional. It provides the illusion of three dimensions, but remains an overwhelmingly static world, hierarchized and feudal, a stage for players whose characters and roles were long ago determined by reminiscence, by history, religion and myth. As such, it is a still-born conception, a privileged view looking into the mythological past, and its impact on the emergent present was always, already non-existent. Thus, although we might not be surprised by any re-evaluation of perspective which claims that 'the subject of perspective, which is said to be "dominant" because it is established in a position of mastery, *this subject holds only by a thread*, however tightly stretched this might be,' we might also turn our attention away from this diversion to something whose influence is more powerful, more ominous in the contemporary world.[3]

So it is with some urgency that we undertake to distinguish the objectivity of single-point or even multiple-point perspective from what is often, if not always, taken to be the same thing, that is, the topology of continuous manifolds, the position of bodies in space at *any moment whatever*. This system is implicit in Kant insofar as the Kantian topology already implies n-dimensions and, eschewing the empirical, an infinity of virtual connections. Perhaps too, the Kantian manifold, the category of relation, is only the most vital, modern expression of an ancient idea, the idea that the power of nature is the divine power to break apart anything that has been connected, transforming every 'and . . . and . . . and' into 'or . . . or . . .or.' When connections are not broken apart, habits form, codes and relations appear where previously there were only continuous connections. Is this not, after all, the millennial view of divinity? It is a conception suggesting that it is the divine task, the ontological task of nature/god to disconnect what has been connected, to keep separate what otherwise might be related, coded, ordered, organized. In such a system, it may be the case that 'the schizophrenic voyage is the only kind there is.'[4] Is it a quirk of fate, a sheer contingency or is it inevitable that the differential relation, which describes the trajectories of the socius, that this same differential relation *expresses*, in the strong sense of expresses, that is, it conjoins its elements to produce, 'the fundamental capitalist phenomenon of *the transformation of the surplus value of code into a surplus value of flux*?'[5] Certainly one can see that when the mathematical, differential equation replaces the barbarian and feudal codes, this is related to a complete breakdown of the subsisting codes and territorialities. This breakdown, the disjunctive synthesis that deterritorializes capital, opening flows of financing, functioning as an axiomatic of abstract quantities, is a sluggish divine power. Its frenetic pace is irritatingly lethargic in the vicinity of attractors in the form of consumer goods. But the structure nevertheless benefits from the guarantee that 'the desire of the most disadvantaged creature will invest with all its strength, irrespective of any economic understanding or lack of it, the capitalist social field as a whole.'[6] But such endless delays, accidents, deviations are precisely the disjunctions that ensure the continuity, that keep the structure from displacing itself at infinite speeds even while ensuring 'the ruin of traditional sectors, the development of extraverted economic circuits, a specific hypertrophy of the tertiary sector, and an extreme inequality in the different areas of productivity and incomes.'[7] All we can do, it seems, is stave off death, which would be deprivation.

Thus, we should not be surprised to find theories of justice attempting to assist us in doing precisely this. When, for example, John Rawls embraces the Kantian view, he argues that political persons must regard themselves as self-authenticating sources of valid claims because they are independent of any particular set of ends or aims. They must remain independent, for any situatedness, any perspective would undercut the reasonableness and rationality of their thinking. This fundamental autonomy results in the establishment of the principle of equal liberty and the priority of individual rights over social and economic advantages, principles of justice, which Rawls finds to be based on the Kantian notion of autonomy or freedom. Indeed, why would we imagine the situation to be any different? Rawls believes that the objectivity and universality of Kantian ethics are its most trivial aspects, and that what really matters is the idea of autonomy or freedom, which is *that moral principles are rationally chosen*. In this matter, the Kantian wish 'that instead of the endless multiplicity of civil laws we should be able to fall back on their general principles . . . [For] the laws are only limitations imposed upon our freedom,' is likewise the wish of the creator of justice as fairness.[8] This makes moral philosophy into the study of the conception and outcome of rational decisions, decisions that will then be acceptable not only to the individual, but to all persons in the society. Presumably this acceptance is grounded in the fact that, for Kant, all 'men' are rational beings who, in Rawls' interpretation, are able to act freely because they are *autonomous*. This can only mean, for anyone who wishes to act on the basis of the freedom guaranteed by this structure, that for any citizen, 'the principles he acts upon are not adopted because of his social position or natural endowments, or in view of the particular kind of society in which he lives or the specific things that he happens to want.'[9] In other words, the principles of justice that are able to be endorsed are those of freedom; they are principles that any rational and independent person in an original position of political equality would choose. Crucial here is the idea, also expressed by Kant, that anyone who allows 'his' actions to be determined by sensuous desires or contingent aims is not free but is subject to nature's laws, which are laws of causality. As we have seen, if one's actions are causally determined whether by natural or social circumstances, freedom, in this conception, would not exist. So, the position from which free citizens choose their justice principles cannot be a perspective, but that position, that trajectory, upon which a noumenal self comes into contact with the world, or rather in which the world contacts each self, shaping and defining personality. Essentially, this view, which is no view at all but an Idea of freedom, is structured from *within* the continuous manifold, insofar as the noumenal world can never be experienced or known, but can only be hypothesized as the Idea, the condition of the possibility of experience and knowledge.[10]

Following from this, it makes perfect sense to define freedom as citizens seeking only what they reasonably can expect to get. They must restrict their justice claims to the virtual realm within the limits of the principles of justice operating in their society because of the manner in which they are chosen (not specified by any perspective) and because they are the perfect expression of rationality, freedom, and equality. That is, as Ideas of reason, they give reality to the supersensible Ideas of god (the *a priori* manifold of the original position), freedom (the unconditioned series generating the principles of justice), and soul (abstractly equal citizens). Yet what if it were the case that when citizens are unable to take their situation into consideration, that is, without a perspective, without a combinatorial network, such citizens cannot verify or provide an account of what is reasonable in 'their' society and even if they did, nothing in this theory would validate their account of what is reasonable? What is under consideration here is that both the n-dimensional, continuous theoretical or ontological world and the n-dimensional, continuous, practical, political world must be carefully circumscribed, limited by an analysis of the kind of power that produces them, their range of applicability, and accompanied by an inquiry into alternative conceptions. Undeniably, the continuous trajectory allows those with the power to adhere to unconditioned principles, to relegate any perspective emerging as *an original spatio-temporalization* to the realm of the private sphere. This is convenient, since it becomes clear that any original spatio-temporalization will be judged to be a private perspective and as such cannot be validated epistemologically, politically or morally (that is to say, empirically) as unconditioned, thus as free. Yet, consideration of particular instances of Western economic organization may lead us to ask if such an epistemology does not constitute the very structure of oppression, a particularly Western structure that so-called second- and third-world societies have had forced upon them by global powers which have the political and economic ascendancy that enables them to reproduce so-called objective freedom.

Asian sex tourism

Anthropologist Lenore Manderson was among the first feminist scholars to make the pilgrimage to Bangkok to observe the sex acts, dances, pornographic tricks, and intercourse that takes place in the sex bars located in the district of Patpong. She may be somewhat unusual, however, in that although she is a Westerner, she disregarded the prohibition against nativism and allowed herself to come under the influence of the codes and concerns of native men and women. What Manderson reports in her early studies exceeds the now nearly familiar descriptions of the routine and disassociated, often drug-aided sex performances of (mostly) young women, many of whom are still teenagers. Manderson traces the organization of two different aspects of the sex industry in Thailand and gives an account of the link between women's public sex performances and traditional Thai cultural practices, images, structures, and understandings of sexuality, maleness, and femaleness.[11] Although the fact that female sex workers use their bodies as a 'means of production' is generally acknowledged by most critics and analysts, it is generally less well recognized that in so doing they fulfill their own purposes as well as those of the customers who buy them and the bar owners who sell them. That is, by using their own bodies as a means of production, young Thai women may fulfill their traditional obligations as mothers and daughters since sex work provides them with income enough to support ageing parents as well as extended families whose size can be vast. In so doing, young women have raised their status within the society. In many of the poorest families, the birth of a daughter might even be seen as an opportunity for social mobility rather than as a burden.

More recently, this is also the case for many Burmese women, who have been described as fleeing a repressive political regime as well as extreme poverty in their homeland, in order to work in the Thai sex trade. Since prostitution is illegal in Thailand, sex workers who are interviewed by foreign scholars and agencies may not feel free to express themselves. Nevertheless, Thai police report that most Burmese women come to Thailand to work in the sex industry by choice. Moreover, many young women from Thailand, the Philippines, Malaysia, and China willingly go to Australia to work, where they are not welcomed with visas, as they would be were they from the UK or Canada.[12] The extent to which women are entering this labor market by choice may indicate that the destruction of local codes by global capitalism is welcomed. All over the world, one sees women, young and old, in public, working, dressing in Western style clothing, embracing the freedom from traditions that have enslaved them for centuries. When Western economists proclaim the 'benefits' of global capitalism, this may not be what they have in mind; however, young women, in particular, seem to embrace the loosening of traditional codes and the personal freedom that capitalism seems to offer. Men too seek some means by which they may break or at least minimize the traditional codes that orient what is or is not acceptable behavior. Manderson argues that for Thai men, the existence of brothels and sex shows has come to provide an institutional means by which local men can briefly step outside marriage without disrupting otherwise highly constrained personal, economic, and kinship ties. Although the duties of Thai women and men with respect to their families and the structure of family relations may be highly problematic or repressive for women and men, nonetheless, as Manderson and others have pointed out, the local attitudes and concerns of Thai women and men are usually overlooked when the use of the body in the production of sex becomes absorbed into Western economies and value structures. Alison Murray singles out the UNESCO report from 1995, on contemporary forms of slavery, that uses terms such as 'trafficking, prostitution and sexual exploitation interchangeably and refers to them as sordid, dangerous and inhuman,' even as sex workers complain of the moral hypocrisy of global capitalism and sexual repression, including criminal penalties for prostitution, as contributing significantly to the exploitation, discrimination against, and negative attitudes towards women's sexuality.[13]

In a second study, Manderson considers what appear to be the 'most flamboyant and excessive aspects of the sex industry,' those created for international sex tourism, in particular, for male tourists from Europe, America, Australia, and Japan. Unexpectedly, when one examines Western representations of Thailand – from the 1970s soft porn film series *Emmanuel* to current international sex tourism brochures – one finds glowing reports of Asian women's love of white men which are symptomatic not of the sensibilities and perspectives of the Asian women, but rather of the strong Western desire to see and exploit Asian bodies, an exploitation aided by extolling the purported 'naturalness' of Asian women's sexuality and willingness to serve. But also, within and accompanying these texts, there are apparent, well defined moral attitudes concerning the necessity of containing Asian male lust, which otherwise would be visited upon Asian women who should be reserved for 'whites,' especially Westerners. In addition, the desire for containment reaches its pragmatic limits when Western men seek to make use of anonymous male and female Asian bodies to create scenarios, in film and on stage, that would serve to liberate Western, white women's so-called, repressed sexuality. What is particularly notable here is that although both local and global aspects of the sex industry commodify, thus subjugate women to the axiomatic of money, the dark precursor that tears apart all traditional coded social relations, it is principally among Westerners (Europeans, Americans, and Australians) that the moral element dominates the market relationship.

In the history of Western thinking about sexuality, the usual structure of this moralism has been to bifurcate and dichotemize bodies and minds. Plato's *Symposium* establishes this quite neatly for us by characterizing the body as an impediment to realization of the Ideas of the good, the beautiful, the true, and the just.[14] Plato's assertion that the 'Idea' of beauty must be the chief example of the so-called eternal Ideas because of its accessibility seems a cruel joke, since the Idea of beauty concerns only beautiful forms which are purely intelligible and intellectual, the sensuous element having been quickly discarded in the ascension to the intelligible realm. In addition, for Plato, access to the intelligible realm implies the necessity of a particular morality, a rigorous and ordered manner of living that ensures that one's intellect is not troubled with bodily concerns, so that consciousness remains unclouded. But Plato's morality is not ours. The methods he uses to guide the soul away from its sensuous nature, bringing it to the point where it willingly leaps across the abyss into a purely intelligible realm are entirely dependent upon having the right philosophical guide and a properly wisdom-loving nature. The method, although compelling, is ultimately unreliable insofar as the circumstances in which the transit takes place are not something available to any and all rational beings. It is not until the seventeenth and eighteen centuries that universal, and therefore presumably foolproof, methods of bifurcation were fully articulated. Aided by the mind-body dualism of the rationalist philosophy of René Descartes, but searching for something less dependent on a benevolent god or pure intuitions, social contract theorists posit a metaphysics of nature accompanied by a naturalistic ethic whose code of conduct is scientifically, that is to say, rationally, derived from a principle of nature. This leads them to formulate a system of rational morality according to which virtue pays off. Kantian practical reason is, in many respects, the accumulation of these positions reformulated so that the rational thought of an individual is not circumscribed by his or her own sensuous nature. If rationality may not be circumscribe by sensibility, then it follows that natural causality is equally problematic. The only acceptable rational framework is that one provided by god, or rather 'his' rational substitute, the space-time manifold cut through by the dark precursor.

In the process of investigating and criticizing this tradition for its effects on women, feminist theorists have often chosen to begin with the observation that the bodily aspects of life, which these philosophers necessarily degrade and malign for restricting freedom, has been associated almost exclusively with the female.[15] Others, not incorrectly I think, have maintained that philosophical constructs which have sought to define women without giving women a voice must be totally undermined and a new language, including new forms of syntax, that expresses women's reality devised.[16] However, it is possible that as important and useful as these critiques have been (and I cannot overstate their value), even these approaches appear to miss the problem at hand. Manderson's work, as well as that of other researchers in the field, suggests a different strategy, one that must be taken equally seriously. For, although there is no denying the blatant commodification of women's bodies which silences women as subjects and agents, there remains the necessity of earning a living to support families who would otherwise be impoverished and suffering. This is not the 'desire' of Western capitalism, for the decoding of flows demands excess, something that the 'Good Woman of Bangkok' does not participate in, except insofar as she, like other sex workers, is an excess, an overcoding of sexuality anticipating the moment when it too will be set 'free.' And that moment arrives quickly. Women's earning capacity in the sex industry is between three to ten times greater than it would be in any other type of employment available to them. Studies throughout the 1980s indicated that a large percentage of prostitutes engage in this occupation to make money for home needs. Among a group interviewed in one study, up to 80 per cent had built houses for their parents and every one was supporting parents and children.[17] Meeting needs dictated by tradition and material circumstances determines lives to a far greater degree than Western theorists and journalists acknowledge. This continues in spite of the destruction of traditional codes, a destruction that women often embrace insofar as it gives them power and independence from men as well as parents.

Thus, in order to study the lives and circumstances of Asian or any group of third-world women, we might want to begin by questioning ourselves and limiting, or at least delimiting, our own power. What presuppositions and values do we take for granted and how does this differ from what Asian or third-world women are seeking? To what extent are their preferences already predictable expressions of trajectories determined by forces of capture whose structure has always, already manifested itself, ordering and organizing not only themselves and their localization, but that of generations before them? Chandra Mohanty has argued, in an essay which the title of this chapter quotes, that:

> a homogeneous notion of the oppression of women as a group is assumed, which, in turn, produces the image of an 'average' third-world woman. This average third-world woman leads an essentially truncated life based on her feminine gender (read sexually constrained) and [on] being 'third-world' (read ignorant, poor, uneducated, tradition-bound, religious, domesticated, family-oriented, victimized, etc.).[18]

This conception of third-world women as decoded, deterritorialized then reterritorialized as commodities, as expressions of the unstoppable force of axiomatization, would be incomplete if they were not also determined to be universally victimized. Such a conception does not merely obscure the economic realities and concrete networks organizing individual lives, it relegates them to the status of details with little or no import, since, as usual, everything has already been determined on a conceptual basis that rules out the sensibilities of living beings, their vulnerable spatio-temporalization, the emergence of points of view constituted as a crowd, and assigns them the status of codes, codes awaiting deterritorialization and axiomatization.

Moreover, this conception is singularly Western, for it is saturated with moralism, indeed it may be thinkable *only* as saturated with moralism. Even as Westerners deterritorialize and axiomatize Asian women for the sake of what they take to be an exotic (meaning erotic) or perverse form of sexuality, they constitute the capitalist form of deterritorialization-axiomatization as something that women desire, not in or as a perspective, but universally. Deterritorialization-axiomatization is constituted as something completely and universally natural to Asian women insofar as the attentions of white Westerners are construed as a desirable (meaning code-free) alternative to what is assumed to be the women's absolute degradation and victimization within their own culture at the hands of vulgar and brutish Asian men or within the more traditional codes of women's social and familial roles. Roughly speaking, the translation is as follows: these women are naturally exotic (meaning promiscuous or highly sexed), so white, Western attention (sexual or sociological, axiomatic or ontological) is therefore morally uplifting, that is, it decodes flows and frees desire. Any judgment of this type can be expressed in universal terms such as, 'one ought to encourage others (including Asian women) toward moral advancement,' terms that disguise the idealization implicit in the judgments of the Westerner and provide a moral screen for the process of deterritorialization and reterritorialization.[19] In fact, this form of universalization is one with moralism. In the guise of moral advancement, it justifies the sex industry and accounts for the way in which Westerners tend to produce naturalized images of third-world women as ignorant, domesticated, and victimized within their own cultures. Rather than focusing on the realities of Asian women and men's lives, their combinatorial influences, their vulnerable sensibilities, their points of view which are crowd-phenomena, the Western view idealizes. Moral advancement is an idealized category that excludes the particulars of Asian lives, cultures, and social structures. Citing Onora O'Neill,

Alisa Carse states that with respect to moral theory, the problem is not theories that abstract:

> It is rather theories that 'not only abstract but idealize. Idealization masquerading as abstraction, produces theories that appear to apply widely, but which covertly exclude those who do not match a certain ideal, or match it less well than others.'[20]

The result of idealization then is that those Asian women and men who are excluded may then be judged defective or inadequate.

Likewise, Western representations of Asian sexuality and sex, which reach far back beyond the popular American film images of Yul Brynner as the King of 'Siam,' represent Asian men as bodies driven mechanically by lust, and therefore also available for deterritorialization and axiomatization by Westerners who nevertheless indict Asian males as morally corrupt and hold them accountable as the source of the moral corruption of women. This accusation of the potential and actual moral demise of ordinary but mostly non-male, and, by extension, non-Western persons permeates modern and contemporary Western philosophy. It is a morality according to which young Asian women are universally corrupted by the promiscuity of Asian men, yet paradoxically remain attuned to and even welcome the desires of 'superior' Western males, those inhabitants of advanced, capitalist nations whose attentions are manifestations of freedom. Western news reports of female Asian sex workers seldom address social or cultural factors converging on women and girls and are unable to discern even the existence of a woman's own sensibility. Instead, the plight of young sex workers is described collectively as the 'paramount moral challenge *we* will face in this century,' and it is especially noted that American women's groups have been shamefully inactive in addressing this moral challenge.[21] It is no surprise then, that white, Western males continue to intervene in the lives of Asian women. When a girl runs away from a stormy relation with her family at the age of fourteen and turns to prostitution to survive, a heroic male Westerner attempts to rescue her, first by buying her from the bar owner where she works, then returning her to her family in a small village with cash to start a business. But the girl cannot be recoded and runs away, back to her desperate life, refusing any further assistance from any humanitarian groups. Stopping the sex traffickers, we are told, has become a hot issue among conservative, evangelical Christians who have pushed the American president to act, to push the director of the 'Trafficking

Office' to 'bludgeon' foreign governments, to force them to curb the practice of prostituting 'under-age' girls or face sanctions.[22] Meanwhile, recent reports continue to emerge of Chinese girls who 'not long ago' had been kidnapped into the sex trade, 'but these days the trade has become largely voluntary,' a system of girls 'working outside,' sending money home, transforming poor villages into 'dazzling pockets of affluence,' tiled villas with air-conditioning and home-entertainment centers.[23] Experts worry that young men are left without mates and note that in these villages, it is girl children, not boys, who are prized. Thus, the problem continues to be articulated in terms of *we Westerners*, and the solutions must come from *us*. Meanwhile, the young Thai prostitute, during her interview with the American, sits listlessly in her room, watching television, paying little attention to the negotiations swirling around her, except to proclaim, '*this* is hell.' The referent of *this* is never ascertained, it is simply assumed.

Given such a situation, what are we to do? If we are to confront and undermine the moralism, inherent in the spread of Western universalization to the Asian sex industry or to any non-Western or Western minority group by means of its link to international sex tourism, a critique based on the commodification of women, their axiomatization, by virtue of their universal deterritorialization from local codes – including traditional roles as well as subjection to male consumption and male lust – is just not enough. Although such a critique challenges the sex industry for its manipulation and exploitation of women, it will never confront the profound moral and ontological justifications for this exploitation. It is difficult to make claims about what may be proposed in place of this compelling if not overpowering structure. One risks, immediately, becoming caught up in the system one is attempting to abandon. Or, what may be worse, one risks a multitude of naïve mistakes and errors. Methodologically, negotiating precariously between pure concepts and concrete realities is perhaps foolish, as structures and concepts are what allow one to make sense of the real to begin with. For this reason we dare not ask about the sense, the meaning, or even the structure of these events, but rather, cautiously, yet of necessity, we may attempt to begin with the sensibilities, the pleasure and pain, the expansion and contraction, diffusion and distress arising from the interconnecting networks, the causal sets, the intuitions, without which no life and no thought emerge.

Moral universalization

Are we at last openly able to address the rationale, in Western accounts, for the unacceptability of recognizing perspectives between and among Asian women and the role this refusal plays in their axiomatization? What happens when networks of relations connecting the combinatorial sensibilities of women, called 'third-world' or 'sex worker,' encounter the structure of morality and the process of idealized universalization that are commensurate with Western philosophy? Can we reconceptualize life and thought apart from universalizing moralism or are we so thoroughly formed by these structures that the best we can hope for is to stay a step ahead? Is our only option to anticipate infinite contacts with affects, percepts, concepts, prospects, and functives? Should we attempt to move, or to be moved, at infinite speeds, torn apart, disjoined, just barely evading the rapidly reforming territorializations, those of capital, but ultimately, those of life in general, the syntheses that dis-join only in order to more thoroughly con-join, at the zero degree, all the elements of the universe? What would remain then, of the Idea of freedom? Instead of that freedom of autonomy in the face of causality, which presumes a belief in the inevitability, the necessity, of *linear* causality to begin with, what may come about when our own sensibilities, our own imagination, moral reasoning and rational understanding are pushed to their limits in a struggle that gives rise, not to good or evil, pleasure or pain, harmony or discord, but to that good *and* bad, pleasure-pain, discordant-accord of our sensible *and* intellectual milieu? Will it help us to resolve these questions to pay attention, as it has been suggested that we should, to the Kantian doctrine of the faculties? By which I mean, that furtive yet presumably explosive moment when Kant introduces what the poet Rimbaud calls 'a long gigantic, and rational derangement of all the senses'?[24] Is this truly the undoing of time as succession, a succession of homogeneous moments, the succession of nature, of linear causality, of dependence and subjugation? Does this derangement, this discordant-accord of the faculties bring us to the same point, the point where we meet with Kant who is brought by his own doctrines to create or discover a new definition of time, one according to which there is no succession of homogenous, temporal moments, thus no determining causality and thereby nothing to free ourselves from other than our own illusions?

If Kant were successful, this new definition would promise to open up a fissure that simultaneously dissolves any transcendental and

unified sense of self, world or god. It would promise too to bring radically into question our understanding of autonomy and freedom, an
understanding which the theory of justice as well as recent, Western
democratic ideals struggle through. Is this, as many have suggested,
not after all a concern with the limits of transcendental Ideas? Are we
done with god, world and soul, and have we now turned in the direction of a much more pragmatic concern that unquestioningly accepts
the demise of the transcendental manifold, yet attempts to fill its
forlorn void with bracing optimism, with rational communicative
freedom, thereby relocating the debate on the same scale but this time
in the vicinity of particular attractors? Should we be speaking here of
global democracy, civil society, the public sphere, the nation-state?
Certainly, it has become commonplace, even or especially among
thinkers who wear a radical mantle that in society some notion of
principles of justice can and must be relied on to determine the distribution of benefits and burdens of citizenship as well as to assign rights
and duties.[25] We have been told that it is 'natural' to think of a concept
of justice derived from what different concepts of justice have in
common. Likewise, when finally, the concept of 'reasonable pluralism'
is admitted in place of simple 'justice as fairness,' it is also natural, we
are advised, for this concept to be *shared by everyone*, although there
is no expectation that they will share religion or morality, even insofar
as these may be purely reasonable doctrines. What is shared in a civil
state structured by reasonable pluralism is the commitment to tolerate
'reasonable' private points of view while keeping them *out* of politics.
Private points of view have no place in the public-political sphere,
which is, also, the sphere of rational freedom, freedom from causality.
Admitting these private points of view remains impossible since
this would unquestioningly open the door to political and moral intu-
itionism and thus to everyday ideas of justice based on each one's own
situation and customs, a primitive system of coding, long-since dis-
mantled.[26] How much more problematic would be an idea of justice
based on one's own sensibilities, one's own ever-changing emergent
perspective which emerges as the perspective of a crowd? Not separate
and opposed to the light that informs and forms it, instead a concept
of justice that emerges out of the very perspective created by those
combinatorial networks spinning out as a vast illuminated spatio-
temporalization, a concept that may or may not be true or false today,
and equally, may or may not be true or false in the future. The reliance
on custom and current expectations is unsatisfactory because it
lacks any criteria for determining which 'competing' interests should

prevail. Admitting so-called private points of view means that different people will give different weight to different interests and this, it is argued, is not satisfactory because should this occur, there is no guarantee that equal rights or liberties, which is to say, acausal freedom, will always prevail in the establishment of social and economic equality.[27] No group or groups, whether on the right or on the left, may be permitted to destabilize the system of equal rights and liberties, regardless of the social or economic benefits, for in the end, it is implied, all that this would produce is adversity, the confusion of competing interests, enslavement to homogeneous temporality.

All reasonable doctrines, it is claimed, do tolerate or advocate reasonable pluralism. Reasonable pluralism remains completely impartial with respect to various private points of view, yet reasonable pluralism dictates some sort of shared basis. This basis is that 'certain ideas that are taken to be implicit in the public political culture of a democratic society,' can be retained.[28] The key word here is implicit because Rawls, for example, has a rather definite notion of what is implicit. Although Rawls will no longer demand that all citizens endorse the moral doctrine of justice as fairness, he will nonetheless maintain that a political conception of justice *is* moral in a modern constitutional democracy. It is moral because it exemplifies certain ideals, principles and standards, norms that articulate the political values of modern democratic institutions.[29] Moreover, having asserted this, it is necessary to maintain that this political-moral conception must operate in one *unified* system of social cooperation from one generation to the next. Even so, the claim is put forth that this political doctrine can stand alone without reference to any moral doctrine insofar as the latter is a general and comprehensive view including conceptions that extend to values in human life, ideals of friendship and family, and generally covers all values and virtues in a precisely articulated system. In short, the principle difference between a political morality and a general morality appears to rest largely with the higher degree of articulation and application of the latter. Whether or not they can be separated as neatly as this remains to be seen.

In addition to differences in their degree of articulation and application, political and general moralities are representative of the difference between public and private culture. Public culture consists of the political institutions of a constitutional regime and their public forms of interpretation such as the courts.[30] Public culture excludes what might be called 'background culture,' religious, philosophical and moral doctrines as well as the culture of daily life, that of social interactions and even of social and economic institutions such as universities and the entire sphere of business, whether local, national, or global. Background culture appears to be similar to the concept of a state emerging from the changing constellation of events, the spatializing and temporalizing influences manifesting themselves in every perspective, yet it is a more limited notion insofar as background culture is most likely constituted by 'individuals.' Certainly, a point of view is not an emergent perspective for Rawls, since the former implies a particular spatial location, which although it may alter, is nonetheless static, whereas an emergent perspective is a changing state, absorbing and emitting multiple influences extending from vast networks. Instead, the liberal individual is defined by the rules of its trajectory such that 'liberals share . . . a commitment to three basic doctrines . . . the doctrines of voluntarism, independence, and asociality.'[31] In other words, the individual both *is* and *exists* alone. Reasonable, impartial, only lightly burdened by affective relations with other individuals insofar as such connections are claimed to be purely contingent, the individual is the model of Sartrean 'good faith.' Thus, the reason for the exclusion of background culture appears be that Rawls takes only political institutions to be a source of implicitly shared ideas and principles while private ones are not. This would be the case, but only on a continuous trajectory, where the rules of the system are one with its political institutions. On this view, a reasonably pluralistic society is defined as one that has a democratic, political tradition, whose citizens are judged to be morally free and equal persons in a well-ordered society regulated by a political conception of justice, a conception whose hidden ontology is one with its concept of the universal and whose private points of view are the scattered and fragmented remnants of universal deterritorialization.[32] This is the meaning of the admission that so-called pure procedural justice is probably best embedded in a Western normative framework, one that tolerates pluralism and advances individualism. In this sense, Rawls is not that far removed from Sartre. In such a system, persons are free to the extent that they both have and apply a conception of justice and a sense of the good as well as the power of reason, and they are equal to the extent that they *make use of* these powers.[33] In other words, freedom is reasonable, impartial and asocial, and equality is transcendence.

It remains somewhat surprising, if not shocking, that the cultural background, consisting of social and economic institutions, should play no role in the theory of the liberal, political state. For, in spite of

Rawls' deferral of culture, there are far-reaching social as well as economic claims upon citizens associated with 'justice as fairness.' Is it not the case, as has been stated above, that particular social and economic claims are implicitly justified and others are *excluded* by the *idealized* moral position on which such a political theory is constructed? The economic and social claims include the following. First, there are social and economic inequalities in society (Rawls affirms that there may be, and that inequalities may be quite large). Second, inequalities must be attached to positions and offices open to everyone. However, this means only that there is equal opportunity but no limit on social status or wealth. Furthermore, the least advantaged members of society must receive the greatest benefit from any social and economic inequalities. Such economic and social claims are always, however, subordinated to the claim to a fully adequate scheme of equal basic rights and liberties for everyone. Equal rights and liberties always trump equal opportunity and the greater benefit of the disadvantaged.[34] Why complain? Is not equality the basis of the democratic ideal of freedom? One might complain because, as one might point out, there is a discrepancy if not outright contradiction in the notion that those who are most disadvantaged can somehow receive the greatest benefits from inequalities, a discrepancy that is never addressed. If the most disadvantaged were to receive the greatest benefits, it is difficult to see how they would remain permanently disadvantaged, unless such gains were always and immediately undermined by the demands of equal basic rights and liberties. If the women of Thailand or Cambodia were able to benefit from their disadvantage, to the point where they were no longer economically, socially, politically or morally disadvantaged, the structure that 'benefits' them would be overturned. Offering equal basic rights and liberties, when these are restricted to moral-political *idealized* universalizations, is meaningless. Moreover, political liberalism's moral position on reasonable pluralism in the liberal, political state appears tailored to correspond to the epistemological claim that political persons regard themselves as self-authenticating sources of valid claims because they are *independent of any particular set of ends or aims.*[35]

This would be the case if so-called individuals are merely effects, the scattered remainders of affects, percepts, concepts, prospects and functives, wrenched from their smothering codifications, then randomly reassembled. This is true equality. No one is at fault if you are female, third-world, sickly, undernourished, denied an education. No one is responsible for the forces that overtake you. In any case, the

Idea is there for you. Are you materially oppressed? Pay no attention, embrace the Idea of transcendent freedom. Just remember:

> bad faith is not restricted to denying the qualities which I possess, to not seeing the being which I am. It attempts also to constitute myself as being what I am not. It apprehends me positively as courageous when I am not so . . . my effort in bad faith must include the ontological comprehension that even in my usual being, what I *am*, I am not it really.[36]

If this is the case for sadness or courage, is it not all the more the case for women, for those who are oppressed, those who are silenced? Any situatedness, which Rawls conceptualizes as a point, a silent, immanent point on an otherwise transcendent trajectory, a point with a particular view (which could be rethought in another system as an emergent perspective), such a situation would, by definition, undercut the reasonableness and rationality of the claims produced by these citizens. This is a convenient definition, particularly chilling when we remember that justice as fairness and political liberalism delimit freedom as citizens seeking only what they reasonably can expect to get, that is, they must restrict their justice claims to within the limits of the principles of justice operating in their society. But given the necessity that in order to be truly just, the entire system of justice as fairness must rest completely on the respect for persons' autonomy or freedom, then it must be clear that individual conceptions of the good, that is, one's personal morality, one's point within the manifold, must necessarily be excluded from the political realm.

Turning back to Kant and to Western representations of Asian women and men, we might see that by excluding the personal points of view, the individual moralities of situated citizens, theorists like Kant and Rawls, although claiming to be neutral with respect to any particular interpretation of the good, can nonetheless impose their own conception of the good. What would this be? Their own interpretation appears to be a transcendental conception according to which the good is equivalent to autonomy, the continual evacuation of any point of view. It has been argued that the refusal to rank particular conceptions of the good implies a strong tolerance for individual inclinations, but this would be misleading. In fact, it implies no respect for individual inclinations at all, coupled with the recognition that they are inevitable. For in the face of autonomy, individual inclinations are little more than articles of bad faith. Bad faith is an immediate threat to the autonomy of one's projects because it is the nature of consciousness to be what it is not and not to be what it is![37]

Autonomy cannot be the simple, unimpeded pursuit of one's own path. In this system, autonomy is keeping one's project ahead of oneself so as to never *be* that project, yet never to be cut off from it either. This conclusion may be supported by the assertion, from Rawls, that the notion of autonomy formulated by justice as fairness is to be found in Kant. In Kant's troika of pure reason, practical reason, and judgment, understanding is given the considerable task of legislating in the faculty of knowledge while reason is dedicated to legislating in the faculty of desire. Judgment, however, is assigned the task of freeing itself in order to set all the faculties in motion in a free agreement. Although understanding, under the provenance of theoretical reason, governs what can be known and the manner of knowing anything, it is practical reason and its rule over the faculty of desire that remains the most powerful aspect of reason insofar as practical reason demands freedom from causality.[38] The causality under consideration here is apparently linear causality, the unending chain of events leads up to an unconditioned first cause although no connection between the first cause and the chain of causes is possible for understanding. While it is true that in the first critique, the conflict between pure thought creating its objects and the necessary condition that thought be bound to sensibility appears to give rise to the conflict of the second critique, the necessity of freedom in spite of the mechanical laws of nature, nonetheless, it is the latter, practical reason (and not theoretical reason) that posits an absolutely spontaneous first cause that stands outside of nature even while theoretical reason, for the sake of understanding, demands that we remain bound to events forming trajectories in the manifold of space-time.

Given the demand of speculative reason, that all our knowledge conform to possible experience, it seems that the idea of an unconditioned first cause would have fast fallen into the realm of illusion, even within the limits of the Kantian system. Yet, we find ourselves making judgments of the character 'Asian men ought to be encouraged toward moral advancement.' In service to this moral end, a particular agenda may then be set in place to the effect that 'Asian men *ought* not to consume Asian women,' or, 'Western men *ought* to control Asian men.' The question here is what principle insists on the 'ought' and what is the status of the subject and the object of the sentence? If the principle of action is based on a subjective ground of determination, what is willed depends on pleasure or pain with respect to some *object*. If the ground of determination is subjective and empirical, *ought* does no more than express the relation of what is desired (not to permit the consumption of women, to control men) to the subject's feeling of pleasure or pain. The subjective ground of determination, however, is merely a material practical principle and can never produce a universal judgment of the kind Western sex tourism and its reformers both make use of since choice arising from a subjective and empirical ground is motivated by the idea of pleasure to be received from some object.[39] Such a system is too unstable to be relied on by Western capitalist production and too many Western reformers have not taken this into consideration. Subjective motives, those stemming from the subject's feeling of pleasure or pain, are different for every person and can never produce an adequate, that is, consistent and consistently profitable industry. As Kant reminds us, innumerable conflicts between opposing maxims are inevitable. Material practical principles (Rawls' private points of view) can never be an adequate ground of choice for the faculty of desire. Merely empirical, they rely on individual needs; they proscribe action but only as a means to some particular end, only as an efficient or immediate cause in relation to a desired effect. They invoke no freedom; they commit the individual to the sincerity of bad faith.[40] However, harmonizing maxims of subjective desire, even if it were possible, misses the point. The point is not to harmonize but to discover a law, a rule for action. No capitalist enterprise involving an estimated 500,000 to 700,000 sex workers employed by brothels, massage parlors, nightclubs, bars, coffee shops, tea houses, barber shops, go-go bars, cafeterias, and on the streets can survive and prosper on a foundation of subjective principles.[41] It is simply too risky; its successes are accidental; moreover, it is judged to be immoral insofar as it lacks autonomy. Without some other more expansive, universal and ideal practical principle that can proscribe a rule for action independently of subjective feelings and individual points of view, the sex industry would collapse, at least as a quasi-deterministic and therefore reliable money-making enterprise.

For philosophy, the stakes are also high. That is, as Kant conceives of it, with only a subjective foundation, reason's positing of freedom as the unconditioned for a totality of conditions is indeed an illusion. An illusion because subjective emotion is not an adequate foundation for the universal 'ought.' Without a universal practical principle, we are subject to nature's mechanical (read efficient, thus linear) causality with no guarantee of an uncaused first cause. The relevant conclusion here may be that capitalism requires, for its successful engagement in the sex industry, a guarantee of universal, objective freedom. How is this to be achieved? According to Kant, we are saved from subjective outcomes, saved from economic uncertainty and international social chaos by our own conscience. Conscience is that painful feeling of self-blame and reproach when our own subjective causality, our sense of ourselves as autonomous, emerging in contrast to the stream of nature's mechanical causality, produces in us a feeling of anguish which culminates in recognition of a sacred 'ought.' Conscience, *good* faith, is that event for which 'to believe is to know that one believes, and to know that one believes is no longer to believe . . . this in the *unity* of one and the same non-thetic self-consciousness.'[42] What then is the ought? According to what standard are we judging our maxims when we suffer the pain and anguish of conscience, the shame of bad faith, the conflict of contradiction that drives our faculties to their limits? What, as intelligible beings, are we to do that will not merely disguise conflict or vainly attempt to harmonize it, but will take us beyond it, transporting us in a sublime passage? According to the rule of freedom, we ought to determine our will according to another standard, not that of sensuous desire but that of the legislative form of maxims.

The legislative form of maxims is structured so as to be completely independent of natural causality; it is truly free and the will that it legislates is a free will. Unlike the maxims of subjectively determined desire, which are empirical, which differ from person to person, and which offer no uniform standard insofar as such a standard would be prior to all feeling, we must be able to discover a practical rule which directly determines the will. How do we locate it? Unfortunately, insofar as we are both free and not free, we cannot know this law immediately, except as *negation*, as the check on self-love and the annihilation of self-conceit. Nothing in our experience is explained by the law of freedom which is freedom from natural causality; as a result, following reason in the direction of an unconditioned outside or beyond the causal series ends in antinomy. How can a maxim of one's own will simultaneously stand as a principle establishing universal law? How can one determine one's own causality through a rule?[43] Go first, Kant counsels, to the accessible subjective maxims, such as, 'I desire submissive women whom I can subject to my will,' or 'I dislike women I cannot subject to my will,' or 'I dislike Asian men, I am unable to subject them to my will.' Then, abstract from all empirical conditions until only the form of subjective law-giving remains, until only the universal is left. If we abstract from every particular object that is the goal of any particular desire, what we are left with is the form of *giving* the *universal rule* rather than any particular object. We are left with pure *a priori* commanding or giving which legislates. This is what Kant calls 'freedom in the strictest, that is, transcendental sense,' insofar as this form is the form of all our maxims, and by giving or commanding universal law, it is the prior and legislative form by which we can judge all material and personal maxims.[44] It is the form maxims must assume in order for capital to be able to take the chaos of material and personal desires and maxims and transform them into profits in the international sex tourism industry.

However, in order for legality or universal, commanded law to be moral law, a further condition must be met: the objective, determining ground of the will must also be the subjectively sufficient determining ground of an action. It must be possible for objective moral law to become an incentive, a motive, a subjective, determining ground of a will belonging to a finite human being subject to a sensible condition and material maxims.[45] Motives are taken to be mere subjective facts – desires, emotions, passions – that *motivate* certain acts. Causes are taken to be objective states of affairs. Their juxtaposition is taken to be a conflict between passion and will. Given this situation, what can a consciousness do? What *is* done? Freedom must move one step beyond, beyond even the leap to the unconditioned in a series of causes. Through the power of negation, the objective determining ground can be made immanent, brought down to the surface. And . . . the subjective determining ground can be made immanent, raised up to the same surface. By means of the *act* of negation, objective will and subjective motives form a continuum. The cause (*motif*) does not determine an action, it appears in and through the action as a project, a project that must always be projected ahead of any consciousness. Freedom has its own structure; it projects itself toward its own possibilities, thus it is the being of this freedom, this for-itself that makes, that does by acting. It makes certain objective structures in the world. Simultaneously, it experiences itself non-thetically, as this project, these acts, and in this discovers its motives. This rational self-love is the recognition of itself as freedom, as transcendence.[46]

Moral law is known only as a negative incentive; this is its transcendent character. It has a negative effect on feeling; it *checks* any and all inclinations, it chokes off all subjective motives. This check on our inclinations suffocates them; it suffocates us, leaving us gasping in pain. Moral law puts a check on selfishness, restricting it while slyly allowing its return in the form of rational self-love, but it is the death-knell of self-conceit (of sincerity or faith) since worthiness must remain a pure effect of *a priori* law. By means of the power of negation, legality rejects every sensible condition, every singular 'I desire,' as its determining ground. Human reality may try to refuse freedom. What I sincerely believe I desire, I may attempt to posit as a subjective determining ground, whether it is a matter of my belief in god, my deterministic conformity to nature, or the formation of my self in society. Such motives are not those of a free being. Freedom coincides with negation; the negation of anything that can be declared human 'being' and the perpetual wrenching away, the negation of every 'self-conceit,' literally, every concept of the self. To be free is to choose project after project; this is the power of will. After all, freedom is the existence of our will and passions insofar as this existence is conditioned by the ontological nihilation of any and all facticity.[47]

Sensibility must be checked insofar as it dares to make subjective determining grounds of choice into objective determining grounds of will, yet this act, as we have seen, does in the end, prove necessary, so self-love, as this is called, must not be obliterated. What is much worse is any attempt by sensibility to make itself legislative, decreeing the subjective conditions of self-love to be the unconditional practical principle, as if it were our entire self. Such self-conceit must be stopped, it must be annihilated. Both sensibilities may be humiliated so that legality may produce something else, something wholly positive. As the law of freedom, legality is the positive object of respect. Legislative pure practical reason gives us a universal law that, in its initial encounter with our subjective maxims, acts by humiliating us for our sensuous nature and for our individual, frequently, if not necessarily, contradictory sensible maxims. Is it not stated, assumed, asserted, again and again, that our sensibilities always contradict one another? Do they not condemn us to confusion, even violence? Or, is something else at stake? Is there some dark precursor always, already at work, frantically fragmenting what it takes to be the primitive connections of sensibility, desperately dispersing them, because it can only think and project life as a continuous manifold on which all relations are relations of proximity and all existence is always projected ahead of itself? If this is the case, if all our thinking and existence is run through and organized by this millennialist fantasy of destruction, we must expect that it is *only out of a negative, destructive incentive that the positive incentive of respect will ever arise.* Again and again, negation is posited as the motive pushing us toward our freedom. Respect, a strange sort of subjective 'feeling' which nevertheless motivates objective legality, convinces us of the necessity and legitimacy of the pure transcendental law.[48]

Respect for moral law as opposed to pure legality is the result of the conflict between our sensuous nature and legality itself, a conflict in which some particular sensuous desires (those involving self-conceit) are annihilated, but others (those involving self-love) are retrieved and made use of in a guarded fashion for the sake of a universal standard. In this manner, they become not only legitimate, but universal. After all, self-love, the tendency to make subjective inclinations into objective rules for the will, is the only route open between law and feeling. Inclination rests on feeling; negation checks inclination and so checks feeling, thus *a priori*, moral law exerts its superior influence on feeling. Is it so surprising that a political theorist like Rawls is in agreement with Kant in the matter of respect? The conception of goodness as rationality is the most important of the primary goods; it is chief among the goods that 'everyone' agrees are fundamental to a liberal democratic state. Self-respect is secured if there is for each person a minimum of one community of shared interests where 'he' finds his endeavors confirmed by his associates, where at least one of 'his' subjective maxims is recognized as transcendental law. So important is this that recognition of law makes possible so-called equality. 'In a well-ordered society, self-respect is secured by the public affirmation of the status of equal citizenship for all; the distribution of material means is left to take care of itself.'[49] The distribution of material means is left to take care of itself because, as we have seen, an equal division of primary goods is irrational in view of the 'possibility' of improving the circumstances of all by permitting widespread inequalities. Those who find themselves disadvantaged are to take comfort in the priority of equal liberty for all, that is, in the guarantee of autonomy granted by moral law.[50] Thus, for Rawls as for Kant, respect for moral law brings us to limit our subjective inclinations, since because of it we submit them to what we ought to do. In subjecting ourselves to the ought, we subject ourselves to law and so become our own unconditioned first cause, undetermined in our actions and intentions by anything outside of ourselves, authors of our own spontaneous, creative, and yet legislative freedom. While it is still permitted to use the sensuous world as a determining ground, this should become less and less likely as we become more and more adept at applying the form of lawfulness in general to what little remains of our sensibility, to what becomes, from the point of view of lawfulness, its multiple contradictions. So really, we ought to just give up our subjective sensibilities along with their multiple and uncontrollable productions. But, as Kant reminds us, because intelligible objects have no subjective reality, their maxims would remain empty of all but the form of lawfulness. We are, in the end, pure subjects of the pure laws of the Idea of relation: connection, disjunction, conjunction. Percepts and affects, prospects and concepts, as well as functives, will of necessity engage us, forming us, pushing us along connective trajectories; attractors will beckon, stabilizing our connections only so that they may be more powerfully torn apart to be conjoined in the delirium of consumption and consummation. Deterritorialization and reterritorialization are the insurmountable laws of the transcendental Ideas of relation operating everywhere.

The idea of lawfulness or pure legality is the law of causality and as such it is the necessary condition of both sensible maxims of desire and of those maxims belonging to *a priori* practical principles. As sensuous, rational beings, human beings are subject to empirically conditioned laws, but as supersensuous, it is the autonomy of pure reason that rules over us. Were we to affirm our purely intelligible existence, our transcendence, as reality and to disdain empirical existence as bad faith, then it would be clear that our intelligible self is a cause with no prior cause, no real and positive existence, no objects of possible experience in a chain of causal links.[51] This is why, we found, incentives or motives are all the more important for the transcendent ego, the intelligible being. Moral law directly 'determines' the will, not as natural (linear) causality, but as an incentive, an incentive that can only be negative. Escaping the in-itself by nihilating oneself toward one's possibilities takes place by means of the tearing apart of connections. The destruction of codes is the condition of autonomy, of free will. So although neither of these aspects of our nature is outside of lawfulness, the form of causality operates with respect to the mechanical causality of the world as the connection between phenomena, and these phenomena await decoding; they motivate our autonomy. With respect to the categories of freedom, causality merely expresses the relation of autonomous will to an independent action through freedom.[52] Legality (operating both in sensuous and practical nature) brings mechanical, causal nature into contact with intelligible nature connecting them *in one reason*. It makes possible the connection between sensible and practical maxims, between individual sensibilities and the acts of an autonomous transcendence. Subjective maxims such as 'I desire submissive women whom I can subject to my will,' or 'I dislike women I cannot subject to my will,' or 'I dislike

Asian men, I am unable to subject them to my will,' will be negated and in their place, we will assert practical maxims that will first take the form of 'Asian women and men ought to be encouraged toward moral advancement.' Kant is clear on this. But then, in order for universal commanded law to be moral law, the objective determining ground of will must simultaneously be the subjectively sufficient determining ground of an *action*; moral law must be the negative incentive; respect, good faith must be the positive outcome of this intelligible act.[53] To make moral law the incentive, we need only to submit ourselves, our formerly subjective maxims, the determining ground of action, to the objective maxims, the determining ground of will. In so doing, we might find ourselves asserting: 'Asian men *ought* not to consume Asian women,' (deterritorialization of traditional codes) and 'Western men *ought* to control Asian men,' (reterritorialization within the axiom of capital). By this means, international sex tourism can bring the alleged chaos and contradiction of individual sensibilities into accord with the legislative and moral demands of universal *a priori* practical reason, encouraging moral advancement. In this universal form and only in this universal form can capitalism embark on its project of universal control and profits, a project commensurate with the autonomy of freedom.

If it is the case that the autonomy of intelligible beings facilitates the axiomatic of capital by means of the politics of justice and reasonable pluralism, many inquiries follow. Questions, possibly demands, regarding the status of the contingency and necessity of these systems would lead us to ask if it is possible that the stranglehold of the universal *a priori* of capital would break either from within or from without? As Kant points out, this system gets and maintains its authority from a particular conception of god. God is the law of the a priori manifold that is presupposed to harmonize conflicting subjective incentives (shame and respect) with the legality of moral law, the unconditioned first cause of nature. God is simply the universal regulator, the law and the unconditioned first cause; or more correctly, God is the *name* of the law. In keeping with the category of relation, there is an important presupposition regarding individual legality; it is the presupposition of individual immortality. But in postulating immortality, we are doing no more than affirming the individual as unconditioned first cause. Freedom, god, and immortality thus are posited as the necessary conditions of the so-called highest good, that is, the pure rational will that obeys the command of reason, the harmony of nature and moral law.[54] Although the moral good is formed by the objects of pure practical reason, 'when reason legislates in the faculty of desire, the faculty of desire itself legislates over objects' and in so doing, represents these objects as realizable in the sensible world as effects of freedom. Moral law then is nothing when separated from such sensible effects.[55] The 'ought' of Asian women and men must be realized in the sensible world; without sensible effects expressing moral law, universal moral law would collapse, but these sensibilities are effects and only effects. They are the effects of autonomous freedoms.

Here, imagination begins to play a fundamental role. Realization of the universal moral good presupposes harmony between practical reason or the suprasensible and sensible nature. The connection between them lies in the prospects of the immortal soul for infinite progress through the intervention of god who is the moral cause of the world.[56] The positing of god and the soul gives objective reality to the suprasensible and to sensible nature. But can sensible nature not posit conditions internal to itself according to which it expresses something suprasensible? Indeed, this is the function of the imagination and it is by means of acts of the imagination that sensible nature comes to express the supersensible. This is the problem that has been expressed as that of generating a higher form of feeling, one that would provide a connection between the chaos and contradiction of individual, subjective, and sensuous desires and the universal moral law expressed through the ought. Certainly, as we have noted, a higher form cannot arise out of mere sensibility, nor can it be intellectual, a function of knowledge. If the latter were the case, there would be an interest – that of the intellect to know itself – but the ought of sexual capitalism never wants to know its object. This is one of the chief advantages for Western men of the Asian sex market and a disadvantage of local Western markets. Having little common language, Asian women and Western men have nothing to say to one another and nothing to know; they are fundamentally disinterested in one another, maintaining only their rational self-interest, a necessary characteristic of political liberalism as well.

What will conjoin individual, subjective desires and universal moral law is pleasure, but only the kind of pleasure that is without interest in the existence of the object. This is a pleasure unavailable to Asian women and men in the sex industry. They are not 'Others' but exist only as decoded material flows, consumables. Nor does this pleasure seek knowledge which is, in any case, absolutely unavailable, for there is nothing to know. The conjoining of individual desire and

166

universal law can be accomplished by means of a reference to the beautiful. We have seen that Plato had long before alerted us to this potential. In the judgment 'some S is beautiful,' or 'these Asian women are really beautiful,' the material existence of the object is a matter of indifference; the materially existing external object need not even be present, no need to worry about the intuition which would always be the intuition of an Other.[57] All that is needed to produce the judgment 'this is beautiful,' is the representation of the pure form, that is, of the object in imagination. As the international sex tourism brochures read, 'Thailand is a land of smiles,' or 'the woman feels very grateful that he [the white Westerner] is helping her family,' and 'everyone has a good time here.'[58] The essential thing is the design – the smiles, gratitude, and good times – because this faculty of feeling, this aesthetic pleasure in the beautiful, has no domain in the world of material objects. It is the reflected representation of the form alone that brings about, 'causes,' the higher pleasure of the beautiful, a necessary and universal beauty, a pleasure that can, in principle, be valid for everyone.[59] Indifferent to the existence of the object, it expresses solely the subjective condition of Western males who exercise their faculties and thereby *consume* the universal Asian woman, even while congratulating one another for possessing such good taste. And beauty, its messy materiality, its glistening spatio-temporalization is emptied.

Yet, insofar as imagination has no authority to legislate, understanding and reason are constituted in a non-empirical, non-intuitive yet subjective free play of imagination and understanding. Here the conflict between shame/sensibility and respect/understanding that characterizes practical reason reappears. We may see now why it is that shame, as Rawls argues, is evoked by shocks to our self-respect, by a lack of respect.[60] The relationship between the faculties of imagination and reason reaches discord, even contradiction, when reason's demands conflict with imagination's power in an intuition of the sublime, an intuition that may arise in but will not be maintained by, a well ordered society. This clash produces the pleasure of imagination exceeding its own limits, though it is mixed in a singular contradiction with pain, the pain of imagination representing to itself the unattainable rational idea. The image of the sublime is untamed, chaotic nature in its wildest and most irregular disorder and desolation; it is free of natural laws governing nature as mechanism, as well as from all constraints and rules of theoretical or practical reason. In any intuition of the sublime, imagination cannot apprehend in a single intuition the absolutely (infinitely) great and so suffers the pain of this inadequacy. Yet, the effort of intuiting all at once what requires an infinite, thus unimaginable time does violence to temporality and breaks up the unity of the faculty. That is, what should be given in a succession is given all at once, annihilating time because it annihilates mathematical and dynamic succession.[61] May we 'imagine' that this fissure is precisely the non-site where the catastrophic event occurs? Such an event, a break, a fissure, is a discontinuous jump that leaps from the trajectory constituted as the moral universal. If such a discontinuity is possible, then what will happen to the autonomy central to Western capital? And what of the axiomatization of Asian sexuality; might this be a trajectory that may then also dissolve?

For Kant, the sublime provides a direct and discordant relation between imagination and reason that ends in pain. Finally, Kant is forced to generate what is not, and cannot be, *a priori* in this relation: imagination's representation of the rational idea, that to which a moral being is predestined.[62] Yet, insofar as the sublime has brought the faculties together in conflict and struggle, it is our initial point of resistance with respect to universalizing morality, but will it become our point of departure from such a morality (a morality with vast implications) as well? In this struggle, it has been claimed, a chasm opens up in the subject whose faculties must function in a situation of fundamental discord. But is the unregulated exercise of the faculties adequate to carry out the critique of Western representations of Asian sexuality and of the well-ordered society as well as to formulate a new structure, one that does not condemn us to the connection, disjunction and conjunction of the capitalist machine?[63]

Notes

1. See Holland, *Deleuze and Guattari's Anti-Oedipus*, p. 80. This is a necessary effect of the massive, generalized decoding of flows. See Deleuze and Guattari, *Anti-Oedipus*, pp. 223–4 (265).
2. Hubert Damisch, *The Origin of Perspective*, tr. John Goodman (Cambridge: MIT Press, 1995), pp. 36, 50, originally published as *L'Origine de la perspective* (Paris: Flammarion, 1987). I count myself among those who have elided homogeneous space and time with single-point perspective when, in fact, they must be distinguished.
3. Hubert Damisch's minutely detailed, scholarly epistemology of perspective is an exhaustive articulation of this view. See Damisch, *The Origin of Perspective*, pp. 388–9.
4. Deleuze and Guattari, *Anti-Oedipus*, p. 224 (265).

5. Deleuze and Guattari, *Anti-Oedipus*, p. 228 (270).
6. Deleuze and Guattari, *Anti-Oedipus*, pp. 229, 228, 230–1 (272, 270, 273–4).
7. Deleuze and Guattari, *Anti-Oedipus*, p. 232 (275).
8. Kant, *Critique of Pure Reason*, A301, B358. Kant goes on to say that if objects in themselves were to stand under principles and principles alone, this would violate common sense. Such violation appears to be what he has in mind.
9. John Rawls, *A Theory of Justice* (Cambridge: Harvard University Press, 1971) p. 252. See also ch. IV, 'The Kantian Interpretation').
10. It is a practical Idea insofar as it is noumenal, that is, outside of experience, prior to experience and merely assumed to exist for the sake of experience or cognition; Rawls, *A Theory of Justice*, p. 255.
11. Lenore Manderson, 'Public sex performances in Patpong and explorations of the edges of imagination', in *The Journal of Sex Research*, vol. 29, no. 4: 451–75 (November 1992). See also Alison Murray, 'Debt-bondage and trafficking: don't believe the hype', in Reina Lewis and Sara Mills (eds) *Feminist Post-Colonial Theory* (New York: Routledge Press, 2003), pp. 417–18. Murray cites articles in *The Nation*, 5 April 1995, and the report from the Asia Watch Women's Rights Project, *A Modern Form of Slavery: Trafficking of Burmese Women and Girls into Brothels into Thailand* (Human Rights Watch, 1993), pp. 67–8.
12. Lillian S. Robinson, 'Touring Thailand's sex industry', in Rosemary Hennesy and Chrys Ingraham (eds), *Materialist Feminism* (New York: Routledge Press, 1997), pp. 253–8; Murray, 'Debt-bondage and trafficking: don't believe the hype', pp. 417–18.
13. Murray, 'Debt-bondage and trafficking: don't believe the hype', p. 416.
14. Plato, *The Symposium*, pp. 229–307.
15. See especially a completely illuminating essay by Nancy Tuana, 'The weaker seed, the sexist bias of reproductive theory', *Hypatia*, vol. 3, no. 1 (Spring 1988): 35–58.
16. I am thinking here of the work of Luce Irigaray, in particular, *An Ethics of Sexual Difference*, tr. Caroline Burke and Gillian C. Gill (Ithaca: Cornell University Press, 1993).
17. Manderson, 'Public sex performances', p. 470.
18. Chandra Mohanty, 'Under Western eyes, feminist scholarship and colonial discourses', *Feminist Review*, no. 30 (Autumn 1988): 61–85, p. 65.
19. Todd May has formulated the concept of the Kantian moral imperative in precise terms, stating that 'as a purely formal matter, the categorical imperative requires a certain kind of anonymity.' (personal correspondence).
20. See Alisa Carse, 'Impartial principle and moral context: securing a place for the particular in ethical theory', *Journal of Medicine and*

Philosophy, vol. 3, no. 2 (1998): 153–69, pp. 165–6. Carse is quite hopeful about the ethics of care which she thinks can ameliorate the problem of idealized impartiality and make a place for the particular in moral theory. Although I appreciate the interventions of the ethics of care, I do not think it restructures ethics in a radical enough manner, that is, it does not definitively propose an alternative to the idealized abstract individual. Carse cites Onora O'Neill, 'Justice, gender, and international boundaries', in M. Nussbaum and S. Sen (eds), *The Quality of Life* (Oxford University Press, New York, 1993), pp. 303–23, p. 303.

21. Nicholas D. Kristof, 'Girls for sale', *New York Times*, Op-ed, 17 January 2004. Admonishing feminists, in spite of their obvious but cautious involvement in such questions, opens the way for moralistic men to take over the situation.

22. Nicholas D. Kristof, 'Loss of innocence', *New York Times*, Op-ed, 28 January 2004.

23. Howard W. French, 'A village grows rich off its main export: its daughters', *New York Times*, Section A, p. 4, col. 3. A young woman is quoted as saying, 'All of the girls would like to go, but some have to take care of their parents.'

24. Gilles Deleuze, *Kant's Critical Philosophy*, tr. Hugh Tomlinson and Barbara Habberjam (Minneapolis: University of Minnesota Press, 1984), p. xi, Introduction in the English version only; originally published in French as *La philosophie critique de Kant* (Paris: Presses Universitaires de France, 1963).

25. Rawls, *A Theory of Justice*, p. 4.

26. Rawls, *A Theory of Justice*, p. 35; John Rawls, *Political Liberalism* (Cambridge: Harvard University Press, 1993), p. xix.

27. Rawls, *A Theory of Justice*, pp. 35–6. Two principles are invoked as necessary to justice as fairness. One, autonomy or equal access to and equal share in fundamental rights and liberties; And two, social and economic inequalities that are acceptable insofar as even the least advantaged members of society benefit (pp. 53, 130–1).

28. Rawls, *Political Liberalism*, pp. 13–14. This includes religious, philosophical, and moral doctrines.

29. Rawls, *Political Liberalism*, p. 11, note 11.

30. Rawls, *Political Liberalism*, pp. 13–14.

31. Alisa Carse, 'The liberal individual: a metaphysical or moral embarrassment?', in *Nous*, vol. 28, no. 2 (June 1994): 184–209, p. 185. Thanks to Todd May for this reference.

32. Rawls, *Political Liberalism*, p. 14.

33. Rawls, *Political Liberalism*, p. 19; *A Theory of Justice*, p. 43.

34. Rawls, *Political Liberalism*, p. 6; Rawls, *A Theory of Justice*, p. 13.

35. Rawls, *Political Liberalism*, pp. 31–2.

36. Sartre, *Being and Nothingness*, p. 111 (107). There is no difference, on this scale, between being sad and being oppressed. All that matters is that one keeps a project in front of oneself (pp. 110–12 (106–8)).

37. Thomas Nagel, 'Internal difficulties with justice as fairness', in Robert C. Solomon and Mark C. Murphy (eds), *What is Justice?* (Oxford: Oxford University Press, 2000), pp. 298–9; Jean-Paul Sartre, *Being and Nothingness*, p. 116 (111).

38. Deleuze, *Kant's Critical Philosophy*, p. 68 (97–8). Presumably, this means freedom from *linear* causality, however, in a world or a universe that lacks any causality, nothing takes place at all, certainly no temporalization.

39. Kant, *Critique of Practical Reason*, p. 21.

40. Immanuel Kant, *Critique of Practical Reason*, pp. 21, 20. This is a prime example of not keeping one's projects ahead of oneself; Sartre, *Being and Nothingness*, pp. 109–11 (105–7). 'The sincere man constitutes himself as a thing in order to escape the condition of a thing by the same act of sincerity' (p. 109 (105)).

41. Manderson, 'Public sex', p. 456. All such figures are approximate as exact numbers are impossible to ascertain. These numbers may be inflated, but they represent the degree of concern among researchers.

42. Sartre, *Being and Nothingness*, p. 114 (110); emphasis added.

43. Kant, *Critique of Practical Reason*, p. 28, 29, 30, 76.

44. Kant, Critique of Practical Reason, p. 27, 29.

45. Kant, *Critique of Practical Reason*, p. 72.

46. Sartre, *Being and Nothingness*, pp. 568, 577, 578, 579 (516, 524–5). 'What can be meant by the statement that I have joined the Socialist party for these causes (*motifs*) *and* these motives (*mobiles*)? Evidently we are dealing with two radically distinct layers of meaning? How are we to compare them? . . . This difficulty . . . has never been resolved' (pp. 576–7 (523)).

47. Kant, *Critique of Practical Reason*, p. 75; Sartre, *Being and Nothingness*, pp. 568, 573 (516, 520).

48. Kant, *Critique of Practical Reason*, p. 75; Sartre, *Being and Nothingness*, p. 565 (513). 'The nihilation by which we achieve a withdrawal in relation to the situation is the same as the ekstasis by which we project ourselves toward a modification of this situation . . . it is impossible to find an act without a motive.'

49. Rawls, *A Theory of Justice*, p. 545.

50. Rawls, *A Theory of Justice*, p. 546.

51. Kant, *Critique of Practical Reason*, pp. 42–4; Sartre, *Being and Nothingness*, p. 564 (512–13). Thus, the significance of motives.

52. Kant, *Critique of Practical Reason*, pp. 54, 57.

53. Kant, *Critique of Practical Reason*, p. 74–5.

54. Kant, *Critique of Practical Reason*, pp. 125, 135.

55. Kant, *Critique of Practical Reason*, Analytic, ch. II; Deleuze, *Kant's Critical Philosophy*, pp. 40–1 (59).
56. Deleuze, *Kant's Critical Philosophy*, pp. 41, 42 (60–1).
57. This phrase is that of an American sex tourist who compares the 'willing' sex workers in Thailand to American women at home whom he refers to as 'bitches.' See the film *The Good Woman of Bangkok*, a documentary written and directed by Dennis O'Rourke (1991).
58. Quoted in Chandra Mohanty, 'Under Western eyes.'
59. Deleuze, *Kant's Critical Philosophy*, pp. 47–8 (69–70).
60. Rawls, *A Theory of Justice*, pp. 442–3.
61. Kant, *Critique of Judgement*, sect. 27.
62. Deleuze, *Kant's Critical Philosophy*, pp. 51, 52 (74, 75).
63. Deleuze, *Kant's Critical Philosophy*, pp. xii, xiii.

5

Passive Restraint

Societies of control

The argument for apparent inevitability of the regulative principles of connection, disjunction, conjunction as an ontological structure is already well known and, somewhat disturbingly, it seems to have been accepted almost without question. It is not only the inexorable judgment of the transcendental idealist, whose ideas, expressions, murmurs, sighs and utterances are given voice throughout the preceding pages of this book, but also that of the skeptical but transcendental empiricist, whose beliefs have been till now barely stated but, nevertheless, quietly insinuated. What allows the empiricist to take up a transcendental, and not merely skeptical, stance is the fundamental concept that all simple ideas may be separated by imagination and united by that power again in whatever form pleases us.[1] Such ideas stand in purely external relations with respect to one another; although empirical in origin, they are organized from 'outside,' embedded in a higher dimension. Is this not a truly transcendental structure? What are the implications of such external relations? What is gained by the swift and repeated association of impressions and ideas? What is lost as the infinite and infinitely accelerated intensities push forward their forces, ready to capture, to overtake and to determine and define whatever events – affects, percepts, concepts, prospects, functives – contingently rush onto each trajectory, giving themselves up to whatever associations 'imagination' has awaiting them. And finally, in the path of such intensities, what of our jagged hesitations, our wild intersecting seperatrices, our intervals of sensibility spilling from illuminated networks into the creation of perspectives, rays of light opening onto the crowds we are? Therefore if, for the transcendental idealist, the transcendental Ideas reveal the regulatory principles in accordance with which we act, then what do we expect from the imagination as posited by the transcendental empiricist?

The universal principles of the faculty of imagination allow for some uniformity, some habituation for perception and cognition. They make it possible for imagination to run along the parts of space and time that have been uniformly connected, but then to separate them, to tear them apart. Disjunction is the fundamental operation of imagination, which is to say, of the transcendental empiricist mind. Continuity of space and time simply constructs the manifold, *as if* it were *a priori* when, in fact, it is entirely contingent. Yet, it is always framed, structured by the habituation that arises from constant conjunction. Imagination can be conceived as the ability to transpose and change its ideas, since wherever imagination perceives a difference among ideas, it can easily produce a separation. Resemblance *connects* ideas, running easily from one idea to any other ideas that resemble it. Contiguity is the effect of the mind running along the parts of space and time encountering, then conceiving its objects. Causation is the judgment that motion or action has been produced by one object in another. Given the *weakness* of the imagination when it comes to the perception of either impressions of sensation or impressions of reflection, it is no wonder that imagination is not constrained by any particular order and form. Memory is said to preserve, but imagination, already dynamically and mathematically sublime, is free to dispense with the order and form preserved by memory. So it is free to tear apart any connection that has arisen, any existing order and form. The sublime, divine disjunction is always, already in play.[2]

It may well be little more than the apparent lack of constraint on the part of the mind, its sublime overreaching, either in the direction of an unconditioned transcendental Idea of reason or in the direction of the uninhibited power of imagination, that gave rise to so-called societies of discipline.[3] 'Respect' for moral law, it has been noted, is nothing more than a fact, a cry against barbarism with no viable philosophical support.[4] That is, what really matter, what have philosophical support are facts that confirm the system of reason. If reason organizes the data of cognition into a system of logical laws that produce general relations, then the system of reason is only as powerful as its predictive success. The system of reason must give to the rational self the capacity to subsume facts under principles, an end that increases the self's capacity for self-preservation by making possible the subjugation of the material, sensible realm to logical laws and general relations. By this means, it is claimed, the material and sensible realm is determined in advance so as to be unable to reform and restructure, and so is efficiently realized in repeatable, replaceable processes.[5] As predictable, as necessarily connected to logical laws and general relations, perception is made to conform to what these laws and relations can classify and confirm. This is the meaning of 'nothing to know.' No knowledge of the transcendental Ideas, but also, nothing new in the universe, only the unending trajectories of predictable behaviors. This is why, if they are rational, individual beings will develop themselves in accordance with these same laws and relations. On this scale, whatever does not contribute to the self-preserving predictive success of the individual threatens to return them to the state of nature whose nasty and brutish tendencies they would fully suffer.[6]

The situation has been no different for the transcendental power of empirical imagination. Here too, the state of nature is taken to be a 'wretched and savage condition,' from which 'men' are protected by furthering their interest in what is *nearest* to them but also, and overriding this, by strictly observing some *universal* and inflexible rules of justice.[7] This, in spite of the assertion that when the mind passes from the idea or impression of one object to the belief in the existence of another, it does so because it is determined by principles that associate the ideas of these objects and unite them in *imagination*, which is, as we know, always ahead of itself, always ahead of memory, able to disconnect and reconnect anything that catches its attention. What, after all, are the interests of imagination? Is it said to be interested in determination, the predictability that lies not merely in relations of ideas but originally in relations of objects?[8] Even as governed by imagination, persons, we have seen, are deemed to be more likely to value what is contiguous to them in space and time. This is because, in matters of the passions and will, proximity rules over all, contributing to the natural propensity to commit acts of injustice. This means that persons exhibit a marked preference for any 'trivial advantage' insofar as it is proximate; this, rather than what is said to be truly in their interest, the maintenance of order in society and the observance of justice, something they do not obtain insofar as they fail to make full and appropriate use of imagination. What is required, in this instance, is to give authority only to those powerfully imaginative persons who do not feel at all, who are as indifferent to those in close proximity as they are to those who are far away. Magistrates, kings, ministers, governors, rulers are among those who are supposed to remain unmoved and indifferent to those closest to them. Unlike ordinary persons, the purveyors of justice must be supplied in abundance with whatever goods they might need, and they may not evince any privileged affection for those closest to them. Thus neither justice nor injustice interests them at all.[9] What interests them is *regularity*; what interests them is nothing but the *observation of rules*, an observation that takes the fullest advantage of the power of imagination to separate whatever has been connected by natural contiguity and to reconnect ideas or impressions in accordance with rules that regulate equity. In service to regularity, such observers will gladly constrain themselves and others to follow rules or to be punished for the failure to follow rules. Lacking an interest in anything but regularity, such persons are designated to be the best to hand out judgments in an equitable manner.[10] Thus, whether justice arises from the attention to logical laws and general relations, from the necessity of conformity to law, or from its only apparently opposing interest, the lack of passionate interest in everything but the observation of rules, the result is the same. Reason affirms self-interest by affirming law and conformity to law.

Nevertheless, in spite of the ever increasing interest in the observation of rules, the conformity to law, it is widely asserted that in Western nations, pre-World War II societies of discipline, in which individuals move from one rule-governed environment to the next, are finished.[11] By the end of the twentieth century, the organization of everyday life as the passage from family, to school, to the factory, farm, or office, and perhaps to the hospital, prison, or the military may well have ceased. This closure has occurred in spite of the obvious fact that people still live in families, go to school, enter a profession, are treated for illness in hospitals and are incarcerated in prison. What has changed, it is claimed, is the structure of the institutions themselves. Whereas they were once driven by rules that guaranteed certainty, the capacity to predict the trajectories and relations of objects in the world, the rules now guarantee only the chaos of probability. Connection, disjunction and conjunction will continue to operate, everywhere, but now what they connect will not be natural nor even conventional, but simply contingent; there will be increasing unpredictability. The self-governing nature of political, social and industrial institutions, their interiority, would then be eclipsed. The endless demands for reform of these institutions may be but the manifestation of their demise as self-regulating entities. If so, they may all fall under what can be called the 'unity of time,' time characterized as a parameter of space (n + 1 dimensions), a characterization organized most recently by a telecommunications system in service to the differential universal, the universal that carries out the threat to delocalize and empty out the interior of all once-private institutions on a global level.[12]

In this way, the public-private dichotomy is also shattered, an event that might be welcomed were it not for the consequences of this particular form of disruption. Driven by the demand for 'just-in-time' market relocations, for live broadcasts, for real-time financial information, for accelerated transportation, the public-private dichotomy has fallen prey to a 'temporal homogenization' in which local and regional activities are easily disjoined, torn apart, their immediacy dissolved. In their place arrive the conjunctions arising from the new universal, the digitalized, global time and global events that have come to be perceived largely through electronic media. Thus 'the old industrial and political complex will already have been superseded by an informational and metropolitical complex, one associated with the omnipotence of the absolute speed of the waves conveying the various signals,' signals provided by or modeled on those of the internet network, one billionth of a second for a one gigahertz computer.[13]

Far from relieving humanity of its suffering at the hands of the Oedipal family or the disciplinary prison, we are warned to expect from this release nothing less than the emergence of new global societies of control. In the self-enclosed societies of discipline, the individual may have been subject to a 'phase transition,' a disequilibrium provoked by external forces, resulting in a leap from one coded, enclosed system to another, requiring a radical adjustment to new or newly emerging situations, but nevertheless, to conditions more or less in equilibrium.[14] But now, we can expect that because of the deterritorialization of each of these formerly isolated interiors, what we are facing is a global system of rules that have developed to accommodate the newest technological form of the ontology which they serve. Nevertheless, the restrictive resources of all the old models of transcendental Ideas will continue to be drawn upon in their regulatory capacity. Nostalgia for the return to states of 'equilibrium' characterizing disciplinary society seem to be chief among the tools utilized to guarantee that such a return will never actually take place. As suggested previously, reason will be concerned primarily with the faculty of desire, determining will according to rules (hypothetical and categorical imperatives) but only insofar as the ground of choice is *not empirical*, not connected to pleasure or pain, but only wholly in accordance with an *unconditional practical law* in relation to which every single subject is passive.

To this end, disjoined images of equilibrium in media, among social and political reformers and the devoutly provident, are necessary to assert to the public that no violent changes have taken place even as old forms of resistance are systematically eliminated. That is, although the factory was organized to produce the greatest amount of goods at the lowest cost realizable commensurate with turning its producers into consumers, its organization as a single isolated system or unit made it possible for those workers to occasionally resist as a unit as well. The corporation, on the other hand, has no similar self-enclosed organization. Instead, the temporality of the factory, its spatially and temporally distinct existence as a steel mill or a tool plant or a shoe factory with its particular demands for overtime or for working with dangerous machinery or enduring the stink of leather and the toxicity of chemicals has disappeared into the homogeneity of cubicles and computer screens that serve as both work stations and as illusory escapes in the form of games, special interest forums, search engines, and pornography sites. Citizens and workers grow increasingly passive. Resistance is incomprehensible since there is nothing specific to resist and no one in particular who is responsible for the seemingly spectral organization of the workplace and the quasi-exploitation of the worker. Every workplace is just like every other workplace. Every child is prepared from birth for employment in the corporate sphere. Every family mobilizes its corporate authority to ensure that the children are able to sit in front of a computer screen for long periods of time. Every school tests and retests every student to ensure that particular bits of universal knowledge have been driven into their brains. Every employee is openly and pitilessly mobilized against every other employee by means of merit pay, by the demand for continuing education or training, and endlessly, by the necessity of increased output. 'In societies of control, one is never finished with anything – the corporation, the educational system, the armed services being metastable states coexisting in one and the same modulation, like a universal system of deformation.'[15]

Let us not, however, assume that it is a simple matter to make and maintain such a system on a global scale; dynamical systems with even a few degrees of freedom (modes of altering) exhibit unpredictable behavior, no matter how accurately determined their initial state.[16] All the more so in a country like the United States whose ethnic and social diversity, as well as geographical and class differences, regularly threaten to expose the thin veneer of the economic-political control over dynamical systems of production, distribution and consumption. Extraordinary steps have to be taken in order to ensure that the old or even new interiorities which can be considered 'private' spheres with private points of view, each with their own unique durations, do not immediately reappear everywhere. Banishment of difficult-to-control non-equilibrium states has required a massive and coordinated attempt in the family, school, corporation and military (minimally) to regulate human activity according to a homogenizing and passifying reterritorialization, one that simultaneously short-circuits apparently foolhardy attempts to engage with either discontinuous or discrete spatio-temporalizations. The question is thereby opened, what is the nature of this short circuit? How and where does it operate? Certain directions or lines of organization have been suggested by any number of theorists.

Jean Baudrillard famously locates the outward manifestation of such a regulatory rule of conduct in the American cryogenization of emotions in a system which blocks interaction with others even while giving the appearance of facilitating it.

> And that smile everyone gives you as they pass, that friendly contraction of the jaws triggered by human warmth. It is the eternal smile of communication, the smile through which the child becomes aware of the presence of others, or struggles desperately with the problem of their presence. It is indeed the smile the dead man will wear in his funeral home, as he clings to a hope of maintaining contact even in the next world. The smile of immunity, the smile of advertising: 'This country is good. I am good, We are the best.' . . . An autoprophetic smile, like all signs in advertising. Smile and others will smile back. Smile to show how transparent, how candid you are. Smile if you have nothing to say. Most of all, do not hide the fact you have nothing to say nor your total indifference to others. Let this emptiness, this profound indifference shine out spontaneously in your smile. *Give* your emptiness and indifference to others, light up your face with the zero degree of joy and pleasure, smile, smile, smile.[17]

Simulation is the essence of America, an effect of its self-absorption brought on by the tragedy of the utopian dream made into a reality which is taken to be the very definition of America. Such observations seem to resonate perfectly and absolutely on an intuitive level, and no demands are made of Americans other than that they serve as an example to the rest of the world of the effects of optimism and indifference. The question of the global nature of the control society is evaded. There is little recognition that simulation is already rampant throughout Europe and the rest of the world, and that under its influence increasingly passive citizens are being rapidly produced, effects of the regulatory transcendental Ideas or of the imagination.

Nonetheless, among so-called democratic nations, it is in the United States that the society of control appears most provocatively, on a large scale; this, in spite of the extent to which its citizens see themselves as the freest in the world. Aided by political and religious demands for universal standards of conformity – including but not limited to belief in god above reason, reassertion of the nuclear family, suppression of sexuality except where controlled by religions, businesses and corporations, all of which profit from it, limitations on free speech, massive spending to maintain and increase the military-industrial complex, and the supremacy of capitalism over every other social and political system – contemporary life exists within an *a priori* spatial and temporal manifold. It is a manifold whose unconscious holds up the reflected mirror-image of god, world and self, even as its inhabitants desperately but vainly flee the reach of such transcendental Ideas. Control arrives in strange ways. It is linked to the spatial and temporal deterritorialization of life, a disjunction that rips apart and empties out the once-coded interiorities of social groups, groups organized largely around their ethnicity and labor. Out of this disjunctive synthesis, one by one, citizens are conjoined; they form a continuous trajectory, a global perceptual progression whose monotony is veiled by the contingency of its participants, the chance happenings and chaotic phases wherein small initial uncertainties are amplified so as to preclude certainty of trajectories. That chaotic systems have no memory and do not evolve is most convenient; they are the white noise that numbs our sensibilties.[18] So we may encounter a former acquaintance, a one-time illegal alien running for political office: 'Wow,' we find ourselves exclaiming, 'I never expected to see you here!' Or: 'Is that a woman driving that race car (or police car, transport vehicle)?' These chaotic outcomes, cited as evidence of diversity, are no more than manifestations of trajectories whose rules do not change, yet whose specific qualities are unpredictable.

In this light, is it accidental that we are fascinated by technologies that accelerate perception, thereby seemingly supplying us with a system of instantaneous stimulus and response that addresses our anxieties over what remains unforseeable? Should we listen to the urban architect who, in referring to the perceptual images of computer and digital technology, argues that 'every image has a destiny of magnification,' which may be said to enhance the 'technicity' of the image insofar as images can be characterized in terms of their intensivity and interactivity.[19] Intensivity and interactivity are terms used so often in contemporary discourse that we have barely bothered to define them or to examine the structure within which they evolve. We assume, perhaps, that they function in a relatively benign manner, yet the implication of the thesis being put forward here is that the pervasive, near universal, acceptance of these terms masks the danger, if not peril, produced by the image they characterize. The intensive-interactive image is inter-changeable, magnifying or amplifying the operation in which whatever is here, present in space-time, comes to be overrun by that which is absent or deferred. This nullification or invasion takes place by means of instantaneous interactivity, the inescapable effect of technological advances in communications, from computers to missiles. As such, it is an image which impresses itself upon us like a burn on our skin or a light searing our eyes. This makes it all the more important to pay attention to what the image is displacing and disqualifying as well as to the consequences of instantaneity insofar as one of the repercussions of the intensive-interactive image is the cancellation of any interval in which we attend to our sensibilities, the sensibilities we absorb from the universe as well as those we emit.

As an image is magnified by technological means, it is able to attract and to hold within its sphere of attraction what otherwise would occupy another time, another space, another perspective, in a network of events influencing and being influenced by one another. The inimitable effect of this deterritorialization and reterritorializa-tion is '*decolonization, decentralization . . . deurbanization . . .* hyper-concentration . . . indicative of a *critical mass* a cataclysmic index of an imminent *disintegration* of the historical city.[20] Today, most of the old 'hierarchies' are disappearing; the power of the center over the peripheries clearly has lapsed. This is a situation that many do not mourn but instead celebrate as a success story for the post-modern if not the *nouveau* anarchist view of the world, for it appears to give rise at least to the possibility of a redistribution of wealth and control. However, it does so only by deterritorializing the former structures, then reterritorializing anarchically. The purveyors of justice must be supplied in abundance with whatever goods they might need and, they may not evince any privileged affection for those closest to them. Thus, justice is placed in the hands of citizens whose 'community' is intensive, interactive and interchangeable, defined by attendance at their choice of sporting event, website, chatroom, cable channel, mall or religious convention, which is to say, by the chaotic dynamics of uncertain initial conditions. The dynamic creation of an endless periphery city results in '*interactive confinement,*' produc-ing independent, local subgroups, '*internal, extraterritorial entities,*' whose purpose is to justify, if not demand, the abolition of the old geopolitical formations, the disciplinary societies, and ultimately the civic rights and political citizenship of other populations in the name of their own subgroup which functions in accordance with its reter-ritorialized images, now assumed to be fundamental.[21] Once again, the failure of memory and the white noise of uncertainty are crucial. In this sense, the arrival of terrorism as a constant threat may be no more than a manifestation of that uncertainty. Still, the diminishment of urban areas as milieus for social and political life needs little enough assistance from the threat of terrorists. Where urban centers have been revitalized (such as the famous Disneyfication of New York City's Times Square), they are primarily entertainment districts, centers of tourism, corporate headquarters and in some cases, urban neighborhoods (in the US the former warehouse or factory turned loft is the new model of chic urban lifestyle). In spite of the lively envir-onments of many of these urban districts, they and the people who populate them are much less part of an intimate cosmological spatio-temporalization, a network of interacting influences, than they are display items for the visitors and periphery dwellers for whom they function only as visual, gustatory stimuli, instantaneous perceptual images.

They are a strange sort of stimuli, one whose influence on one's own sensibility is discarded in the infinitely fast rush of images. Instead of opening influences between networks of influencing events – between one mingled perspective and another, between groups of persons or between persons and their milieu, absorbing and emitting informa-tion, flows of energy and matter, radiating light – the new urban center exists in order to populate the moment. It exists in order to fill each moment intensively with a greater number and density of diversions, enticements, images; percepts, affects, concepts (prospects and func-tives to a much lesser degree if at all), each intensifying through its con-tingent, that is, unpredictable, conjunction with others. The increasing speed of information, the immediacy of information, eliminates space and time as the field of freedom, the zone of indetermination for life. As velocity vectors (the average speed and direction of any change of state) are driven faster and faster by high energies that approach the speed of light, a local and global 'state of emergency' emerges as a mundane feature of daily life.[22] Locally, the deterritorialization of civic centers is especially notable when one considers that most of the actual work in these districts is carried out by second- and third-world immi-grants, legal and illegal, who often send their earnings home to support their families in poverty-stricken, unstable periphery nations whose agricultural and industrial production are confiscated for export or which have collapsed under the so-called competitive and open market treaties demanded by global competition.[23] Like their peripheral, suburban brothers and sisters, the residents of metropolitan zones work in businesses dominated by the 'instantaneous interactive capacities of technologies that privilege henceforth the multinational monopolistic *intensivity* to the detriment of the *extensivity* of national capitalism.'[24] Although many might rejoice in this collapse, as it points to the elimination of any difference between first-, second- and third-world inhabitants by bringing the latter out of the cold and into the newly created plane of immanence, since every space-time has become interchangeable with every other, there is no sensibility and no perspectives are created in and through this development. It is a sublime structure; each first-world participant must have no *interest* in the actual existence of the second- or third-world others. Infinite and infinitely accelerated intensive interactivity supercedes interest. Thus communication, even conversation, between first- and third-world populations is unnecessary; they live and work together in silence.[25]

What is intensive is an effect of interactivity, and what is interactive is interchangeable. What is displaced is the image that may be created out of combinatorial networks, what has been called *la longue durée*, the ongoing, but discrete durations of spatio-temporalization in which the emergence of spatiality and temporality are one with the sensible and creative situation.[26] The deliberate distribution of disinformation, along with overwhelming amounts of useless information, throws individuals off balance so that, for example, even those immigrants who have entered the US legally may suddenly find themselves deported. Everyday, new stories appear in the newspapers involving women, men or adolescents who have been deported to countries they never knew or countries where they will be subject to political prosecution and sometimes torture.[27] Their deportations are justified by 'crimes' as heinous as traffic violations, a bounced check, a late green card or visa application. In principle, there is nothing to distinguish these relatively benign civilians from any other so-called criminals with whom they may be fundamentally interchangeable. The decision to deport these persons is automatic, an effect of

Momentary law, legislation of the instantaneous, special courts, government by decrees, by ordinances, state of emergency, all [of which] serve as *indices of a transpolitical intensivity destructive of the permanence of laws, of the continuity* [la longue durée] *of laws, of the persistence of the civil state,* permanence disabled henceforth by the instability of employment situations, of housing, the frequency of 'across-the-border' exchanges, and flux, signs of the decrepitude of a *civil peace*, whose avant-garde technologies continuously threaten one's rights and for which the notions of *terrorism and conspiracy against the State* are a telling institution.[28]

In a society of control, passifying reterritorialization guarantees respect for utterly relentless penal laws. Otherwise expressed, obeying the 'moral' law frees one from the fears of hell and those who obey absolutely are willing to submit to any tyranny as long as all others are made to submit as well. In any case, only those at risk, those who do not follow the law fundamentally and absolutely, regardless of the arbitrariness of the direction, only these resist, albeit blindly. For the rest, calculation and planning, intensive and purposive activity, arbitrarily determined rules are all signs of their election.[29]

Utopia or dystopia?

If the transition to a space-time manifold characterized by 'intensity' is the condition of the possibility of the society of control, then what has been written about Disneyland can probably be applied to all of the United States, if not the world. That is, that insofar as simulated spaces like Disneyland have often been presented as the very image and model of utopia, a site of freedom and pleasure, they may instead operate as dystopias. Their organization and functioning may well be symptomatic of the entire society of control. For far from being a land of pleasure and smiles, an imaginative playground for children, adolescents and adults, we might consider the extent to which, by means of such logistically constituted illusions, the society of control has masked itself as a site of freedom and equality when in fact it serves a much more disturbing function. That is, it has become dedicated to the production of consumable collective images, which create and maintain the system of ideas and values used by social, political and economic forces to maintain their dominance and somewhat secondarily, to promulgate their values, since 'values' are only in service to dominance. It is no secret that the visitor to 'Main Street' is not a spectator but a participant in a mythical story that represents past and future, estrangement and familiarity, comfort, welfare, scientific and technological progress, consumption, superpower, all overlaid by a universalizing morality that guarantees profits, just as it does for international sex tourism.[30] If this applies to Main Street, Disneyland, then it applies every bit as much to Main Street, USA and perhaps it is not an exaggeration to claim that like the propaganda films of Leni

Riefenstahl, much of America, if not the world, has become 'an artificial universe that look[s] entirely real.'[31]

Imagination and imaginary images are, of course, a trademark of utopia. Along Main Street, imagination operates by associating ideas and images from movies and cartoons with actual sites populated by men and women disguised as film and cartoon characters. If this has the effect of constituting the imaginary of the citizen with 'a fixed, stereotyped, powerful fantasy,' then what is interesting is that the citizen actually pays and seeks to pay for images that are inert, blocked and recurrent.[32] This is further reinforced by the limitation on the citizen's possible interpretations of his or her interactions. The narrative trajectory is completely laid out in advance and structured by regulative Ideas. Every section of Disneyland, for example, is completely interpreted for the visitor. The cartoon places and characters as well as the organization of the various segments around 'Main Street' all contribute to constraining the visitor to a trajectory governed by a set of rules and a signifying attractor from which the visitor can make no escape.[33] Perhaps the rest of the United States is rapidly becoming no different. On Main Streets around the country, if not the world, the inhabitant, as well as the visitor, is often progressively coerced, forced into circumscribed pathways, limited in her or his interpretations and almost always, eventually mastered, restrained by the cultural imaginary intensively and interactively presented to him or her, to the point where behavior and responses become so passive that they might be characterized as purely masochistic. It is not surprising that tourists are satisfied with the fake representations of countries and cultures constructed in amusement zones from Las Vegas to Epcott, insofar as the guided tourist trails of Venice or Paris or Beijing or Teotihuacan are scarcely any different, neither alien nor uninterpreted.

Yet, what in these structures allows the claim that they verge on masochism? We have referred to the insight of Wilhelm Reich that his own clinical studies provide ample evidence that various psychological manifestations attributed to the death instinct are caused by something quite different, that masochism in particular is not an effect of the death instinct, and that in fact, there is no such thing as a biological striving for unpleasure, hence that the death instinct is a fiction.[34] The clue for the genesis of masochism comes instead from the work of Krafft-Ebing, whose research indicates that being hurt or being beaten is not at all the immediate goal of masochism. Enduring harm is but a link in the overall experience of self-depreciation making pleasure possible. Thus, rather than positing the existence of an organic drive for pain, something rather different and more subversive appears to be taking place. 'What the normal person perceives as unpleasure, the masochist perceives as pleasure or, at any rate, as a source of pleasure.'[35] The process by which this arises, it has been noted, can already be discovered in organisms on the simplest level of life – protozoa. Protozoan life consists of cycles of alternating tension and relaxation operating to gratify hunger as well as sexual needs. However, it is often the case for protozoa that previously dissolved substances form precipitates, which harden and block the cycle of tension and relaxation. This is not the ascendancy of a death instinct; it is, however, a limitation of pleasure functions insofar as the block operates to prohibit life processes, particularly the gratification of hunger and sex. Somewhat similar results have been obtained more recently for juvenile green iguanas; placed in a 'situation of conflict between two motivations' – that of food and that of warmth – they were able to compare the two sensory modalities, trading off necessity for comfort but only as long as the offered food was not necessary to their survival.[36]

On the human level, the solidification of life processes (such as hunger and sexuality) is taken to be always accompanied by anxiety. Anxiety appears to be greatest when sexuality is inhibited and lowest when the individual experiences sexual satisfaction. Were there a death instinct, particularly one driven by a biological striving for unpleasure, one would expect that anxiety would occur in precisely the opposite circumstances. Adolescents would have no anxiety while old people would have nothing but anxiety insofar as their approaching dissolution in death would dominate their psychology because it dominates their biology. Should we demur? Is it the case that anxiety is socially constituted? We may say that anxiety is describable as the effect of the world upon the body, but it is an affection produced by constriction and stasis, a painful affect and percept, a constraint deflecting the light rays of combinatorial networks, leaving the body submissive and reactive, torn apart and forcibly rejoined, subject to *passive restraint*.[37] The greater the stasis, it is argued, the more likely it is that sexually related fears will become manifest as affective anxiety and they will form structures associated with death. Anxiety arises, minimally, when the feeling associated with sexual pleasure, the diffusion of pleasure, is blocked. In human beings, the principle irritant producing constriction and stasis is not precipitates, it is morality. Far from being an organic drive, passive restraint may be a social restriction on pleasure. Sexual pleasure will be regulated; it must give way to the sublime moral law which dictates that no interests may come into play. The implication then, is that pleasure-negating moral law and not the death instinct leads to the acceleration of the process of death.

Excerpts from the case history of a male patient (see Chapter 3) reveal a great deal. The patient's father is described as psychopathic and sadistic, a man who severely beat the three-year-old child for soiling himself and for minimal displays of infantile sexual curiosity. Such a beating could not fail to reach the genitals. Obviously, the child's castration anxiety was not misplaced. The child's intense anxiety and fear of punishment later developed into an extreme form of masochism. This masochist is not a failed lover who will not tolerate the Other's objectification of himself. He or she approaches pleasure like anyone else, as a positive activity, but the fear of punishment and extreme anxiety interfere to prevent the experience of pleasure.[38] Masochistic self-punishment is a pathetic defense against an anticipated extreme and painful punishment resulting from seemingly arbitrary moral prohibitions, restrictions and judgments handed down by parents and society. In part, as a result of his punishment and in part, as a manifestation of his profound grief and emotional distress, the patient also experienced a deep disappointment in love regarding those persons who were loved intensely and who subsequently harmed the child or did not gratify the child's love. The patient's constant complaints have been expressed in this way:

> His complaints had the following layers of meaning, corresponding to the genesis of his masochism. 'Look how miserable I am; please love me' – 'You don't love me enough, you treat me badly' – 'You must love me, I shall force you to; or else I'm going to annoy you.'[39]

The masochist is unable to assert a zone of indetermination that would liberate him from the feeling of suffering that corresponds to this high tension and anxiety. The stronger the demand, the less likely there is to be satisfaction, with the result that the masochist remains caught in a structure of passive restraint, unable to free himself from his pain and suffering.[40] Thus, it is the parents' violently aggressive responses, their regulative morality asserted over what is nothing more than a child's infantile sexual curiosity or actions which produce the masochistic state.

But this is not all. The parents' harsh and moralistic reaction to the child's sexual curiosity is also related to his eventual and ongoing failure at sublimation when that word is taken to mean, creative contributions to civilization. The 'inhibition and repression of genital exhibition [in childhood] leads to severe impairment of sublimation, activity and self-confidence in later life.'[41] This means that in avoidance of severe anxiety, the masochist is more likely to pursue a conformist path in which she or he does not stand out. Such a personality, as even the afflicted patient describes it, is often 'bureaucratic' and, one can imagine, pedantic, demanding, and self-deprecating as well. Perhaps now, it is becoming a little clearer why passivity is ideal for societies of control, why certain persons, referred to as masochists, cannot relinquish the passive restraint that organizes their behavior, and why they continue to seek situations in which they are passive and must submit to the demands of a dominating master or mistress. Moreover, insofar as the masochist, formed by sex and pleasure negating morality, seeks to be loved but generally feels unloved, and responds to this with anxiety, conformity, and pedantic behavior, to the degree that these formative influences are culturally induced, then we may be facing a situation in which the masochistic tendencies of an entire population are engendered within the context of societies of control.

Freudian psychoanalysis accounts for masochism in terms of a conflict between eros and thanatos in which the latter, the death drive, gradually wins out and completely absorbs the life drive, thereby enforcing the need to be punished and to suffer. As such, it presumes that the instincts or drives exist within *isolated* systems of matter and energy.[42] The emphasis is on masochism, wherein the instinct for aggression, in opposition to sublimation, becomes inwardly directed and linked to sexuality. In this situation 'man's natural aggressive instinct, the hostility of each against all and of all against each,' clearly stands in the way of the creation of civilization.[43] This is so much the case that it begins to appear that sublimation (acts of the ego and super-ego) are little more than aggressiveness internalized and introjected.[44] The ontological limits of this system may not have been particularly apparent to psychoanalysis. That is, the principle of the conservation of energy has the status of a natural law, an ontology giving energy the status of 'being,' what is. But the second 'principle' of thermodynamics, that of entropy, '*that which truly changes when everything is apparently returning to the same form*,' remains a law of observation in a *descriptive* science, linked to the 'boundary conditions' of specific problems.[45]

Thus the psychoanalytic characterization of masochism irks the cultural theorist because it takes the social and cultural structure, an observation within a *descriptive* science, to be an ontological law. The descriptive scientific view prevents the reduction of masochism, arising from passive restraint, to a biological will to self-destruction which fails to answer the question of how it is that suffering is associated with pleasure. Not surprisingly, much of this arises from our disinterest in making sense of pleasure, our disinterest in understanding the degree to which the gratification of pleasure, and not the desire to be punished, is the principle orientation of living beings existing within the system of masochism in societies of control. Recent physiological investigations of human and animal subjects tend to affirm that pleasure serves as the common currency in the trade-offs between clashing motivations. The displeasure of frustrating one motivation being accepted for the sake of a larger pleasure obtained in satisfying another one. In one set of experiments the subjects tended to maximize the algebraic sum of their sensory pleasure or to minimize their displeasure. The conclusion made here is that in a situation of conflict of motivations, one can predict the future choice of the subject from the algebraic sum of affective ratings of pleasure and displeasure, given by the subject, to the conflicting motivations.[46] In the case of the 'pathological' masochist, it is not the act of being beaten, whipped, or bound that is in itself pleasurable, but rather, there is the hope that this particular ideal of punishment will be adequate to overcome psychic tensions produced by the social restrictions placed on the individual, to allow the masochist to feel the pleasure of sexual excitation and gratification. Thus, the masochist is like anyone else – she or he seeks pleasure, but unlike the non-masochist, this pleasure is often blocked, and every sensation that could be pleasurable is instead the opposite, it is unpleasurable.[47]

Is there not something like this masochistic structure operating within the society of control, ultimately rendering it dystopic? Corporate controlled amusement parks, but also every redeveloped downtown in every major and minor American city, attempts to produce an image of desire and free will by means of passive restraint. Promotional literature provided by multiple city governments on their websites and in the media contain images of happy and excited children delighting in the fun and enjoyment of some city center, zoo, museum, amusement park or mall. Adults appear to be smiling and content, gratified that their children's desires are so harmlessly met and that their own childish sentiments and yearnings are humored and satisfied. In these advertisements there is no question but that America's Main Streets are an exciting adventure for thousands of families who are not merely pleased but thrilled to find themselves in these magical places which are intended to provide citizens with the very image of fun, imaginative play, and relaxation. Nonetheless, as the darker view of numerous social critics implies, as a visitor to one of these sites, one's trajectory falls increasingly under the control of the images and language made available by the advertising campaign designed to promote and guide, thus to control the entire experience.[48] And it is not just cities, amusement parks and resorts that present themselves in this way. Brochures and websites for college campuses, for the military, as well as for corporate recruitment often present an image of these institutions as having the power to transform one's life. All that is required is that the individuals submit themselves to the organization and order that has been prepared for them.

Of course, as every adult knows, there are always undesirable aspects to the fantasy of escape with its overtones of innocent play, excitement and adventure, whether those of the resort or those of the social institutions. With regard to amusement sites in particular, there is the cost of travel to such destination resorts as well as the climbing price of admission and meals, particularly for a family with several children. Then there is the matter of placating tired or impatient children as they wait in long lines, often in sweltering heat, so that by the time one reaches the specific ride or amusement, it is a relief to collapse and buckle oneself into the cushioned seats, contentedly, passively restrained. As the entire family consumes more processed food and sugar, everyone grows cranky, tired, dirty, and stressed, so that the visit becomes as much a matter of pain as of pleasure. Of course, everyone returns home from the vacation proclaiming that they had a great time, as if a certain amount of punishment were the necessary condition of enjoyment! This feeling may have more to do more with the regulative codes that they have purchased, than with their real experience, insofar as visitors to these sites generally fail to realize that what they can say about them is almost completely limited to the descriptions provided in the promotional materials which bring them there and guide them through the experience. This is the case whether one is visiting Disneyland or one of the great museums of Europe. In Paul Virilio's view, these contemporary institutions make use of the techniques of the cinematic spectacle. They bring together disparate images of past, present, and future and of multiple continents into one comprehensive representation, a single intensive image. Each entertainment provides an intensive image of an America or Europe where before and after, future and past exist only to make the present disappear. This is a vision of America or of Europe that never has and never will be the present, just as colleges and corporate headquarters built out of concrete and brick try to evoke images of ivy-covered traditional institutions in their promotional materials. Such images serve as a screen for the actual environments and experiences which these sites and institutions offer. In the contemporary world, perhaps it is no longer appropriate to refer to this as imagination, perhaps it is in fact nothing more than anticipation, foresight and production of simulations.[49]

So it seems that the experience of passivity and punishment is promulgated nearly everywhere in the contemporary spectacle-institution. One need only reflect on the manner in which at every amusement park, visitors are almost always seated and bound, held in place with seatbelts and sometimes shut in behind sealed doors where they are passively, if not forcibly, fed images, sound, lights, and motion. Specific entertainments include even more powerful prohibitive elements. At Disney, a structured narrative of pirates places those waiting to embark in a dark cave where the first thing they see are the imprisoned brigands. Their spoils are draped with the skulls and skeletons of other pirates who were killed when the forces of good wreaked punishment and revenge upon them. The scenario proceeds to show the visitor that the punishment has been incurred as a result of the pirate attack on a merchant ship. This wanton act apparently leads to the pirates being attacked, their eventual defeat, imprisonment and (for some) death. Of equal importance is the scene of pirates feasting and reveling in the pleasures of their treasures. Not surprisingly, some drunken pirates are shown chasing women and embracing them in sexually suggestive poses. The reading of scenes is constrained by the regulative and universalizable moral law that for pirates, crime does not pay; they may be said to have embarked on the schizophrenic voyage.[50] Their trajectory is defined by the breakdown of the subsisting codes and territorialities, a breakdown in which they are mere instruments since, as we have noted previously (in Chapter 4) 'the desire of the most disadvantaged creature will invest with all its strength, irrespective of any economic understanding or lack of it, the capitalist social field as a whole.'[51]

The activities of the merchants, however, are universalizable. Recall that if the principle of action is based on a subjective ground of determination, what is willed depends on pleasure or pain with respect to some *object*. When the ground of determination is subjective and empirical, *ought* does no more than express the relation of what is to the subject's feeling of pleasure or pain. The subjective ground of determination remains a material practical principle; it will not result in a universal judgment of the kind required by corporate powers. Actions based on subjective and empirical grounds are motivated by the idea of pleasure to be received from some object.[52] Subjective motives arising from the subject's feeling of pleasure or pain are different for every person and can never produce a profitable industry. Piracy is legitimate only when it operates independently of one's *interests*, that is to say, pleasure and sex are not to be pursued. Thus the female figures must be represented as victims, not as willing participants and the interest-driven pirates must be punished even as the merchants are vindicated by their revenge. Given the reality that this scene is primarily for children (although adults are well represented on these rides), the passive acceptance of these scenarios on the part of all visitors implies that parents agree with the trajectory as it develops. In fact, it is an entirely predictable trajectory, reason enough, one suspects, to call it 'fun,' or better yet 'good fun,' since fun usually consists of repeatable, predictable, universalizable behaviors that, insofar as they are universalizable, must be good. Even when some degrees of freedom are admitted, and chaotic, non-predictable, trajectories result, they will not be subjective and empirical, based on one's interests, since none of the elements constituting them involves one's pleasure or pain; one's own sensibility never enters the equation.

One can only suspect that this morality echoes and reinforces the one enforced at home. Here, however, nothing is left to chance, the mere possibility of a creative or original interpretation is negated by the regulative moral principles, the demand for universalization. Moreover, the images that are intensified in this 'entertainment' are quite possibly those of death, superpower, violence, destruction, and annihilation. As such, it is a image of war. The fact that this narrative sequence is repeated on a miniature scale in so-called Fantasyland, a part of the park specifically produced to attract very small children, only reinforces the claim that these images are meant to be a means of control, one that intends to teach and reinforce a certain morality which equates pleasure and sex with death, destruction, and annihilation. Other Fantasyland rides manifest this same regulation. Author Kenneth Grahame's outrageous story of the car-driving maniac Mr Toad in *The Wind in the Willows* is transmuted into a morality tale.[53] The irrepressible and devious toad, once jailed for audaciously stealing and driving a car madly through the countryside, is, in this version, shown not merely in jail, but taunted by menacing red devil-toads goading him with pitchforks in toad hell. Clearly there is no other way for societies of control to interpret freedom of movement; mad behavior is always subject to the laws of vision machines where to be seen is to be subject to the machine of control. Such is the price of the diffusion that is pleasure. Any sensibility indicative of a free-wheeling, pleasurable life must be regulated, lest any human children be led astray, unable to differentiate between fictional toads and non-fiction actions in a society where the sensible interiority of children's stories as a genre disappears and they must now be read as homogeneous with real-time events and acts.

Given this situation, is it the case that amusements and entertainments are regularly constructed in order to conceal from citizens the fact that what we experience as real is already fake? Is the theme park presented as an imaginary adventure, in order to reinforce the pretense that the rest of America and the world are somehow real, when in fact most of the world, the United States in particular, is hyperreal and simulated? Is it the case that there is no false representation of reality, rather, there simply is nothing real left at all, that all of America and perhaps most of the rest of the world are fake, all of it is a simulacrum? To hide this fact is no more than a last-ditch attempt to save the reality principle.[54] Of course, the value of this move itself is in need of evaluation. Psychoanalysis claims that the ego, driven by self-preservation (reality), replaces the pleasure principle with the reality principle, which determines that pleasure should be postponed and discomfort tolerated, thus that the road toward pleasure should be indirect.[55] Pleasure must be set aside for the sake of survival. Baudrillard's complaint would appear to echo this one, that there is too much pleasure, that fakeness and fantasy serve the pleasure principle and that it is too late to 'save' the reality principle. What if, however, we consider another position? All that is 'fake' and 'fantasy,' insofar as it participates in the structure of masochism, is in fact deadly. It is death itself and its imperative is that henceforth, there shall be no direct pleasure in the form of attunement to one's own sensibilities, whether this be sexual, intellectual, social, aesthetic, economic or politic. The thesis of the necessary abandonment of sexual pleasure is perhaps emblematic of the abandonment of all the others insofar as it may be simply the most deeply intimate and personal of these sensibilities, the most sensibly one's own.

In order to formulate this thesis more precisely, we might attempt to examine the extent to which the repudiation of sexual pleasure has come about on both the personal and the social level. In 1933, Reich believed that only 'the smallest minority of masochistic characters also develop a masochistic perversion.'[56] But in the society of control, masochism appears as a general characteristic organized by societies of control. Character analysis is the heart of the method that counters the psychoanalytic suppositions, because its aim is to liberate sexual energy from the moral constraints of society, which, according to this perspective, frequently redirects sexuality into anxiety. Restrained and misdirected sexual energy not only limits sexual gratification, it also directly limits culture by making less energy available for sublimation; culture arises not from the repression of sexuality but from the combination of sexuality with other influences, its diffusion in the world. Even Freud recognizes that sublimation creates culture, knowledge, arts, and sciences, and presumably it is women's inability to tolerate sublimation that places them in opposition to civilization and makes them so much more likely to be neurotic because, unlike men, women cannot endure the frustrations of sexual life called for by the activity of creating a culture.[57] This perhaps, gives us a first hint about beauty, that beauty may be the effect of the diffusion and combination of one's own emanations with rays of light emerging from near and far. Existing as illuminated perspectives, it is entirely likely that much more beauty exists than we can now imagine.

In addition, if it were the case that women cannot endure any frustrations of sexual life, one would expect that anxiety related to masochism would appear primarily among women, yet as Sacher-Masoch's notorious but illuminating *Venus in Furs* implies, this need not be at all the case. The conditions conducive to masochism, such as the authority to train another person to dominate oneself, are more likely to be found among culturally 'male' behaviors, although female masochists certainly do exist. Additionally, with respect to sublimation, both men and women engage in cultural creation of a certain type. Perhaps the key to masochism lies with the *contractual* relations between the sexes that permit the male to fashion the woman into a despot. Thus, he acts in accordance with cultural norms and perhaps can even be said to engage in the creation of a perverse social contract, an anti-morality according to which he educates the woman, dresses her for her part and prompts her harsh words and behavior, punishment for his supposed brutish but natural state. The contract between them is thus a cultural artifact created by both in order to guarantee her willingness to allow him to submit to her.[58] Perhaps it is an aspect of the masochist's demand for love. However, insofar as the masochistic contract is part of a search for the transcendental Ideal and seeks to provoke a mystical frame of mind, it would appear that once again, it deflects sexual gratification into religious or mystical sentiments and such sentiments themselves inhibit the creation of culture and replace literary, scientific, philosophical and artistic creation with idealizations at best and dogma at worst.

For our purposes, the significant effect of these structures is that, whether directly or indirectly, the more anxiety there is among individuals in society, the less cultural and intellectual life will be created. This may be why Reich recognizes that not everyone is capable of sublimation, and thereby he insists that in shifting the therapeutic emphasis from sublimation to direct gratification, the range of therapeutic possibilities is greatly increased. This explains also why Freud, for whom health amounts to learning to live with a maximum amount of misery, is satisfied with sublimation while in Reich's analysis, health requires the establishment of a satisfactory genital sexual life and only secondarily, its accompanying sublimations. Indeed, some principle is at work, possibly the principle that when desire is no longer viewed as the desire for something, it functions machinically, that is, as a life force, to desubstantialize and demystify sexuality. 'If desire is repressed, it is because every position of desire, no matter how small, is capable of calling into question the established order of a society . . . there is no desiring-machine capable of being assembled without demolishing entire social sectors.'[59] Surely, as its authors claim, an amusing hypothesis. But machinic desire, connecting one organ to another, is not pleasure, and force remains part of the chaotic trajectory that allows unpredictability while leaving itself open to the ontological force of the transcendental Ideas, to the detriment of one's own sensibilities, one's connections with all things emitting and absorbing light.

If sexual gratification is a condition of sublimation rather than something opposing it, then masochism, the inability to achieve sexual gratification, directly benefits the creation of a universalizable imaginary under the control of corporate interests in the societies of control. For if sexuality and sublimation are foregone, leaving only anxiety and masochistic behavior, then Main Street is prepared to satisfy this worldwide perversion. Numerous globalized companies, for example, now own and control large blocks of property in major cities, retail stores in malls around the country, hotels, destination resorts, small cities, as well as major news outlets, film and publication companies, even toy manufacturing. The image of Main Street has expanded to include a great deal of the world so that no one is untouched by the hand of corporate control. But one need only visit, be educated by, work for, or be confined to any of the thousands of sites and institutions that are now part of the society of control whose homogeneity makes it possible to bring together otherwise disparate times, places, and historical periods. The purpose of all this control appears to be profit. Less pleasure guarantees more profit, less interiority homogenizes the processes which produce profit. But this makes the control no less vicious, virulent, and deadening. All of what have been called the formal components of masochism – disavowal, suspense, waiting, fetishism, and fantasy – are taken up by the corporation and used to stimulate the masochistic tendencies of a moralistic society. The aim here is to discourage the creation of new realities, new spatio-temporalizations, and to direct the visitor into the morality of consumption in place of the ethic of sexual gratification and cultural sublimation.

For Reich, disavowal is the attempt to master one's tension and anxiety by fully inadequate mechanisms that tend to cause even more tension and unpleasure. In substituting the culture of control for the anxiety over one's desire for sexual pleasure and creative sublimation, one only reinforces the sex and pleasure negative morality of one's parents, substituting a more universal punishment, one packaged as clean, idealized fun, but one with a moral imperative to leave behind creative impetuses for the security of the culturally sanctioned and thereby profitable consummation of goods and services. Suspense arises out of the central conflict between sexual desire and the fear of punishment. The sensible being can still imagine free sexual pleasure, perhaps she can anticipate letting herself become diffused by intense sexual pleasure, but then she suspends this, fearful of the consequences, at first merely parental sanctions, but over time, those of a society increasingly unable to tolerate creative life. Suspension of pleasure is related to waiting and the fantasy that perhaps as the masochist waits for punishment before advancing toward more intense sexual pleasures, the fantasy that being beaten or the reality of being punished for one's sensibilities will be enough to allow him or her to relax the feeling of anxiety and to experience sexual gratification, as well as to engage in the creation of meaningful cultural sublimations. But the waiting goes on forever. In place of pleasure, sensible and intellectual diffusion, one is given tourism, the tour of the regulated site where what one can say, do and feel is organized by passive restraint.

In place of family, education, employment and healthcare, each and every citizen is organized into a single, intensive and homogeneous system of control until fetishism is all that is left to the masochist, and increasingly, as we all come under the regime of moral passive restraint, it is all that is left to all of us. Fetishism is, of course, the other name for consumerism. Clothing covered in logos, cellular phones and beepers that keep one constantly in touch with one's labor, movies whose plot lines are only thinly disguised repetitions of previous movie plot lines, rock bands whose members and music are entirely organized by recording companies, stacks of tee shirts advertising corporations, restaurants, clothing manufacturers, internet companies, and tourist destinations, indiscernible sports teams moving from city to city in search of a bigger stadium and a more profitable market, tourists flocking to consume Times Square, the new sanitization of pleasure, or to the simulation of foreign countries in Epcot and the simulation of cities in Las Vegas, media increasingly in the hands of a few ultra conservative global corporations featuring stories on health and lifestyles to the exclusion of politics, hunger, war, or disease; designer housewares in discount stores, bigger and bigger sports utility vehicles, and accessories for every aspect of one's life, including and especially the new bigger and better desire shops where one can buy stereotyped sex videos and clichéd toys for doing it all by oneself; tourism without going anywhere.

It is all about tension and discharge, Reich claims. The masochist fantasizes being beaten in order to bring about the relaxation that he or she was prohibited from bringing about any other way. But usually, the relaxation of tension never happens. The masochist's anxiety is so great that he or she never allows anything unexpected to take over, no involuntary increase in excitation is permitted. In fact the masochist avoids increases in pleasure and finds it intolerable to let these sensations take their course.[60] In place of creative sexual gratification and sublimation, the masochist repeats the unpleasurable experience again and again and again. What better outcome for a consumer society in an environment of manipulation and control? Driven by our compulsion to repeat, we turn our cities into theme parks, we prepare children from birth for hours of mind-numbing labor in front of a computer screen, we train worker-slaves not thinkers in the universities, and those whom we have failed to subdue in the family or in the educational system can be restrained by the military or the system of prisons. If all else fails, poverty, poor housing and nutrition, and lack of healthcare will ensure that every last citizen is subjected in the society of control. Thus, we seek passive restraint and its accompanying restraint of pleasure, which is, is it not, death itself?

Is this all? Is this all there is? Throughout these pages, I have tried to indicate that it does not end here, not with passive restraint and not with the dark precursor. Sensibility is everywhere, yet moving so fast, at infinite speeds, forced on by affects, percepts, concepts, even by our prospects and functives, that we miss it. Little in our thinking or in our experience prepares us for it. Yet, it is there. Sensibility is there, pleasure and pain are its reality, and beauty is its sign. So let us make one more attempt, in a final chapter, to locate this sensibility, this slow-down and to absorb and emit its waves, its scent, its sound, its touch, taste, and sight.

Notes

1. David Hume, *A Treatise of Human Nature*, p. 10. It is precisely the weakness of imagination, relative to memory and original impressions, that gives rise to the liberty of imagination.
2. Hume, *A Treatise of Human Nature*, pp. 9–13.
3. See Michel Foucault, *Discipline and Punish, The Birth of the Prisons*, tr. Alan Sheridan (New York: Vintage Books, 1979), originally published in French as *Surveiller et punir; Naissance de la prison* (Paris: Éditions Gallimard, 1975).
4. Max Horkeimer and Theodor W. Adorno, *Dialectic of Enlightenment*, tr. John Coming (New York: Herder and Herder, 1972), p. 85, originally published as *Dialektik der Aufklärung* (New York: Social Studies Association, 1944).
5. Horkeimer and Adorno, *Dialectic of Enlightenment*, p. 83. Thus, reason paves the way for the slave owner, the entrepreneur, the administrator.
6. The obvious referent here is Thomas Hobbes, *Leviathan* (Baltimore: Penguin Books, 1968), wherein nature is not only nasty and brutish but is also the source of the natural right of self-preservation, even if this means 'take all, kill all.'
7. Hume, *A Treatise of Human Nature*, p. 534. This view of nature justifies self-preservation at any price (the right of nature to kill all and take all) but may also be an attempted refutation of mathematically derived determinism and the reassertion of free will, freedom both of passion and of reason.
8. Hume, *A Treatise of Human Nature*, pp. 89–90. The implication is that the so-called uniformity of nature is undemonstrable.
9. Hume, *A Treatise of Human Nature*, pp. 494–5. Selfishness and scarcity provoke the demand for justice, but most ordinary persons are incapable of fulfilling the demand.

10. Hume, *A Treatise of Human Nature*, pp. 534, 535, 537, 531. Intimacy with the notion of 'regularity' would nonetheless fail to produce greater probability or predictability.

11. Gilles Deleuze, 'Postscript on control societies', tr. Martin Joughin, in *Negotiations* (New York: Columbia University Press, 1995) pp. 178–82, originally published in French as '*Post-Scriptum sur les sociétés de con-trôle,*' in *L'Autre journal*, no. 1 (May 1990), reprinted in *Pourparlers* (Paris: Les Éditions de Minuit, 1990): 240–7.

12. Paul Virilio, 'Continental drift', in *The Virilio Reader*, ed. James Der Derian, tr. Michael Degener, James Der Derian, and Lauren Osepchuk (London: Blackwell, 1998): 183–95, p. 192.

13. Paul Virilio, 'Continental drift', pp. 192–3. For example, a one gigahertz computer performs the switch from '0' to '1' in about one-billionth of a second. More gigs yield faster switches. The speed of light is a constant 299,792,458 meters per second.

14. See, for example, Per Bak, *How Nature Works, The Science of Self-Organized Criticality* (New York: Springer Verlag, 1996), pp. 28–9. 'Systems in balance or equilibrium, by definition, do not go any-where . . . apparent equilibrium is only a period of tranquility, or stasis, between intermittent bursts of activity and volatility . . . called *punctu-ated equilibrium*' (p. 29).

15. Deleuze, 'Postscript on control societies', p. 179 (243, 242). This is one with the axiomatization that drives capital.

16. Bak, *How Nature Works*, pp. 29–30.

17. Jean Baudrillard, *America*, tr. Chris Turner (London: Verso Books, 1988), pp. 33–4, originally published in French as *L'Amérique* (Paris: Grasset, 1986).

18. Bak, *How Nature Works*, p. 30.

19. Paul Virilio, 'Critical space', in *The Virilio Reader*, ed. James Der Derian (London: Blackwell, 1998): pp. 58–72, pp. 58, 61, originally published as *L'Espace Critique* (Paris: Christian Bourgeous, 1984), pp. 155–81.

20. Virilio, 'Critical space', p. 58. Virilio makes it clear that these develop-ments, possibly unstoppable, are not welcome.

21. Virilio, 'Critical space', p. 59. Virilio has in mind situations such as the homelands established in South Africa in the 1970s. I am thinking about contemporary life in the United States.

22. Virilio, 'The state of emergency', in *The Virilio Reader*, pp. 51, 52, 56–7.

23. Chapter 11 of the NAFTA trade agreement authorizes the rights of corporations over those of nations and states and enforces the rights of multinationals to set up businesses wherever they wish regardless of environmental and economic costs to the local and regional populations.

24. See Virilio, 'Critical space', p. 59. Urban zones are, then, no more relevant than colonial empires.

25. I have in mind the illegal 'aliens' as well as the disenfranchised indigenous or ethnically disadvantaged workers who work, everywhere in the so-called first world, as maids, gardeners, dishwashers, janitors, caregivers, car-washers, street-sweepers, and so on.

26. I am transposing Virilio's insights into my own ontological framework. See Virilio, 'Critical space', pp. 59, 60, 66. Virilio notes that this 'crisis' is 'curiously analogous to the fractional character of our recent conceptions in the domain of theoretical physics' (p. 60).

27. See, for example, Nina Bernstein, 'A mother deported, and a child left behind', *New York Times*, 24 November 2004, Sect. A, p. 1.

28. Virilio, 'Critical space', p. 60. I have previously discussed this issue in 'Time Lost, Instantaneity and The Image', in *parallax* 26 (January–March 2003): 28–38.

29. Horkeimer and Adorno, *Dialectic of Enlightenment*, pp. 87–8. Horkeimer and Adorno have in mind the fundamentalism of Sade.

30. Louis Marin, 'Disneyland, a degenerate utopia', *Glyph*, 1977, p. 54. American students and adults tend to view Marin's essay warily. Disneyland, they argue, is simply entertainment and not to be taken seriously. They are most likely right that it does not 'cause' dystopic sentiments; however, this does not imply that it may not simply reflect them.

31. Marin, 'Disneyland, a degenerate utopia', p. 54.

32. Marin, 'Disneyland, a degenerate utopia', p. 56.

33. Marin, 'Disneyland, a degenerate utopia', pp. 58, 59. I am reframing Marin's essay to de-emphasize the psychoanalytic 'imaginary,' in order to emphasize the empiricist imagination and the regulative transcendental Ideas.

34. Wilhelm Reich, *Character Analysis*, p. 208. See Chapter 3 for an initial exposition of masochism.

35. Reich, *Character Analysis*, p. 210.

36. Marta Balasko and Michel Cabanac, 'Behavior of juvenile lizards (iguana iguana) in a conflict between temperature regulation and palatable food', in *Brain, Behavior & Evolution*; 1998, vol. 52, issue 6: 257–61.

37. Reich, *Character Analysis*, p. 213. Reich opposes any concept of a death instinct.

38. Reich, *Character Analysis*, p. 213. This harrowing experience is akin to torture. The masochist's anxiety cannot be underestimated.

39. Reich, *Character Analysis*, pp. 232, 236.

40. Reich, *Character Analysis*, p. 232. Another way of approaching this would be to say that the masochist operates at equilibrium in a closed system. New matter and energy would have to enter to destabilize the equilibrium for any change to occur, but even this might not be adequate to dislodge the masochist from the attractor around which they cycle endlessly.

41. Reich, *Character Analysis*, p. 232.
42. Sigmund Freud, 'Project for a scientific psychology', in *The Standard Edition of the Complete Psychological Works of Sigmund Freud*, tr. James Strachey (London: Hogarth Press, 1966), 1: 295.
43. Sigmund Freud, *Civilization and Its Discontents*, tr. James Strachey (New York: W. W. Norton, 1961), pp. 66, 69.
44. Freud, *Civilization and Its Discontents*, p. 70. 'The tension between the harsh super-ego and the ego that is subjected to it, is called by us the sense of guilt . . . *Civilization, therefore, obtains mastery* over the individual's dangerous desire for aggression' (pp. 70–1, emphasis added).
45. This excellent and meticulous characterization of thermodynamics is provided by Rémy Lestienne, *The Children of Time, Causality, Entropy, Becoming*, tr. E. C. Neher (Urbana: University of Illinois Press, 1995), pp. 115, 116, originally published as *Les Fils du Temps* (Paris: Presses du CNRS, 1990).
46. For details of these experiments carried out with humans and animals, see Michel Cabanac, 'Pleasure, the common currency', *Journal of Theoretical Biology*, 155 (1992), pp. 173–200.
47. Reich, *Character Analysis*, p. 217.
48. Marin, 'Disneyland, a degenerate utopia', p. 55.
49. Virilio, 'The state of emergency', pp. 47, 50. Thus the speed at which a society operates indicates the kind of civilization it constructs (p. 51).
50. Deleuze and Guattari, *Anti-Oedipus*, p. 224 (265).
51. Deleuze and Guattari, *Anti-Oedipus*, pp. 229, 228, 230–1 (272, 270, 273–4).
52. Kant, *Critique of Practical Reason*, p. 21.
53. It has been renamed 'Mr Toad's Wild Ride', See Kenneth Graham, *The Wind in the Willows* (Avenel, NJ: Lithium Press, 1987).
54. See Gail Weiss, *Body Images, Embodiment as Intercorporeality* (New York: Routledge Press, 1999), p. 73; also Jean Baudrillard *Simulations*, tr. Paul Foss, Paul Patton, and Philip Beitchman (New York: Semiotext(e), 1983), p. 25.
55. See Sigmund Freud, *Beyond the Pleasure Principle*, tr. James Strachey (New York: W. W. Norton, 1966), p. 24 and *The Ego and the Id*, tr. Joan Riviere (New York: W. W. Norton, 1960), p. 45.
56. Reich, *Character Analysis*, p. 218.
57. Freud, *Civilization and Its Discontents*, pp. 44, 50, 55.
58. Deleuze, *Masochism*, pp. 20–1.
59. Deleuze and Guattari, *Anti-Oedipus*, p. 115 (138).
60. Reich, *Character Analysis*, p. 241.

6

In the Realm of the Sensible

Darkness and light

Sitting before the computer screen, we gaze at the display of digital photographs, souvenirs of summer. A few of the images appear to have a sequential or serial character. I am trying to make you laugh, so I click, click, click, one image after the next. We throw them up on the screen, viewing them at first simultaneously, then one at a time, but quickly. Your shoulders jerk back and forth; the laughing mouth lights up the image then quickly evaporates as we move forward then backward, forward and backward again, symmetrically, through the series, replacing one image with the next as quickly as possible. It is so awkward, still, we exclaim, 'Look! It's like a movie!' Yet, it is not quite like a movie because the movement is too slow, too jerky. Its not true animation, not a continuous sequence of moving images. It remains a set of discrete images, images that influence one another, images that have their effect on us, but not quite like a film whose continuity is made possible by the minutely differentiated, sequential attitudes of the frames that make it up – twenty four immobile frames per second. Moreover, as we click through the photographs, one or another in the array stops us. 'Ah,' you exclaim, 'that one is you.' The slideshow stops abruptly; you survey the image, a pure contingency – one that does not interest me at all. Thus, in the midst of our display of discrete moments and halfway attempts to produce continuity, something else emerges. As photographs, individually and devoid of attempts to reconstitute movement, a few, a very few of the discrete images engage either me or you; one or the other of us cannot stop looking. Later, you stop the slideshow at one photograph in particular. It is the social, historical, and cultural *discontinuity* of this image that seems, at first, to be so jarring, so improbable. It is the image of the seemingly impossible co-existence of you and the vacant, decaying shell of the once unknowable and menacing Palace of the Republic, in front of which, on this day, crowds are gathered to watch the Brazilian and Italian women's teams play beach volleyball on sand courts splayed out over the former parade grounds of the dark empire. Although this profusion is surprising, even to we who have posed for and taken this photograph, it is not this discontinuity but only the lopsided stance of your torso that arrests my attention. This is the detail, this is the personal attitude reflected in the image that captures me as I gaze at you, your eyes shielded by dark glasses.

But mostly, these are just pictures, reminders of a place, a day, the cloudy sky, the rebuilt, fallen capital. The unsuccessfully serial images of you or I from grimace to grin, from grin to grimace are so discretely separated from one another that running through them in reverse order absolutely reveals their individual character. Our attempt to bring movement to these images *from outside* ultimately fails, and they do not seem to attract us except as information, most lacking even the discontinuity implicit in the photograph where I stand, amused, in colorful attire, with my hand clasping that of the giant Marx who sits, placidly, next to an equally giant standing Engels. To make a movie, to produce the illusion of mobility, we need something else. We need thousands of frames that exist as immobile states, this frame and that; we need minutely sequential frames and much more movement.[1] This is possible with film, for which movement may be generated by the apparatus, by the mechanical film projector, but such movement remains outside and external to the sequential images, which are constituted as a string of inert states. For traditional film-making, cinematographic movement consists in bringing together many sequential images, many successive attitudes to reconstitute mobility. Yet, our experiment with stringing together a few, clearly discrete therefore neither sequential or successive photographic images leaves behind some uncertainties. What if we do not want merely to constitute movement from outside, by means of an external and awkward film apparatus? What if we would like to produce an image that, in some manner, exists in the midst of multiple combinations of images and influences, at the very interior of things, as you once existed in that dark world in the midst of coercion and uncertainty, threats and promises? If this is what we mean by 'animation,' not just the external stringing together of a sequence of behaviors, then making use of the cinematographic apparatus, we will necessarily fall short; we will fail. The reasons for failure, however, are far from clear.

The film-making and film-projecting apparatus, it has been claimed, abstracts from visible figures some movement that is impersonal, ideal, simple. It has been characterized as movement in general, featureless movement, empty, silent and dark, without the light that emanates from your figure in the discrete photograph, the light that impels me to look, to see you, so familiar, yet a completely new and strange being, a revelation. If we attempt to recombine this general, abstract movement – twenty four frames per second – with the average and mundane images among serial photographs, or even with the discontinuities or the absolutely unique and remarkable individual attitudes, the results are bizarre. In fact, do not the discrete photographs, because they will never be able to be made into a film, do they not have an influence, an impact, unknown in film? Is it possible that I will never see a film that I love, a film that *'fills the sight by force,'* that influences and recreates my sensibilities as certain luminous photographic images do?[2] How has this happened in spite of our good intentions, in spite of all the attempts to make film real, to make it come alive? How has this happened, not only for our half-hearted, failed productions but also for the finest, high production-value film showing at 'a theater near you'? How have we managed to merely juxtapose proximate realities, placing ourselves outside the light that sears our eyes and goes to the heart of things? How have we missed the reality of motion and in its place left a string of ideal, uniform, invisible motions, a weak and pathetic approximation of the existences we sought to capture, devoid of any temporal articulations of their own? Is it possible that all our vision, and even all our knowledge is like this, that in order to know *anything*, we place ourselves outside of it and thereby lose it?[3]

Perhaps we have been lead to believe that what is at issue here is the distinction between continuity and discontinuity, and that all of our attempts to bring mobility to either successive frames or to discrete photographic images are centered around the transformation of discontinuities into continuities. If so, then we are mislead. Discrete images are simply not able to be transformed into continuous images. Even discontinuous images are unable to be transformed into continuities. Let us begin with the latter in order to follow the implications of these statements. For mathematics, the relation between continuity and discontinuity is asymmetrical. Discontinuity may be defined as a discontinuous transformation of a continuous series. It is a break, a gap that implies the impossibility of remaining within the existing system and the absolute necessity of escaping it. Moreover, there is no going back; it is impossible to run the tape of discontinuity forwards then backwards. In this sense, a discontinuity is catastrophic. Not because it is destructive, but because like the break between the dark empire and the social and cultural mix that has irrupted out of that break, it is final. Once a discontinuous transformation occurs, you are elsewhere; you exist on another space-time manifold, another set of initial conditions, another set of affects, percepts, concepts, prospects and functives constitute your reality. The cinematographic apparatus cannot string together discontinuities; this is an impossible act. What then does it do? We have learned from Kant that understanding and reason are limited with respect to what can be known. What can be known must be able to conform to the spatio-temporal manifold of our faculties. Beyond this, lies a nearly unlimited realm, the realm of what can be done. It is no exaggeration to say that intellect is almost wholly interested in what can be done and in the results of its activities. This is the point of the *Critique of Practical Reason*.[4] Moreover, given its limitations, intellect is only able to represent its actions in terms of their ends and to represent ends as points of rest on a given manifold. Thus our actions are represented to ourselves as movement from one point of rest to another. Most importantly, 'in order that our activity may leap from an *act* to an *act*, it is necessary that matter should pass from a *state* to a *state*,' an unmovable, material surrounding the frame of our acts.[5] And although the frame of our acts *seems* to be continuous, this is only in accordance with the scientific conventions dominant up to the mid-1920s. Thus it seems that the overwhelming direction of the critique of cinematographic knowledge is one that attempts to find a structure to express our acts as heterogeneous, *internal* and *absolutely new* – an original moment of a no less original history – rather than as homogeneous, external, deterministic and probabilistic, in the manner of continuous, smooth space, a structure that is expressed by classical dynamics, whereas the former criteria are expressed by quantum, the one theoretical structure in physics that expresses uncertainty.[6] But given that a clear formulation of uncertainty would not have been generally available until at least 1926, a philosopher who wished to conceptualize discrete images and motion within a system of uncertainty – a structure out of which emerges the absolutely new – such a philosopher had few theoretical resources. Thus the importance of theories of perception, where such concepts can more easily be situated, particularly in relation to human beings.

The role of perception may be said to be to serve the intellect, to assist in carrying out actions. For intellect to succeed, prior to grasping any objects, perception seems to be simply the perception of qualities: color, sound, touch, each persisting in an immobile state until replaced by the next quality. Yet further analysis allows us to postulate that even the most immobile quality consists of trillions of oscillations and that it is their repetition that leaves us with the sense of permanence. This is why perception condenses. 'The primal function of perception is to grasp a series of elementary changes under the form of a quality or of a simple state, by a work of condensation.'[7] Moreover, there must be continuity between those entities that oscillate impassively, with few oscillations, and those for which every perception is a gestalt-like consumption of trillions of such oscillations dedicated to action. Thus, for every gestalt, for every stable view, a trillion instabilities. And although everybody is changing at every moment and what is real is movement or change, *perception* only perceives form, a 'snapshot view of transition,' potential motion only, thereby solidifying into immobilities what is otherwise nothing but movement and change. Changes in situation reflect the profound changes accomplished within the whole, changes hidden in the shadows, the 'penumbra.' In this aspect of our sensibility, we fail completely as narcissists. For most people, alcohol and entertaining distractions are evidence of the extreme discomfort and tedium we would suffer were we to attend to the complex relations of even our simple acts with their myriad motions.[8] Perhaps this is why we overlook the motions and imagine the meaning, which we suppose will be discoverable at the end point as the form of each act.[9]

Paradoxes of immobility

So it is not so strange that the limitations imposed by cinematographic movement and the knowledge we derive from it remain mired in confusion. Given the vast variety of interactions that are encompassed by change, given that, on a certain scale, all is change, a single account of becoming, a single, general abstraction can, at best, represent change from one immobility to another. This is why the Bergsonian argument perplexes us. How can it be that we may grasp *change itself,* change from *within,* myriad, complex interactions, along with the successive states *in* which these complexities might potentially, at any moment, become immobilized? That is, what structure might allow us to grasp change from within rather than from the outside, from inside and not from the situation of a dynamical system, a pure exteriority, a trajectory assembled from contingent affects, percepts, concepts, prospects and functives? Is it not the apprehension of change itself, in all its complexity, that makes it possible to conceive of immobility, in the same way that the apprehension of what is, what exists, makes it possible for us to conceive of 'nothing' and the 'void'? 'Nothing' is conceivable only as the annihilation of what is and as such seems to require that we first conceive of positive existence.[10] Likewise, immobility, this immobilized state or that, is similarly the *imaginary annihilation* of motion. But from outside, on the manifold of smooth space-time, such states are taken to be real, individual events, no longer merely potentially immobile, but really or actually immobile and all efforts on our part to reconstitute change out of real or actual states, which is to say, immobilities, leads to paradox.[11] Multiple expressions of the paradoxes of motion exist: the dichotomy, Achilles and the tortoise, the flying arrow, the stadium. It is likely that these paradoxes, attributed to Zeno, form a group addressing a multiplicity of questions: motion between given limits, limits of indeterminate and indifferent lengths, one single mover realizing a motion, a comparison of two movers in motion, the impossibility of relative motion as well as of absolute motion, the impossibility of motion in space or in time when either are conceived of as indivisible points. Moreover, the first pair of arguments combats the idea of the indefinite divisibility of the continuous, while the second pair opposes indivisibility.[12]

For our purposes, let us work through just one paradox, that of the flying arrow, as emblematic of the problem at hand. Its argument is as follows: (1) Anything occupying a place just its own size is at rest. (2) In the present, what is moving occupies a place just its own size. So (3) in the present, what is moving is at rest. (4) What is moving always moves in the present. So (5) what is moving is always – throughout its movement – at rest. In other words, 'time' is composed of moments or instants; it is a series of *immobile* 'nows.' Stated in terms of space and motion, since the arrow is at rest at any given point, the arrow is motionless at each point, motionless during all the time it is moving.[13] The moving arrow is 'never moving, but in some miraculous way the change of position has to occur between instants.' 'Every attempt to reconstitute change out of states implies the absurd proposition, that movement is made of immobilities'; it forms the basis of the 'cinematographic' mechanism of our ordinary knowledge, a mechanism that makes motion an illusion.[14] This is an old problem, one for which Bergson's concerns are illuminating. Can the arrow ever *be* in a point? Can a moving arrow *be* in a position that is motionless? Can we say anything more than that a moving arrow *might* stop at some point in its course, but if it did, would it not be at rest and would there be any further movement? Is not a single movement just a movement between two stops? What happens in this paradox? What is the source of the illusion? Is it that, 'the movement, *once effected*, has laid along its course a motionless trajectory on which we can count as many immobilities as we will?'[15] If so, it is a count that can proceed to infinity. Are we to simply dismiss the moving arrow as the misconception of mathematical physics inappropriately applied to nature or can some sense be made of this paradoxical model? Perhaps we have assumed too quickly that we understand the paradox when in fact we do not. Take, to begin with, the concept of a motionless trajectory, what really are we referring to? Although the paradox is ancient, modern mathematics continues to conceptualize it.

We have seen that mathematical idealization posits a geometrical model (see Chapter 1). This model, called *state space*, is posited for the set of *idealized* states of any phenomenon – thus our first possible misconception. According to the mathematicians, 'the relationship between the actual states of the real organism and the points of the geometric model is a fiction maintained for the sake of discussion, theory, thought, and so on.'[16] Within state space, changes in position can be represented by points that when connected, form a curved line. Each point is an implicit record of the time at which an observation is made within the geometrical model. This is the definition of a *trajectory*. A time series may also be represented across multi-dimensional space, meaning, a series of state spaces each one situated vertically at a unique designated time. Representations of trajectories in geometric state space or of the time series (called a graph) of the trajectory were already in use in the middle ages. The modern innovation, introduced by Newton, was the addition of velocity vectors, that is, the ability to calculate, using differential calculus, the average speed and direction of any change of state.[17] Trajectories determine, calculate, accurately predict velocity vectors, the average speed and direction of a change of state. Velocity vectors may be *derived* at any point, that is, at any *time* along the curve. Inversely, velocity vectors can also determine, calculate, accurately predict trajectories using the process of calculus known as integration. Thus, if every point in a given state space were to be mapped in this manner, the state space would be filled with trajectories.[18] Over time, which is to say, at many different given points, points that are connected and represented as trajectories, each point will have the exact same velocity vector (the average speed and direction of any change of state), as the vector specified by the dynamical system. There will be no surprises. The system determines velocity vectors. Secondly, and equally important, the space that is being described here, the space of a dynamical system is smooth space; it is continuous, without jumps, breaks, leaps, without corners, as trajectories are smoothly curved.[19] Thus, if a dynamical model is called for to describe some observable behavior, the model will consist of a *manifold* or state space and a vector field; it is a model for the habitual tendencies of the situation as it *evolves* from one state to another. This charting of evolution is what makes the model dynamic. But insofar as the system yields qualitative predictions of long-term behavior, its evolution is deterministic. This is what makes it useful.

It is precisely trajectories and velocity vectors that are at stake in the acknowledgement that our ordinary knowledge has become cinematographic, and that cinematographic motion is an illusion. It is precisely this view of reality that Bergson would seek to limit to its appropriate sphere, to separate it from other views of reality, views that take seriously the words 'creative,' and 'evolution,' especially when they are characterized by an explosive evolutionary force, a '*grand éclat*' which is not possible in continuous, smooth space but requires minimally, a discontinuous transition onto another manifold and maximally, a discrete transition, which would be, an emergent state, unpredictable and unknown. Nevertheless, Bergson's hesitations concerning the continuous, dynamical manifold have been criticized as 'overhasty'; and the idea of a creative explosion has been covered over by a vast, articulated 'encounter' between movement, the physical reality in the external world and the image, the so-called psychic reality in consciousness, between these two and the cinematographic image, a dynamical model of observable behavior.[20] Like the dynamical model, the cinema may be said to consist of a manifold and a vector field. It is a model for the habitual tendencies of the situation as it moves from one event to another. It yields long-term predictions, it is useful for action. And although such dynamical systems have been contrasted, again and again, with the phenomenological view, they are utterly commensurate with the position expressed by 'The Film and the New Psychology,' for which, objects and lighting form a system – not through any operations of intelligence – but through the configuration of the field that organizes itself in front of 'me.' Henceforth, philosophy will be in harmony with cinema; thought and technical effort are said to be heading in the same direction.[21] Or, as this has been more recently expressed, a theory of the cinema is not about cinema but about concepts, concepts that are every bit as practical, effective or existent, as cinema, and we are admonished that 'there is always a time, midday-midnight, when we must no longer ask ourselves, 'What is cinema?' but 'What is philosophy?'"[22] Indeed, that is the question. What is philosophy? What is the relation between cinema and philosophy, cinema and the real? Philosophy and the real?

Hoping only to entertain ourselves by gazing at some photographs, we have instead become mired in problems. But we might wish to attempt to sort through some of these questions so as to return to those photographs. If two such outwardly different philosophies as phenomenology and the philosophy of difference are in agreement that dynamical systems provide a model for cinema and cinema provides concepts for philosophy, then perhaps we need to pay a bit more attention to these systems. We said, dynamical systems consist of two principle elements. First, a manifold, that is, a playing field or space on which the motion of the system takes place. Secondly, a vector field, which is simply a set of rules that tell us where to go on this space from where we are now. If we follow the rules, beginning with the system's initial state and moving from space to space, from location to location, this route is our trajectory. Once the manifold, the initial state and the rules are given, our trajectory is completely fixed. We will unquestionably reach the end-point of the trajectory, called the attractor. So important is this end-point that the behavior of dynamical systems is largely fixed by the number and character of the attractors, and so it is precisely with the attractors that dynamical systems become interesting, insofar as many attractors are unstable and allow for some unpredictability even while deterministically following the established rules.[23] Everyone has seen films whose characters, plot and ending are, if not absolutely predictable, nonetheless hardly surprising. 'Romantic comedy,' 'horror film,' 'film noir,' 'chick flick,' 'action film,' even 'art film,' or 'independent,' each of these terms seems to describe a well known genre of films, many of which ultimately offer few surprises. So many films move inexorably from a particular starting point consisting of characters, plot, visual and sound effects, to a particular end-point (attractor); the particular story line (trajectory) is little more than an effect of the starting-point. In most cases, we are merely grateful that sequels are usually limited to two, otherwise we would find ourselves trapped forever in a limit cycle, a cyclic orbit in which the same or similar characters and events are repeated over and over, the true formula for pornography. In every case something is happening, but mostly, it is excruciatingly predictable and repetitive.[24]

This is the model for perception that the phenomenologist Merleau-Ponty appears to be opposed to in his discussion of the phenomenal field. 'For centuries,' goes the argument, perception appeared to be quasi-teleologically directed to an end; every instant could be coordinated with the previous and the following instants, and every perspective could likewise be coordinated with every other in an orgy of monadic and intersubjective experience constituted as a single unbroken text.[25] The continuous manifold of dynamical systems used to observe the body yields a notion of geometrical space indifferent to content; a pure movement, a setting of inert existence in which each event could be clearly related to physical conditions producing changes of location. It matters little if the object is never completely constituted, for the natural object is still an ideal unity. Moreover, the gestures, expressions and acts of a subject had now to be resolved into a series of causal relations, thereby bringing experience 'down' to the level of physical nature and converting the living body into an interiorless thing. Nor are emotional and practical attitudes of living beings spared. They too are able to be mixed into the vat of psychophysiological mechanisms, namely elementary impressions of pleasure and pain bound up with nervous system processes. Intentions are converted into the objective movements of the nervous mechanism, sensory experience becomes a quality traceable from nerve endings to nervous centers, as the body is transformed into an object, a machine among machines, both one's own body and that of others.[26] Such are the boundaries of dynamical systems – bound to their vector fields and attractors.

The phenomenologist is right to argue that this view of the world as predictable was already collapsing, but only insofar as it was globally applied to all observable phenomena. Nature is geometrical only within limited macrocosmic systems. The experience of 'chaos' is cited as a phenomenon that changes everything.[27] In the face of this chaos, as defined by the second law of thermodynamics, there appears a demand for a return to philosophy and to the philosophical *act* of returning, returning to a world in which *actual* experience precedes the objective world and somehow serves as its basis. Of course, if we stop with classical science, which after all begins with Newton and Leibniz, the deterministic, causal world it describes does indeed appear to have long ago collapsed, or at least to have been circumscribed to a limited field of stable behaviors. That phenomenology rushed in to fill the void may appear to be an appropriate corrective. But what is it that phenomenology proposes in place of deterministic, dynamical systems and is it any different to the corrective that mathematics itself proposes? That is, has phenomenology along with certain other enormously influential contemporary philosophies – and here I am thinking of nothing else than the philosophy of difference and intensities – have these philosophies themselves been caught up in what can be called a *limit cycle*, an attractor that operates when the rules of the system cause a given trajectory to repeat itself cyclically, to pass through the same series of points forever? Is this the meaning of cinematographic movement; is this the true consequence of what Bergson refers to as the view from outside?[28] At first this seems most unlikely, as Merleau-Ponty clearly proclaims:

> Nature is *not* in itself geometrical. Human society is *not* a community of reasonable minds and only in fortunate countries where a biological and economic balance has locally and temporarily been struck has such a conception of it been possible. The experience of chaos, both on the speculative and on the *other* level, prompts us to see rationalism in a historical perspective which it set itself on principle to avoid, to seek a philosophy which explains the upsurge of reason in a world not of its making and to prepare the substructure of living experience without which reason and liberty are emptied of their content and wither away. We shall no longer hold that perception is incipient science, but conversely that classical science is a form of perception which loses sight of its origins and believes itself complete.[29]

Yet, by the time these words had been written, classical science had long since superseded itself in the direction of the unforeseeble, the uncertain, and the absolutely new. Acknowledging that it would be difficult for life to emerge and survive in a structurally unstable world, where no situation and no pattern could be counted on to repeat itself with any regularity, mathematics also recognized that not all phenomena are structurally stable, nor are they continuous. Not only are dynamical systems open to contingent factors, but discontinuities abound. Moreover, from the perspective of some other structure, one that might be said to take its view from within, on microscales, nothing is continuous, nothing is static, space and time are themselves discrete; they are not constructed *a priori* but arise as the spatio-temporalization of the absolutely new. Let us begin with the simplest of these ideas, the idea that some things are not stable even though they are continuous, the system that is accurately named, deterministic chaos.

Simply stated, 'Newtonian determinism assures us that chaotic orbits exist and are unique, but they are nonetheless so complex that they are humanly indistinguishable from realizations of truly random processes.'[30] Sufficiently complex dynamical systems require as much informational input as they can provide informational output, in other words, strictly speaking, nothing can be predicted if the input information has to be equivalent to the output information. Under these conditions, if the rules of combination do not alter, in some sense, determinism remains, but predictability is lost. In truth, Merleau-Ponty's corrective does not always venture this far. Seeing its utility, he sometimes retains the structure provided by classical, deterministic dynamics and sometimes, his corrective goes elsewhere. To start, there is the argument that classical psychology errs by positing the visual field to be a sum or mosaic of sensations, each of which is caused by a single local retinal stimulus. As a corrective, the visual field is now posited to be much less a mosaic than a *system* of configurations. Similarly for sound, melodies are not the sum of notes but a structure of interrelationships. The absolute value of separate perceptual elements is contested in the light of the perception of forms, the structure, grouping, or configuration of any perceptual field and this is the case not only for individual senses but for the perceptual field as a whole. The unity of perception is not, therefore, an effect of memory or intelligence and not an *a posteriori* synthesis.[31] Moreover I do not *think* the world in perception, it organizes *itself* around *me* so that I am always searching, and what I am searching for is what the world *means*. Movement and rest are, in some way, subject to the manner in which the body situates itself, the position *it* assumes, but movement and rest also distribute *themselves*. These words remain ambiguous, if not contradictory. Is it the case that some hidden intentional consciousness is still at work? After all, Merleau-Ponty's perceiver is always situating himself, situating his body and always, attempting to ascertain the meaning of what he encounters. It does seem to be the case that as an *a priori* organizing principle, consciousness, that is, intentionality disappears, yet it does so only to re-emerge in an altered form. Beneath the objective idea of movement, there will be a pre-objective experience from which it borrows its significance, an experience in which movement is still linked to the perceiver, an experience in which movement is a variation of a subject's hold on 'his' world. Ever vigilant to the tricks of intellect, Merleau-Ponty warns that in asking the question 'what is movement?' and in assuming the critical, scientific mode, we are preparing ourselves to reject appearances for the sake of truths, but to do this is to risk concealing the *genesis* of movement, reducing movement as a phenomenon by decomposing it into the accidental attribute of a moving body, a change in purely external relations between a moving body and its surroundings, eliminating the very idea of a body *in* motion.[32]

Certainly it makes sense to oppose this. A moving body that would remain the same throughout its motion returns us to the moving arrow, to motion as a series of continuous but separate positions successively occupied in a series of continuous but separate instants, a cinematographic illusion. Moreover, the argument goes, every time I walk, I do perceive movements, while I do not perceive identical moving objects, stable external landmarks or relativity. The 'appearance' that is lost by taking up the critical attitude is the 'shift' or transition between 'two instants and two positions,' an appearance necessary to the genesis of movement. A stroboscope flashing alternately on two lines set at a right angle to one another reveals a single line moving continuously and symmetrically, back and forth. But speed up the light or slow it down and the line jumps from one position to another. At certain speeds, there is an appearance of smoothly continuous motion; at other speeds, one perceives the motion to be much more erratic. To conclude, however, that this experiment shows that the perception of positions varies inversely with movements, is not to deny that perception is an effect of movement, particularly since this experiment may be perfectly described as a classical dynamical system, it is simply a matter of continuities spaced more or less widely apart. Nor does this allow for the conclusion, nearly incomprehensible in this context, that 'dynamic phenomena take their unity from me who live through them and who effect their synthesis,' incomprehensible since without the flashing light, nothing would be given to perception, a perception so clearly reliant on the speed of light.[33] If the two lines are white or colored and are placed on a black background, then once again, utilizing a stroboscope, the background, that is, the space through which the movement extends, is never illuminated. But even though this may be evidence, as is claimed, that the perception of movement does not require the successive occupation by a moving body of every position between start and finish, nevertheless, is it not a perfect example of continuity operating in the same dynamical system? The cinematographic illusion may, then, have less to do with the successive occupation by a moving body of every position (something cinema in no manner can achieve) but rather, with the continuity of deliberately, successive snapshots that are virtual immobilities, frames in a given manifold. Thus slowing down motion to the point of imperceptibility says nothing about continuity and perception; rather it is a recognition of the limits of human sensibility.[34] That movement cannot be accurately described as a system of relations external to an object in motion, without leading to paradox, in no way implies that movement cannot be described as a system of relations period. It is entirely a matter of scale. Clearly, when Merleau-Ponty says movement, he means continuity. The greater distance between two lines in proximity is still movement for him, but when implied continuity disappears so does movement. Thus the discrete transition of photons or particles from one room to another does not for him constitute movement because movement can only take place within a continuous system whose rules do not allow either discontinuous or discrete transitions.

What about the possibility that there is an internal relation of some sort operating in the system of movement? Is there an alternative to the multiplicity of fusion and interpenetration of consciousness, the position attributed to Bergson, at least when precisely the opposite claim, that movement is nothing but flowing-matter with no point of anchorage nor center of reference, is not being laid down from other quarters?[35] What happens when the magician transforms himself into a bird? 'There must be some internal relation between what is abolished and what comes into being: both must be two manifestations or two appearances, or two stages of one and the same something which is presented successively in two forms.'[36] But what exactly does it mean to say that there is an internal relation of something presented successively or in two continuous forms? Let us look at this more closely. 'If I try to describe love or hate purely from inner observation, I will find *very little to describe*: a few pangs, a few heart-throbs – in short, trite agitations which do not reveal the essence of love or hate.'[37] As feelings, love and hate offer practically nothing. Superficial, able to be dismissed, trite and trivial; they yield little but awkward or embarrassing clichés. But if I think about my love and hate as a modification of my relations with others and with the world, as an effect of those relations; if I think about my love and hate as I would think about the behavior of someone I just 'happened to witness,' then the meaning of these behaviors will be perfectly clear. Love and hate are types of behavior, they are styles of conduct, entirely visible from the outside, on the face, in the gestures, constituted, as are all systems of deterministic chaos, out of the contingent modifications, the variations in one's relations with others and with the world. Others, in every sense of the word, are 'directly manifest to us as behavior'; others are incapable of constructing the world because it constructs them, they are a structure, thrown into the world, or perhaps more accurately, thrown together by the world, consisting of 'externally related terms,' words and meaning, bodies and behavior.[38]

What we have discovered regarding perception can now be applied to film and vice versa. In film, the succession of scenes creates a new reality that is not merely the sum of its parts. In film, there is a certain order of shots, and a certain duration for each in that order; cinema being a system of measurements. Music, sound, noise also contribute to the expressive force of this montage. Characters are created out of vocal and visual components, parts that add up to more than a whole, not simply through expository dialogue, but through tone of voice and the dramatic interactions between characters, scenes, lighting, sounds, each of which consists of myriad components. In all this it is the ensemble that produces the expression. Here, understanding serves imagination and the idea that is the film issues from its many component parts, parts that emerge into a whole, pushed forward by the rhythm, the temporal structure of the film, the temporal and spatial arrangement of its elements. Thus cinema produces a world that is more exact, which is to say, more predictable than the real world, but a world like the real world insofar as we do not have the thoughts of its inhabitants – we have only the conduct or behavior, a world in which dizziness, pleasure, grief, love, and hate are ways of behaving, visible only from the outside.[39] In short, what does it mean to say that consciousness is thrown into the world except to acknowledge that there are material flows, the expressed as mind and body, body and world, self and others, love and hate?

Cinema and philosophy

Perhaps this overstates the case. No doubt between the phenomenology of the visible and the invisible and the philosophy of differentiation-differenciation, there is a greater gap than this comparison allows for, but insofar as this is the case, it is a gap that yields the structural similarities all the more compelling. In the philosophy of difference,

> the model would be rather a state of things which would constantly change, a flowing-matter in which no point of anchorage nor center of reference would be assignable . . . it would be necessary to show how, at any point, centers can be formed which would impose fixed, instantaneous views. It would therefore be a question of 'deducing' consciousness, natural *or* cinematographic perception.[40]

Seen through the eyes of phenomenology, the new psychology does view the world from outside, through conduct and structures of behavior. And, it does form centers by asking, again and again, 'what does the film *signify*: what does it mean?' This incessant question is given the strange answer that 'the film does not mean anything but itself'; the idea emerges from the structure of the film, from the temporal and spatial arrangement of elements.[41] Were the phenomenologist able to give up the power to tacitly decipher the world, there would be much less distinction between this position and that of his critic who argues that the cinema lacks a center of anchorage and horizon, thus nothing prevents it from moving away from perception, away from a centered state of affairs to an acentered state, suppressing the subject's anchorage along with the world's horizon.[42] What is at stake here begins with what was called the new psychology. It begins when images could no longer be placed in consciousness and movement no longer separated in the world; the qualitative and intensive world opposed to the quantitative and intensive, overcoming the duality of image and movement, consciousness and thing.[43] Or, as Merleau-Ponty articulates this, movement does not presuppose a moving *object*, a collection of determinate properties; it is merely something that moves. And, if not an object, then why not simply, *something*, something colored, something luminous, something in between the object that moves and pure movement. This color, this luminosity would be the excluded middle. Between the propositions that there is an object that moves and there is not an object that moves, there is something, rather than nothing, but something excluded by binary logic.

Yet, in the same breath, Merleau-Ponty takes this back. If motion must either have or not have a moving body, then let us not dare to deny the logic of the excluded middle, and let us instead posit a pre-logical, pre-objective world that foregoes the unity of a Kantian actor, but nevertheless unifies.[44] And so we have, not an alternative ontology, but the classical dynamical system in relation to which philosophy both cowers and preens, as its pre-objective, condition or its emancipated but deterministic chaos. Phenomenology does not make the leap into non-sense and contradiction which is the very foundation of the philosophy of difference whose Kantian subject knows nothing, but does all or is done to by the infinity of affects, percepts, concepts, prospects and functives. But this philosophy too will not take the risk of the excluded middle. Its encounter with non-sense and contradiction are a short-term encounter, the incitement sending the acentered, fragmented subject into the flux of deterministic chaos, the dynamical system, the plane of immanence whose contingencies are infinite but whose rules are fixed. So have we articulated something new if we claim that matter and movement are identical, but in a manner that foregoes spatio-temporalization and makes of every matter-movement a 'bloc of space-time,' part of an infinite series of such blocs corresponding to the succession of movements in the universe, the universe transformed, now, into an infinity of cinematographic movements, where in place of movement from within, there are states, bodies (both subjects and objects) and action, everywhere action, in all possible directions and dimensions, always tearing apart whatever has connected itself, whatever habits have formed, then conjoining these fragments into a shattered universe on a single plane of immanence.[45] For these ontologies, as for Kepler and Galileo, time has no natural articulations, we can and ought to divide it as we please. If no moment has the right to set itself up as a privileged or essential moment, the one that represents all the others and is retained in memory as the essential moment, then like the succession of film frames, time isolates any moment whatever, putting them all in the same rank. As in film, the successive states of the world could be spread out all at once without having to alter the ontological conception.[46]

And we can still speak about time, but units of time, since for modern science, as for cinematographic knowledge, time is an independent variable, a parameter of the spatial manifold useful for calculating the positions of real elements of matter at any moment whatever if their current positions are given. Time is then a 'mobile T on its trajectory . . . [so that] to consider the state of the universe at the end of a certain time t, is to examine where it will be when T is at the point Tτ [to the power of t], of its course.'[47] From this point of view, events do not happen, rather, events are already mapped on the trajectory; we simply encounter them along our way; the emergence of events, spatialization and temporalization, the unpredictable would be an illusion. Events would be nothing more than continuous snapshots, successive images, indifferent images, insofar as the partitioning of space and time must be given equal rank, thus the succession of images would be simply the illumination of points on a line given all at once. But alternatives can and have been offered. In contrast to the concept of the snapshot, a successive image in a determined trajectory, a virtual immobility, let us propose the concept of the discrete photograph, which would be an effect of an 'uncertain art,' a science of desirable or detestable bodies, that *animate* the spectator by means of discontinuous elements and discrete effects.[48] If film photography is the invention of chemists, then digital is the invention of physicists, yet what does not alter is the role of light. The photographed body is expressed by the action of light; its luminescence touches the viewer with its own rays, so that the photograph is a literal emanation of light. Light-sensitive silver halogens make it possible to recover and print the luminous rays emitted by a lighted object. Image sensors sample light coming through the lens, converting it into electrical signals. Its grid of electrodes, exploiting the photo-electric effect, release electrons when exposed to light, the light that emanates from objects. Voltages are measured, amplified, converted, stored, but sensitivity to light ensures that the photographed body touches you with its own rays and so truly gazes at you, influences you in a profoundly sensible way.[49]

In a dynamical system, every trajectory is defined by laws that specify the movement and interaction of particles. The rules are given, what may be contingent are the particular particles themselves, that is, which particles enter into any given trajectory? Which affects? Which percepts? Which concepts? Which prospects? Which functives? This cannot be predicted, thus every configuration of particles produces a different world. But what do not alter are the rules themselves, rules that specify the movement and interaction of particles. Moreover, in these systems, space and time are given, not emergent, and in principle, reversible. They are the pre-existent manifold, and time is a fourth dimension, a means for differentiating different spaces, but it is not a spatio-temporalization, not the creation of a new spatiality and temporality. So again, we ask, what if it were possible to theorize a world in which different observers 'see' partly different, partial views of the universe, partial views which nonetheless overlap? Would this imply a dependence on the location of the observer, on the observer's unique duration, not the flow that constitutes her, but the information that constructs her perspective – her spatio-*temporalization*? Recall again the image of a cone, the image of Henri Bergson's concept of ontological memory, that memory created by the imperceptible influences of events in the world on a vulnerable sensibility. Under the sign of this cone, in a system that affirms relativity, the entire past coexists with each new present in relation to which it is now past.

> Memory, laden with the whole of the past, responds to the appeal of the present state by two simultaneous movements, one of translation, by which it moves in its entirety to meet experience, thus contracting more or less,

though without dividing, with a view to action; and the other of rotation upon itself by which it turns toward the situation of the moment.[50]

All of this occurs, we have noted, as if these memories were repeated a vast but not infinite number of times in the many possible contractions of any past life, but always altering, altering in each so-called repetition under the influence of intersecting networks of events. These *different planes* are myriad in number but not infinite. They stand in relations of simplicity and contiguity, influencing one another and influencing the present for the sake of action or *restraint*. For any present, for any perspective emerging from this past, there is the influence of the many layers of the past and of many interactions, networks of interacting events. This is, once again, what has been referred to from the beginning of this volume as *the past light cone of an event*. But what if we multiply these influences and effects? What if, as we have noted, the causal past of an event consists of *all* the events that could have influenced it? The influence travels at the speed of light or less from a past event to the present; really, it *is* the present. So it is light rays consisting of photons that form the outer boundary of the past of an event and make up the *past light cone of an event* – the past that arrives at the present and by arriving, creates the space and time in which that event happens as well as the event itself. What if we push this a little further by utilizing a concept and an image in theoretical physics? What if, rather than a single cone, every perspective and every event consists of a multiplicity (not an infinity) of cones linked to one another, 'combinatorial structures,' that have been called 'spin networks,' networks giving rise to self-organized, critical behavior? According to this conception, the causal structure of events evolves and the motion of matter is a consequence of that evolution, that spatio-temporalization. This gives us the opportunity to reformulate our hypotheses, our preconceptions about what may or may not be real in the universe. It allows us to reconsider the hypothesis that the real arises in a manifold consisting of smooth or continuous space-time; it allows us to postulate that smooth and continuous space-time are useful illusions. It allows us to consider the universe from the perspective of a different structure, a structure according to which the world can be said to be composed of discrete events, events on a very small scale, but nevertheless, events that are discrete with respect to both space and time on that very small scale. And so we ask: under such conditions, what would be observed, what would be discerned? 'The photograph does not call up the past,' it does not restore the past, it is not a memory, not a reconstitution, it is at once past and real.[51] It is a spatio-temporalization that fascinates the one who looks, that attracts the one who looks, that makes her the reference, that generates her astonishment. When I am drawn to and wounded by the beloved image, it evokes, not only the question, why is it that I am alive here and now to see, to sense this light radiating from your body to mine, but what is this world, this universe, that intertwines its events, that spatio-temporalizes itself, radiant and diffusive in myriad directions making it possible, once again, for beauty to emerge?

The continuum of differentiation-differenciation is the field of pure immanence. As a system, its primary processes are not the same as those we are attempting to introduce here. These latter processes involve the construction of a vulnerable duration, a sensitive contingency, an ontological spatio-temporalization, an ever-changing perspective in the heterogeneity of space and time. Such a perspective, if it is thinkable, if it is real, could manifest itself as a sort of history, not a linear, causal chain, but a complex causality, layers and layers of events, always susceptible to realignment, to patterns and particles resolving their scintillation and constructing an ontological memory below the speed of light. These primary processes, imperceptible, ephemeral, evanescent, influence one another and in this, they influence the sensibility of human beings. This is not perception, for it does not yet imply typical perceptual prerequisites, thought-like mental processes such as description, inference, and problem solving, no matter how unconscious or non-verbal.[52] Nor is it a pre-perceptual hovering at the edges of dynamical systems, mysteriously tied to their logic, the mostly binary logic of excluded middle. Rather, given that this is something much more difficult to situate, it is much more likely to be overlooked. It is the manner in which events (including very small events) influence and alter one another and so influence and alter human sensibility, all sensibility. These influences are not the objects of perception nor of consciousness; they cannot be experienced as increases or decreases of power, as the raising or lowering of intensities. They are, in some sense, passive and primary. If they are noticed at all, it is insofar as they are *felt*, felt as pleasure, felt as pain, as diffusion and expansion or dissolution and distress. Their influence on sensibility comes via the sensory system, but as ontological not personal memory. It is manifest in the exceptional absorption and emission of each event-organism – purely contingent, subject to alteration, but circumscribing what is characteristic of each sensibility as an original spatio-temporalization. So it is the way you emerge in the photograph, in the midst of multiple combinations of images and influences, at the very interior of things, as you once existed in that dark world in the midst of coercion and uncertainty, threats and promises. It is an absolute, immediate, non-conscious consciousness, an ontological unconscious whose existence no longer refers to an individual or to a being but is unceasingly suggested in the reflection, refraction and dispersion of light.[53]

Sensation comes from the past

Nothing, we are told, travels faster than the speed of light. It is an irritating invariant that provokes us to impatiently assert our demand for infinite speeds. And perhaps, given the realization that whatever is seen, heard, perceived through smell, and even what we have touched or tasted – given that all these sensations come to any sensibility from out of the past – perhaps the demand for infinite speeds reflects a creative refusal of cosmological limits. Or, just as much, a refusal of sensibility, of combinatorial networks and influences, not only for human beings, but for all things. Given this attempt to consider the place of sensibility among human beings and by extension, under the name of 'influence,' to non-human beings and events, much more needs to be said about epistemological structures.[54] It is undeniably the case that the phenomenological notion of flesh, the reversibility of feeling and felt, two hands clasped together, world and body exchanged as correlates is still 'too tender,' in need of 'house or framework . . . 'sections' . . . the pieces of differently oriented planes that provide flesh with its framework, foreground and background, horizontal and vertical sections, left and right, straight and oblique, rectilinear or curved.'[55] Yet, the phenomenologist of perception knew this too – and sought a solution not unlike that of the philosopher of differentiation-differenciation. Yet, what are the consequences of the solution that has been offered? These latter, differentiation-differenciation systems, with their continuous dynamical, n-dimensional trajectories have been called 'sophisticated random noise generators,' for only at critical points where transition from predictable periodic behavior to unpredictable chaotic behavior takes place does complex behavior show itself, although even here, the complexity is not robust.[56] Nor does chaos produce spatial, scale-free, fractal structures; chaos does not explain complexity, neither in the form of emergent behaviors nor as emergent structures.

The speed of light, 300,000,000 meters per second; the speed of sound in air at 20 degrees Celsius, 343.599 meters per second; the speed of scent, much faster than previously assumed, as much as 200 meters per second, the speed of touch and taste, perhaps unmeasurable, but not instantaneous.[57] Each of these wavelengths affects not only human sensibility but every non-human receptor as well. So, should we be content with a theory of percepts and affects that insists on their independence from all states in order to make them stand on their own? Under what limited circumstances do such percepts and affects stand on their own? Events in the world, conceived independently of human beings, conceived as elements interacting, differentiating on a pure trajectory within a plane of immanence are intelligibly conceived of as blocs of sensations. Pure blocs of percepts and affects, independent of the state of any receptor, are forces beyond the strength of any who encounter them – noumena, beings-in-themselves, beyond the lived, beyond the sensible, existing in themselves.[58] From a certain point of view, that of dynamical trajectories, that of the continuum of differentiation-differenciation in the field of pure immanence, '*affects are the non-human becomings of man* (sic)' and percepts the '*non-human land-scapes of nature.*'[59] So, we might recall what was said previously, that chaotic systems have no memory and do not evolve, that they are the white noise that numbs sensibilities both human and non-human. This, because under the regulative principles of connection, disjunction and conjunction, not only all life but all movement is fixed, subject to n + 1 dimensions, an eternal now not merely freed from the past, but literally without a past, without a future, aiming only for what cannot be predicted, for 'an extreme contiguity within a coupling of two sensations without resemblance.'[60] An extreme contiguity which would be, of course, a non-human becoming for 'man,' not even for *le genre humain* (humans, humankind).

Thus into a picture of a stable and predictable world, a world defined by the conservation of energy, a world begging to be disrupted and disturbed by the white noise of chaos, enters the second law of thermodynamics. Thermodynamics studies the transformation of energy and the laws of thermodynamics recognize that although 'energy is conserved,' when energy is defined as 'the capacity to do work,' nevertheless, nature is fundamentally assymetrical, that is, although the total quantity of energy remains the same, its distribution changes in a manner that is irreversible. So, for example, although human beings long ago figured out how to convert stored energy and work into heat, the problem has been to convert heat and stored energy into work. Otherwise expressed, how are we able to extract ordered motion from disordered motion?[61] When a system is heated or when it is heating its surroundings, it is stimulating incoherent or disordered motion, energy tends to disperse and so to lose coherence. The philosophers of differentiation-differenciation posit a universe in which, for every act of breakdown, for every loss of coherence, there is a 'little order to protect us from chaos.'[62] It is, they argue, because we are constantly threatened with loss – with a universe apparently moving continuously in the direction of disorder – that we hold on so tightly to our ideas and fixed opinions. Conceding that, were there not some 'objective antichaos,' some order in things themselves or in states of affairs, there could be little order in ideas, they nevertheless proceed to search for what they take to be the true causes of this order.[63] According to the first law of thermodynamics, a glass of cold water could spontaneously heat up, an old person could become a baby, energy could not only spontaneously localize and accumulate in a tiny, little spot in the universe, but it could do so coherently. Any mechanical system, any room full of molecules, is time-reversible, meaning the velocities of all particles could simultaneously reverse and the system would retrace its steps, moving backward in time.[64] Energy, highly localized and stored in the coherent motion of atoms could reflect the reversal of chaos and entropy; if so, it would imply change in the direction of greater order and organization.[65] The question becomes, how to achieve this highly improbable order and organization – how to create order out of chaos.

The philosopher, the scientist, the logician and the artist, it has been ascertained, must do more than empirically associate ideas, as empiricism yields no more than opinion, no more than pleasant dinner conversation and debate. The philosopher, scientist, logician and artist return from the land of the dead, that is, they return from the dispersal of energy, the degradations of quality, but in order to do so they need much more than *opinions*. The philosopher, in particular, must have not merely associations of distinct ideas but '*reconnections through a zone of indistinction in a concept.*'[66] Thus it is clear that no mere opinion, no empirical association of ideas will save the philosopher from dissipation, from chaos. Ideas may be associated as images and they may be ordered as *abstractions*; but much more than this, in order not to be mere opinion, Ideas must be *mental objects, determinable as real beings* in an *open Whole*, a plane of consistency, which is, however, conceptualized as a *single wave*, present everywhere at once. And, even as its peaks and troughs are multiple, they are never the less absolutely identical, giving way to a global homogeneity more absolute than any ever conceived. Extended to larger and larger values, such a system is no longer open but closed since it encompasses everything.[67] So of course the Whole, the wave, will be observer independent as well. So, it appears, philosophy is free to embrace chaos, defining it as the infinite speed of birth and death taking place on a plane of immanence, a single wave present everywhere and at once, giving consistency to chaos, giving rise to an *infinity of consequences*. Whatever is, whatever exists, is a consequence of the One-All, the homogeneous wave, present everywhere and at once.

Science, on the other hand, is burdened by the plane of reference, the referenced chaos called nature, the requirement that its hypotheses are testable, which means, it is burdened by the reality of physical existence. This reality is bogged down by invariants, most notably, the speed of light, which has been disparaged as the freeze frame, the deadly slow-down, the dirty laundry, the fall-out consisting of infinite consequences that limit or border science and reassure it as it confronts chaos. If functions derive their authority by reference to states of affairs, things, or other propositions – prospects lack even this as the realm of the logicians is deprived of any specific characteristics that would refer it to another dimension.[68] Lacking the context supplied by either the states of affairs of science or the lived world of affection, percept and action, logic recognizes and what it recognizes is not even truth but something much more 'impoverished and puerile,' the recognition of truth in the proposition.[69] Thus the proliferation of logic supplements like fuzzy logic which allows for set membership values between and including 0 and 1, shades of gray as well as black and white, and in its linguistic form, imprecise concepts like 'slightly,' 'quite' and 'very.' Under these conditions, the extent to which opinion proliferates depends on the reference – states of affairs, objects, bodies, lived experience – the former producing clear truth values, the latter leaning toward opinions. Often, in order to say anything interesting at all, the logician recognizes and thereby extracts a pure quality from a lived situation and identifies him or herself with a generic subject experiencing some common affections. Discussion follows concerning the choice of the abstract perceptual quality and the power of the generic subject affected by it. 'True opinion will be the one that coincides with the group to which one belongs by expressing it.'[70] But is this not always the case when logic considers only empty reference – simple truth value? And truth value, it serves only the function's references and those references are states of affairs, objects and bodies or lived states, all in a structure of probabilistic but smooth and continuous space-time, where the rules of the system are deterministic even if opinions change. Confined by the law of non-contradiction, logic is always only about truth value, probabilistic at best, but it is never concerned with uncertainty – such a logic would require admitting the excluded middle – something the philosophers of differentiation-differenciation simply do not consider.

And art – what happens with art? Art, like science, does not struggle with the whole of chaos as does philosophy – art is said to place a little bloc of chaos in a frame, forming a composition of sensation or extracting a bit of sensation. Art does not create, it *preserves* and is *preserved* – and what is preserved is a bloc of percepts and affects *independent* of and exceeding any living being, standing on its own, that is to say, without reference, without resembling any object, simply expressing a pure sensation – freeing it from objects and from states of a subject.[71] Thus art creates nothing – it preserves the non-human becomings of *man* and the non-human landscapes of *nature*. And artists – they are beings who sacrifice all to becoming – even if it destroys them. What is this becoming for whose sake artists perish? The affect and the percept are consequences of the single universal wave that is everywhere and everywhere is the same; they are extracted from it in the purest possible form; their origin is not in human or animal life, not even in nature, but in the chaos of the One-All. And what is this isolated bloc of becoming?[72] Perhaps, we would still call this view of origins the unconcealment of Being.[73] But what is the nature of the Being that is unconcealed? Rigorous mathematical treatment of the concept of disorder assigns constant rather than increasing disorder to any isolated system. In other words, when a system is isolated, disorder does not increase; when two previously isolated systems interact – their combination yields greater disorder than either when they are left alone and isolated. So affect and percept, isolated blocs of becoming are thereby screened from the cruel second law. 'But the relentless increase of entropy does not apply to a single "free-running" system – such as the entire universe.'[74]

The artist is said to add varieties, beings of sensation, analogous to those variables of the scientist, the logician, and the philosopher; expressions of the single wave of infinite chaos. The philosopher's variables are concepts, those of the scientist are functions, those of the logician are prospects, and those of the artist are sensations. What are the implications of this notion of artistic varieties? Is it deeply creative?

Is it the expression of the chaos or the uncertainty that is the universe or is it one more tool in the philosopher's box? Is the artist the means by which the triple organization of perceptions, affections and opinions are undone and replaced with percepts and affects, blocs of sensation – even if the effort of this process destroys the artist? What matter, since what remains for the philosopher is the language of sensations, a stammering, singing language, a style producible by no other means? Any other origin for the work of art, any origin relating to nature or to the human, would return us to the realm of opinion. This is the situation, we are told, that phenomenology falls back into when it tries to make *flesh* the perceptual and affective *a priori* of lived experience, the transcendent function that determines the limits of experience, that traverses the lived in the here and now, and that constitutes the embodied experience of living sensation. Flesh is both world and existence within that world, the reversibility of feeling and felt that precedes the intentionality of consciousness and makes it possible. But flesh, we are told, only measures the temperature of becoming, 'flesh is too tender,' it remains both a pious and a sensual notion, an affront to the law of non-contradiction.[75] Embodied flesh, incarnated flesh of the World, transcendently pious yet sensuously lived. Tied to experience, flesh is the *Urdoxa*, the founding or original opinion, but still an opinion insofar as it is the body's orientation in the world, the habituation of an embodied being for whom the parameters of the world are defined by foreground, background, horizontal and vertical sections, left and right, straight and oblique, rectilinear or curved, and beyond these nothing but chaos.[76]

From this point of view, embodied phenomenology never reaches a high enough level of abstraction; it never makes the passage from the finite expression to infinite expression; its lived flesh yields to the transcendental world flesh but remains as such tied to opinion, for only as the infinite consequences of the single wave might flesh express the infinitely varied infinities. In short, it is too empirical. By contrast, molecular becomings – blocs of sensation seized from the One-All by the death artist – are called cosmic or cosmogenic forces. They are forces by which the body disappears into color or into matter, simple enough on the molecular level. Such non-human forces are everywhere in the universe, overtaking the transcendentally organized human or animal or plant body, the body of perception, the body of opinion. If for phenomenology, art is the way in which humans give birth to perception making it possible to perceive a world, it may then also be said to be that which opens up a world but sets it back on earth. Through art, earth emerges as native ground, but the work of art is forgotten in the process of understanding the world.[77] For the philosophy of the variable, art, insofar as it is limited to the sphere of sensation, performs a similar function. It does not create concepts, strictly speaking, it does not create at all – its sensations are becomings, consequences of the single wave in the realm of the finite that reaches up to the level of the infinite. It is the sacrifice demanded by the cosmos, the price paid in order that philosophy not succumb to the slow-down, the deep freeze. Rather than things or objects, art gives us intensities, affects and percepts that sweep through our world, sweeping away the habitual ways of knowing, but always in conformity with the rule, the rule of the One-All.

But let us consider for a moment another kind of slow-down – not the absolute deep freeze but one that takes place effectively within the very structures we inhabit and that constitute us. Let us dare for a moment to exist within the interval, to remain within the effective slow-down between perception and action and let us consider the following. In the discussion of thermodynamics 'we have not considered the consequences of a *flow* of material through systems. Ordinary thermodynamics concentrates on closed systems, in which matter does not dribble in or out; but the living body is *open*, and matter is ingested as food, drink, and air, and in due course is discarded.'[78] If, as was noted above, the philosophy of difference is predicated on *real beings* in an *open Whole*, a plane of consistency conceptualized as a single wave, present everywhere at once, then its multiple peaks and troughs are absolutely identical, giving way to a global homogeneity more absolute than any ever conceived. Moreover, extended to larger and larger values, *infinitely* extended, such a system is no longer open but closed; it encompasses everything. Is it then a closed system that we encounter, within which philosophy, science, logic, and art express the infinite consequences of the one universal wave?[79] This is entirely possible from the scientific point of view – that is, even in a closed system, there may be and are local reversals of chaos which appear as emerging structures, but always at some price. Like the artist who is consumed by the effort of preserving the blocs of sensation that she cuts out of the triple organization of perceptions, affections and opinions, local abatements of chaos can be said to compensate for their organization with the generation of a certain amount of chaos elsewhere.[80] A bit of oil, for example, does not disperse and dissolve when dropped into water, but the appearance is deceptive. Dropped into water, the oil molecules are immediately surrounded by water molecules, each of which rests in a delicate molecular structure – the water molecules are more organized in the presence of oil, thus there is an increase in the order in the world and a decrease in entropy, a decrease that counters the increase in entropy caused by dropping the oil into the water in the first place.[81] Is this not the image of the artist who carves a bit of sensation out of the cosmos and gives it to the philosopher but at the cost of her own health and life? But such theories can be deceptive, based on nothing but phenomenological necessity. There is nothing preventing us from considering another possibility – that the thermodynamic model of independent subsystems does not apply to most of life – that since the universe began atoms have not spread themselves out uniformly but stubbornly cling together to form heterogeneous clusters of stars, planets, galaxies. Moreover, the relentless sense of *loss* that we are said to experience is only a consequence of combining previously separate subsystems leading inevitably to decrease in the number of those subsystems.[82] Let us therefore dare to propose another image for philosophy, one long ago discarded by the philosophers who embrace the dark precursor.

The field of flowers

'It was a place where dogs would lose their quarry's trail, so violent was the scent of the flowers. A stream cut deep through the grass of a meadow that rose at the edge to fall sheer in a rocky ravine into the very navel of Sicily. And here, near Henna, Kore was carried off.'[83] It was a place that would attract a young girl, virgin daughter of two gods, beloved child of Demeter, born of a violent coupling with brother-father Zeus whose nostalgia for the radiant light out of which all life emerged found perverse expression and whose acts, although they were the acts of a god, could never approach the everything of she/he who had been the 'first-born' of the world, the first appearance emanating from light.[84] Some claim the girl picked poppies, identifying her with their soporific qualities, their red color promising resurrection after death. Others, perhaps more attuned to the continuous usurpations of the male Gods who, of necessity, fixed upon Kore's eye, these others who may also have been more attentive to the sensibility, the mind, of a young girl, daughter of the goddess of three worlds – the heavens, the earth, and the caves beneath – these others assert that the girl, Kore, was looking at a narcissus, or perhaps it was a lotus, a lily or a rose. For them, 'the psyche as flower, as lotus, lily, and rose, the virgin as flower in Eleusis, symbolizes the highest psychic and spiritual developments . . . the birth of the self in the Golden Flower.'[85] In any case, the accounts of the Greek poet say it was a narcissus, so overwhelming, so seductive, 'a thing of awe . . . from its root grew a hundred blooms and it smelled most sweetly, so that all wide heaven above and the whole earth and the sea's salt swell laughed for joy.'[86] Obviously, a flower begging to be picked.

Perhaps the flower was a narcissus and she was about to pick it. If 'Kore was looking at a narcissus. She was *looking at the act of looking.*'[87] She is said to be looking at the flower of the youth, Narcissus, who, it was prophesied, would live to a ripe old age only if he never came to know himself. But this did not happen. Spurning all others, Narcissus was condemned to fall in love but denied the possibility of consummation. Seeing his own image in a spring 'clear as silver,' undisturbed by animal or plant, the already heartless, self-absorbed boy saw himself and came to know himself. Unlike the double-sexed goddess-god, Phanes-Eros – who, men say, is the off-spring, the luminous male principle, the divine son of Persephone-Kore – unlike Phanes-Eros, Narcissus is unable to copulate with himself. Moreover, in seeing and knowing himself, Narcissus does not gain understanding. Self-love merely enhances his pridefulness. Overly proud, overwhelmed by self-love, overcome by grief, he plunges a dagger into his own breast. Little wonder that narcissus came to be used in the ancient wreaths of Demeter and Persephone, also called Kore.[88] For, if to look at and to pick narcissus is to look at and to pick the act of looking, it is to see it and, through seeing, to understand. So Demeter-Kore may well be the expression of seeing and seeing as understanding. But for Persephone-Kore, for this girl, understanding was, at the beginning, denied. Wandering alone on a sunny morning amid clusters of blossoms, Kore stops to look and reaches out, touching the flower, pulling at the stem. Precisely at the moment when she reaches out to pluck the flower, precisely at the edge of her own look at the act of looking, at the edge of under-standing through seeing, the earth opens and she is taken away by an unseen power to a dark, invisible place. Is this not the fate of many young girls? In the full light of the sun, at the very instant when they begin to look at the act of looking, on the verge of seeing and of coming to understand through sight, are they not also swept away by some unseeable power, a power that sees itself in them but which they cannot see? And unlike Persephone-Kore, most do not return.

Why does Hades, who sees and understands nothing of the world above, why does he come from the underworld with his golden chariot and four black horses? He who is made imperceptible by the gift of the Cyclops, the helmet that conceals him, why does he come to earth to abduct Kore?[89] Is Hades the descendent of the serpent Ophion, created with the wind by the 'Goddess of All Things,' the naked Eurynome? Eurynome, wide-wandering goddess, the visible moon, diffuse light. Eurynome, exhaulted dove, the first and only, the universal goddess who arose from yawning Chaos, danced with the wind, and gave rise to all things. Eurynome, the dove, tumbles above the waves and is fertilized by the wind. Out of the union of dancer and wind is hatched the Universal Egg, from which all things emerge, a cosmos set in motion by the Goddess and forever transforming itself, its seven planetary powers now ruled over by the Titanesses whose interests the Titans serve and safeguard. But Ophion soon exasperates the goddess, claiming to be himself the author of the self-created universe, until she, incredulous, 'bruised his head with her heel, kicked out his teeth, and banished him to the dark caves below the earth'[90]

And now it is Hades who claims supremacy in the dark caves below the earth; the other world, an invisible world defined as isolated, separated and silent.[91] In the myths reported by men, this new Ophion returns to the earth, but not to see and not to understand through sight. On earth, once again, a snake wraps itself around a goddess. In the myths recorded by men, Hades returns to the self-created and visible world where formerly only deities ruled the seven days of the sacred planetary week: the Sun to illuminate; the Moon for enchantment; Mars giving growth; Mercury giving wisdom; Jupiter giving law; Venus granting love; Saturn granting peace.[92] There are no dark powers, no isolated, separated, silent, deathly powers among the *conceptions* of the goddess, Eurynome. The snake wanders in the caves beneath the earth; it is nothing more than wind whistling through cracks and crevices. Banished, defanged, not a god, for gods give, they do not take anything away. But men, Hesiod, Ovid, ensure the return of the once powerless, defanged creature in a much more despotic and dangerous form. They make him a sightless God who seeks a vision of himself. Perhaps then, we should note that for them, Eurynome, Goddess of All Things, has vanished from the cosmos she brought forth; she is the first goddess to disappear, but will not be the last.[93] For these men, poets and philosophers, Darkness is first and from Darkness springs even yawning Chaos. And from Chaos springs not illumination, enchantment, growth, wisdom, law, and love, but Doom, Old Age, Death, Murder, Sleep,

Discord, Misery, Vexation, Nemesis, and later, Terror, Anger, Strife, Vengeance, Intemperance, Altercation, Oblivion, Fear, Pride, and Battle. What little can Sleep or Joy, Friendship or Pity do to ameliorate the force of the dark planetary powers now unleashed?[94] And for them, for the philosophers, Nature is now the 'God of All Things,' *he* who does not bring forth but who *separates*, who *separates* earth from heaven, water from earth, the upper realms from the lower, unraveling all elements. And this unraveling is called 'setting in due order,' but it is an endless task in a cosmos set in motion by the Goddess of All Things, a cosmos ceaselessly transforming itself through the powers of illumination, enchantment, growth, wisdom, law, love, and peace.[95]

Perhaps then, given the arrival among men of the idea of setting the cosmos in due order, we should anticipate and acknowledge the importance that comes to be placed on the eternal model of the cosmos, that which always is and has no becoming, from which the world order is created in a *symphony of proportion* according to which what fire is to air, air is to water, and what air is to water, water is to earth. It is a structure that arises from a symphony of self-love ('he who framed the universe . . . wanted everything to become as much like himself as possible') and it produces a symphony of proportions consisting of Originals and their imitations. As such, Different is to Same as men are to Gods, and female to male (female being the inferior nature, the poor imitation, the formerly male soul that fails to live a good life).[96] Given all this, it is not surprising that Hades emerges from his separated and silent realm, from the realm of the invisible, into the field of flowers, into the visible, to abduct the daughter of Demeter, daughter of the 'triple goddess of the cornfield,' whose priestesses initiate the young and newly wed into 'the secrets of the couch,' but who takes no husband herself, who remains independent of all dark powers.[97] Perhaps we should not be surprised that the separated and silent world, the invisible world asserts itself, asserts what have been called its 'rights' over the visible world, meaning over the visible body of a young girl about to reach out and pluck the act of looking, about to take this open flower, this opening to understanding for herself. Where do these rights of the invisible over the visible arise? What justifies such rights? Are they also the effect of the symphony of proportion?

We have been told, 'I'm sure you've noticed that when a man looks into an eye his face appears in it, like in a mirror. We call this the 'pupil' (kore), for it's a sort of miniature of the man who's looking.'[98]

If an eye is to see itself, it must look into a mirror or an eye. Moreover, the best part of the eye is said to be the part with which it sees, and this is likened to the best part of the soul, said to be the part that knows. The best part of the eye and the best part of the soul are said to resemble the divinity, perhaps because the pupil is thought to be that part of the eye that gives vision, and the intellectual soul is that part of the soul that gives understanding. In spite of a general injunction against the senses which disturb the proportions to near breaking point, sight is acknowledged to be a great benefit to humankind. 'None of our present statements about the universe could ever have been made if we had never seen any stars, sun or heaven.'[99] Our capacity to see Nature is the gift of vision. And from the human ability to observe day and night, months and years, equinoxes and solstices, has come the invention of number, the idea of time, as well as numerous inquiries into the nature of the universe. And from these pursuits have arisen philosophy! Thus from vision – understanding, and not the reverse. But the philosopher is rather blind to this relation. He reasons that vision is the effect of particles shot out of the eyes, the *pure fire* that flows through the middle part of the eye, that part which is close textured, smooth, dense, so that pure fire and only pure fire passes through. From the contemporary perspective, 'it is difficult to imagine now why Plato did not try to settle the matter with a few simple experiments.'[100] But his conception of vision was inextricably linked to the mixing of fires, like coalescing with like, the pure fire from the eyes coalescing with daylight, mixing and forming a *homogeneous* body, a medium that is able to transmit the motions of whatever comes into contact with it. The homogeneous body transmits motions from objects that contact it or that it comes into contact with; it transmits these motions through the eye straight into the soul! Fire meets fire, and *Kore*, the young girl about to pick a flower, must be blinded, lest vision lead to understanding. She must be abducted so as to become the pure, virgin opening onto knowledge of an Other self. Eyefire and dayfire mix, homogenize, and convey directly whatever they come into contact with to the invisible soul, the only thing said to properly possesses understanding, by which is meant, self-knowledge.[101]

And the soul? The soul is conceived of as a dark box, part of a *camera obscura* consisting of a pinhole opening through which passes one single ray of light; a single ray cuts through the *kore*, the tiny pupil, and is projected onto a screen for *direct* viewing. To see clearly, the soul must be completely dark, dark as the unlit and invisible place from which the God, Hades, emerges; it is the dark place into which the pinhole opening of the eye projects inverted images of the objects outside.[102] This is what the philosopher calls understanding, but it is little more than a view of the self, a view of the tiny image of oneself in the eye of the other, the very image of what is called self-knowledge. Precautions are put in place to ensure that nothing will enter the soul that should not enter – no diffuse or scattered light, scattered like flowers in a field. The motion of fire that gives sight is described as a *direct* motion; the internal fire travels through the homogeneous medium; it *strikes* an external object, *pressing against it*. It is a motion that may be called *ballistic*.[103] The *camera obscura* operates in accordance with the principles of the dark soul, the soul that knows what the eye perceives, but what the eye perceives is oneself. Contemporary perception theory agrees with the ancients that the mind does not record an exact image of the world but in fact creates its own picture.[104] Nevertheless, it can be argued that perceptions are neither arbitrary nor illusory; that they are unaffected by knowledge of ourselves or knowledge of the world. 'Within the range of stimuli to which our senses are attuned, our perceptions of the sizes, shapes, orientations, stabilities, and lightnesses of things turn out to be . . . as the students of perception say, *veridical*.'[105] Our so-called direct perception of the world must be mediated by the senses but as veridical, our perceptions do correspond to things in the world when those things are considered objectively, meaning, independently of viewing conditions, meaning, something obtainable through some form of measurement. However, the question remains, *is* vision direct perception, as has been claimed? Geometrical optics tells us that light does travel in straight lines, but the 'law of refraction,' operates due to the requirement that the speed of light can be constant only in a perfect vacuum. Strictly speaking, if a ray of light passes from something like a glass of water (a dense medium) into air (a less dense medium), the ray of light will refract or bend. Light does travel more slowly in a denser medium and mediums do vary, they are not, as the philosopher hypothesized, homogeneous. Bending, refraction is inevitable and is the basis of image formation by all lenses including those of the eye.[106] But this is not all.

Shadows and light

The Goddess Eurynome, dancing in the wind across the sky, sets the sun in place to illuminate the daytime sky and the moon to illuminate the night-time sky. Eurynome, wide-wandering goddess, the visible moon, diffuse light. Eurynome, exhaulted dove, the first and only, the universal goddess who arose from yawning Chaos, danced with the wind, and gave rise to all things. Eurynome, the dove, tumbles above the waves and is fertilized by the wind. Out of the union of dancer and wind is hatched the Universal Egg, from which all things emerge, a cosmos set in motion by the Goddess and forever transforming itself, its seven planetary powers now ruled over by the Titanesses whose interests the Titans serve and safeguard. But Ophion soon exasperates the goddess, claiming to be himself the author of the self-created universe, until she, incredulous, 'bruised his head with her heel, kicked out his teeth, and banished him to the dark caves below the earth'[107] Eurynome is both the Goddess of All Things from whom all things emerge and the transformative, dynamic element, the creative element, setting the cosmos in motion and impelling it toward change.[108] In the cosmos set in motion by the Goddess, it is the luminous moon and moonlight that form the background against which the sun and the cosmos stand out, light being the fruit or flower of the night. Ancient cultures calculated time from light of the stars and the planets, especially the moon. From this point of view, the light-bearing goddess of the night was identified with the moon and the moon was identified with life.[109] Such was the basis of the great mysteries of Eleusis, a celebration of the phases of the luminous moon, the joyful birth of the new moon, following the dark-moon, when the light of the heavens, the flourishing girl, Kore, is abducted by the death-sun.[110] Darkness corresponds, then, to the disappearance of the moon, its luminous, reflective rays, and death, the darkening of the moon, *comes from the sun.* The winter solstice celebrates not only the return of Kore to Demeter from the caves of Hades, but also rebirth, Kore giving birth to the moon, the full moon, and the transformation of the girl Kore, 'by achieving union on a higher plane with the spiritual aspect of the Feminine, the Sophia aspect of the Great Mother, and thus [herself] becoming a moon goddess.'[111]

A daring proposition? Dare we propose that the true transformation, the return of Kore to Demeter and to the moonlit earth, is her transformation from girl to goddess, from sunlight to moonlight, an 'immortal and divine principle, the beautific light . . . [so that with] Demeter, she becomes the goddess of the three worlds:' the heavens, the earth and the caves beneath?[112] This conceptualization, speculative and, at its inception, untestable, is grounded in the idea of transformation. There is a transformation of material or natural elements, a quantitative and qualitative transformation in which something new is achieved, something that, like the moon, illuminates the heavens with its reflective light and by means of this reflective illumination, transforms all, not once, but again and again. Its limits are found, perhaps, in the ancient idea of the cosmos as finite and bounded, having actual edges beyond which . . . nothing, nothing to sustain an object's structure. In such a cosmos transformations are limited, possibly little more than repetitions or maximally a finite number of variations. Still, is there any reason to believe that the universe created by the Goddess is not at least *unbounded*, a sphere that is finite in area but delimited by no boundaries?[113] Nevertheless, what matters for the moment is the Goddess floating, dancing with the wind above the water, the transformational aspect of this conception, for which it may prove to be of the greatest importance that, whether it is called *cosmos* or world-order, there is no severance of the connection between the concept and the reflective moon, the luminous aspect of the night.[114]

The philosophers too began with a concept. What the Goddess has consigned to the dark caves below the earth diffusely lit by the reflective rays of the moon, they raised up to the highest heights. What had been lowest will be highest; what had been little more than the sound of the wind whipping through the caves below; what had no being and so no gift-giving, planetary power; the invisible realm of Ophion and Hades, the dark realm of the death-sun, this will be the model for a cosmos made in the image of being. No longer a cosmos undergoing transformation of its natural elements, but *mimesis*, a world made, guarded, and limited by a nameless *demiourgos*, now little more than a maker, a craftsman.[115] The philosophers therefore begin with the eternal *a priori*, with *sheer being*, '*that which always is* and has no becoming.'[116] No becoming, no *genesis*, meaning no dawn, no dawning, no engendering, no generation, inception, opening, no origin. If it is only visible and perceptible, the cosmos lacks sheer being. If it has come to be, it is grasped not by understanding but only by opinion. But the cosmos has a cause. It is not simply set in motion out of its own material and natural elements. It has a maker, a father who makes it from fire and earth bonded together by water and air according to rules of proportion which are applied to these materials. Such rules belong to the *a priori* realm of what is stable, fixed and transparent to understanding, in the hope that what is ruled over will have the same fixed and stable character. Nonetheless, there is something disturbing, something wide-wandering in these heavens (*ouranos*), for we are told that the god 'took over all that was visible – not at rest but in discordant and disorderly motion – and brought it from a state of disorder to one of order . . . he made it a single visible living thing, which contains within itself all the living things . . . *one* universe.'[117] For the Goddess, who is Goddess of All, the 'All' is first, the sun arising from the night sky that is the totality of all things. For the philosophers, the discordant particulars precede the whole, and although the universe resembles a Living Thing, of which all other living things are parts, disorderly elements and unrest somehow crept into the maker's world, from where it is not clear. What is clear is that the maker orders them.[118]

This brings about a paradox. The begotten universe lacks eternity; it is a shrine for the gods, a copy of an everlasting Living Thing, but not eternal. The maker must nevertheless master the media. He makes a *moving image of eternity*, moving according to number, but as unified, eternal. He makes 'time,' using the planetary powers, but not to bestow the gifts of illumination, enchantment, growth, wisdom, law, love, and peace. When the philosopher's god kindles a light in one of the heavenly bodies that moves in a circular motion, it shines over the cosmos for the purpose of setting limits and standing guard over the numbers of time. The Sun serves as the measure of the slowness and quickness of all the other bodies; its circle providing the measure of a day and night; its cycle the measure of a year. And beneath the stars the maker made men to whom were shown the laws of this cosmos and to whom were given sense perception, as well as love mixed with pleasure and pain, fear and spiritedness. Those who fail to master these emotions are reborn as women or wild animals.[119] And the wandering Goddess of All Things? What becomes of her? Stripped even of her lunar reflection, she is the wet-nurse now made invisible, dragged down to the dark and invisible realm of the death-sun, the intelligible realm where she can, at best, provide a necessary, *a priori* fixed space with no characteristics of its own, *chora*. An indeterminate space for whatever comes to be, for those things that resemble and imitate self-knowledge, that which remains forever unmoved by persuasion, that which keeps its own form unchangingly.[120]

And strange to say, for 'men' (made from left-over fire, earth, water and air, impure but not discarded) – whose purpose in this eternity remains a mystery, since the maker wanted everything to be as much like himself as possible – for men, some adjustments are needed. There is the necessity of visibility, the eye being a condition of the possibility of inquiries into the nature of the universe. The eye that sees by the light of the sun remains subject, in this account, to something else, something other than vision and the principles that govern sight. 'The god invented sight and gave it to us so that we might observe the orbits of intelligence in the universe and apply them to the revolutions of our own understanding.'[121] Crafted by 'Intellect,' the eye allows us to stabilize our own understanding through the symphony of proportions, through *mimesis*. Thus the human being may imitate the unstraying revolutions of the god – but only by seeing them first. And yet, self-knowledge seems to require something else. Not a view of Nature, but a view of the self, perhaps a view of the soul? For this it is helpful to look into the kore, the pupil of the eye, to capture the young girl, in order to come to know oneself. The question remains, for self-knowledge, why look into the kore of the eye; why not simply gaze into a mirror which, after all, would give one a much clearer image of oneself rather than a tiny doll-like image, an image reminiscent of a young girl? Perhaps the fascination with gazing into the eye of an other is due to the suggestion that to know itself a soul must look into another soul. Looking at the pupil allows another eye to see itself. Kore is both 'girl' and 'pupil,' that part of the eye in which one must look in order to see oneself; to see oneself in the eye of the girl who does not yet see and understand makes it possible to know oneself. To look into the kore is to look into that Kore who reaches out to pluck the flower. She exists 'on the brink of meeting a gaze in which she would have seen herself. She was stretching out her hand to pluck that gaze.'[122] Hades asks brother Zeus for a living woman. Zeus, the god who does not set the cosmos in motion, who can only reproduce what he has devoured – the skies, sea and earth along with the Titanesses and Titans – this god devours the cosmos, then spits it out, an act of mimicry, not of creation. Henceforth 'the world from end to end is organized as *mimesis*; resemblance is the law.'[123] This same god whose own power is nothing but *mimesis* is eager to acknowledge the reality of a second world, a separate and silent world of resemblance. He is ready to embrace the dark realm of an invisible mind, to let the power of shadows and darkness invade and overtake the world of the enchanting moon goddess, the Goddess of All who danced with the wind.

The visible and the invisible

The earth splits open and Kore is plucked so to be taken away by Hades. Did Kore's eye meet that of Hades? Did her eye meet the eye of Ophion risen up from the world that until that moment had been invisible to her and who remains invisible under the vaunted helmet? Or, does the invisible Ophion, the god Hades, not see himself in the eye of Kore? Is this not his only reality? Far from recognizing herself in that invisible eye, is it not Hades who needs and seeks recognition, who can only find himself in the pupil, in the kore of Kore, daughter of the triple-Goddess? 'But Hades wanted Kore as his bride, wanted to have a living person sitting on the throne beside him . . . in the kingdom of shades, there is at least one body, and the body of a flourishing young girl at that.'[124] The necessity of this move may prove to be multiple. If Hades sees himself in Kore's eye and Kore sees nothing but his shadow, then indeed, vision is the prey. The beautiful visible world, the world granted by the powers of illumination, enchantment, growth, wisdom, law, love and peace is invaded by the invisible world. Someone and something are taken from the visible to the invisible. The 'girl,' young and flourishing, is abducted from the beautiful, visible world transforming itself through its material and natural elements and she is dragged down to the shadow world. 'The eye pounced from the shadows to capture a girl and shut her away in the underworld palace of the mind.'[125] Is the invisible realm, the realm of shadows, the realm of Hades, of death, one with the unchanging mind? How can this be? Are not the sun and sunlight thought to be the very image of the Ideas or forms and the intelligible world? And if death and the unchanging mind are one, then what of the so-called divine Ideas? What of philosophy itself? Is it possible that the love of 'Sophia,' the goddess 'Wisdom,' has been transformed into a love of death? Sophia is also the flower. And what if it is the flower, Sophia, that Kore reaches out to pluck? What then? 'Vessel of transformation, blossom, the unity of Demeter reunited with Kore, Isis, Ceres, the moon goddesses, whose luminious aspect overcomes . . . nocturnal darkness, are all expressions of this Sophia, the highest feminine wisdom.'[126]

It has been asserted that 'the Olympians developed a new fascination for Death.'[127] Is not the reality that men, the philosophers and poets who told the stories about the Olympians, these men developed a new fascination for Death, a fascination not present in the earliest stories of the creation, the stories of the Goddess of All Things? Perhaps the fascination with death is related to the philosophers' and poets' fascination with the world of shadows. 'The everlasting correctness of things seen, perceived rightly, has banished not only the darkness of night but also the fires of noon. The *episteme* begins it surveying, measuring, and calculating on the basis of *shadows* projected by/upon surfaces, screens, and supports.'[128] The living, flourishing girl, ready to embrace vision and understanding, to affirm visibility and the beautiful world transformed in and through its material and natural elements and tended by the goddess Demeter, this girl is swept away by a shadow to the world of shadows, a world where nothing happens, where nothing changes. What would Kore have seen of Hades made invisible by his helmet? Only his shadow. So it has been noted that the divine Ideas or forms, absolutely invisible themselves, are able to be detected only by the light that they stop, that outlines them, the light they block or cut off.[129] Certainly it is true that the strange prisoners in the cave, when forced up the rough, steep path into the sunlight, would be pained and irritated, able at first to see shadows and nothing more. Only at night would a former prisoner be able to see and so to study the stars and the moon and only after a long time would 'his' eyes adjust to the light so as to be able to see and to study the sun.

But perhaps we misunderstand this tale when we forget the warning of the philosopher that 'the visible realm should be likened to the *prison dwelling*, and the light of the fire inside it to the power of the sun . . . the upward journey and the study of things above [are] as the upward journey of the soul to the intelligible realm.'[130] The visible realm – all visibility – is on this account a prison. The invisible realm in which one's eyes are blinded is the intelligible realm. If a person were to turn from the study of what is divine to the human realm, their sight would indeed be *dim*. The visible, human world, the beautiful, self-created cosmos of the goddess would be difficult for them to see insofar as they would be unaccustomed to using their eyes at all! Vicious, clever people are said to have keen vision. Their sight is not inferior at all insofar as they are able to sharply distinguish all that they survey. How much more keen must be the vision of these individuals who live in the realm of that which is *coming to be*, what is *becoming*, as opposed to those who see nothing because they look only at *true things*, which is to say, they do not look with their eyes at all, but only with the intellect. For such an individual, the return to the cave is the only possibility of seeing at all; their eyes function at all only in the deepest shadow. Indeed, there in the cave, they see vastly better than the people who dwell there.

Poor vision as well as insufficient, strained views wreak havoc throughout the cosmos.[131] When Zeus drives his winged chariot looking after and putting in due order the heavens, the gods follow him to a place beyond the visible heavens, a high ridge whose circular motion carries them round and round. It is a strange place, without color, shape, or solidity, where Justice, Self-Control, Knowledge are each invisible to the eye, yet are visible to intelligence.[132] Souls that cannot move themselves fast enough and with enough self-control, fail to 'glimpse' these truths. Not only that but they trample and strike one another, their wings breaking, their plumage shredding in a heavenly image of carnage and destruction. So they fall, fall, fall to earth where they are burdened by earthly bodies, hence mortality, finally losing the wings of angels to foulness and ugliness. They are the victims of a weak memory and of senses 'so murky that only a few people are able to make out, with difficulty, the original [Idea] of the likeness they encounter here.'[133] Initially it seems that only 'if it does not see *anything* true' does a soul fall to earth 'burdened by forgetfulness and wrongdoing,' and yet, 'a soul that has seen the most will be planted in the seed of a man who will become a lover of wisdom.'[134] Thus in spite of having seen some truth, glimpsing some Reality, some additional souls are still condemned to earthly existence. How then does this account of souls – both those crippled and opinionated and those close to things divine – how does this accord with the claim that *every* soul is immortal, for what is *psyche* if not something self-moved that never ceases to move and so is immortal? As a source of motion for itself and other moving things, immortal soul must not be able to be destroyed, otherwise it would never start up again. Absent immortality, the cosmos itself would collapse, never to be reborn.[135] Absent immortality, no souls would ever glimpse 'Reality.' Perhaps this is why some souls are looked after by philosophers who are not, strictly speaking, mortal but who are in some sense divine and immortal and grow wings. Those philosophers stand outside human concerns and draw close to the divine. They are said to practise philosophy without guile, they look after the boys – philosophically; perhaps it is only these souls, the philosophers and the boys they look after, who will ever return to the realms where Justice, Self-Control and Knowledge reign. The rest, it appears are condemned, punished in places beneath the earth.[136]

So it has been argued that, strictly speaking, non-philosophers, those who are truly mortals, do not, indeed cannot, *look* upon the invisible Good since such 'beings' have their ideal inscription only in the *psyche*. A young girl, daughter of the triple-Goddess, who wanders through fields of flowers is thought to be too close to the light which is too close to the senses. Her *guileless virginity*, her *flourishing body* are not left undisturbed; she is not to be allowed to come to understanding through vision in the flourishing cosmos of the Goddess. Little wonder that Hades looks into the pupil of Kore to see the soul, for he would make her the soul, the psyche, the receptacle of his self-knowledge. Little wonder too that the image of the sun, useful in pointing to the power of Truth, nevertheless 'must fall once more below the horizon. [Its] rays of light, *flashing*, burning, glaring, must cease to harry the Truth – *aletheia* – unchanging in the guileless virginity of the *logos*.'[137] But is this so? The philosophers make claims. They say the maker looked at an appropriate form for each thing made, that these things once made exist in time, that time is a moving image of eternity. They articulate a hierarchy of imitations, reflections that *chill the light*, shielding us from the capacities of light to diffract and to vary our perceptions. May we not question their claims? May we not, like Kore, return from the dark, invisible realm to the daylight of sight and diffused reflections, from vision to understanding (*Sophia*)? Or are we to be confined to the direct passage from the visible to the invisible, from the so-called prison of vision to the self-knowing realm of the intelligible, a passage that may be nothing less than the passage from life to death?

Light and mimesis

If Kore's return is possible, it might require that we pay attention to the characteristics of light. 'Light interacts with matter in all sorts of ways.'[138] White light is a mixture of different colors, each with its own frequency; short wavelengths have very high frequency, long wavelengths have low frequency; their energy is proportional to the frequency. Light is not only what can be seen, from visible red to blue, to violet; it exceeds the visible in the direction of what is (for human beings) outside the limits of visibility: ultraviolet, x-rays and gamma rays. For each of these, the frequency of light is higher and higher. When the frequency becomes lower and lower, light goes from visible blue through red, to infrared (heat), to radio waves. Although this explanation implies a view of light as an oscillating, electromagnetic *wave*, light behaves like particles with wave properties; these particles have been given the name 'photons'. 'Light is something like raindrops – each little lump of light is called a photon – and if the light is all one color, all the 'raindrops' are the same size.'[139] Five to six photons are adequate to activate a nerve cell of the eye, where energy is transformed into messages sent to the brain. When light dims, *photons are still present*, there are simply fewer of them, messages are still being sent to the brain and energy is transmitted from photons to nerves. Were their eyes more sensitive, human beings would be able to see even the dim light of one color appearing as intermittent flashes, equal in intensity. And, although light appears to travel in straight lines, attempts to squeeze light through a small opening so as ensure that it follows a straight line have the opposite effect; the light spreads out, it disperses, it scatters. Like many observable phenomena, the idea that light moves in straight lines is a convenient but crude approximation, for even the light that reflects off a mirror spreads, strewn in many directions.[140]

Unable even to risk looking into a mirror, Ophion-Hades, the snake, gazes directly into the eye of Kore seeking to see and to know himself. Her retinas focus the light, keeping it from dispersing. Looking directly into the darkest part of her virgin eye, he sees and he seeks . . . and what he seeks there is the reflection of his own soul. Looking into the virgin pupil, seeing himself, 'the lover takes pleasure in seeing [gazing at] his beloved' which would be, himself.[141] Still, the philosophers claim that, 'people with bad eyesight often see things before those whose eyesight is keener.'[142] The eyes of any philosopher who turns from the study of divine forms in the invisible, intelligible realm to human life, 'his' eyes are filled with darkness, his eyesight dimmed.[143] Moreover, the craftsman and his followers operate, always, within the *'matrix of appropriation.'*[144] The god 'makes' the being, the form of each thing: heaven, earth, Hades. But even the work of the god is an imitation, every 'being,' Sun, Moon and Stars, a moving *image* of eternity. The apprentice philosopher, less skilled in *mimesis*, uses a mirror to imitate each thing that the god makes. But, better not to look at what is made, better to have bad eyesight or no eyesight at all. Better to seek and to see one's soul only, in the virgin eye of the Kore.

Unlike the wide-wandering goddess, Eurynome, who is the visible moon, whose constant motion and diffuse light illuminates all things, the philosopher's god is

> the result of systems of mirrors that ensure a steady illumination, admittedly, but one without heat or brilliance . . . and the presence, the essence of forms (usually translated under the name of Ideas) will be determined only by the light they have stopped, trapped, and that outlines them. The force of ideas, and their hold on memory, will be a function of the intensity of light that they are able to block or cut off.[145]

But if we are truly seekers after wisdom, should we not inquire into and examine the evidence that form perception is or is not innate? Animals reared in the dark lack normal maturation of the visual nervous system, thus are inappropriate to test form. Tests of form perception on animals and humans with 'normal' visual nervous systems reveal that the perception of forms appears to be capable of releasing instinctual reactions in a variety of species. Human infants show definite preferences for certain objects at which to gaze. In the first month, they prefer to view patterns of discrete elements like checkerboards over simple, uniform shapes such as squares and circles, as well as drawings of the human face rather than other drawings of the same shape and size. However, they also appear to show preference for faces whose features are totally scrambled to the point of losing their face-like qualities. It should not surprise us then, that newborn humans prefer to look at areas of the greatest variation or discreteness. In other words, they show a decided interest in discrete over uniform shapes. Thus, to the extent that there are innate perceptions of form, it is discrete patterns and variable or changing forms that are innate rather than uniform patterns and forms.[146]

These conclusions might well be considered together with studies of the effects of past experience on the perception of form. In addition to the tendency to perceive borders, to group together parts or units of figures that appear to us to be aligned, as well as those that are proximate and those that are similar, human perception tends to group figures that move together at the same speed and in the same direction, as well as components that constitute a closed figure.[147] Thus, even for familiar objects, *recognition* occurs only after shape has been perceived. Recognition and the identification of forms as recognized imply contribution from past experience but perception comes first. So it appears that, based on studies of perception, memory does not determine the perception of forms. Memories can only even be accessed based on their similarity to a *present* perception; 'the process proceeds from lower levels of sensory processing toward higher cognitive levels.'[148] And once again we are led to surmise that from vision – understanding – and not the reverse.

What is philosophy?

Let us see and understand then, two images of philosophy. There is the powerful and dark image that lurks nearby, one whose shadow is cast over the cosmos to this very day. It is the image of the snake made god. It is the image of the continuum, the perfection of the undifferentiated, the one, the image of he who wanted everything to be as much like himself as possible.[149] Thus, it has been argued that for the apprentice philosopher, for the 'man' in the cave, only death will lead to something more, to something beyond the realm of shadows, of blocked light and direct vision. Is the philosopher the messenger of death since 'were it not for the words of the philosophy teacher who talks to you about immortality, who would be preoccupied with such an issue?'[150] Conception, rather than the transformation of the light that enters the eye into energy that is transmitted to the brain, conception instead finds its proper meaning as the re-birth into truth, a truth situated in an eternity beyond appearances, in the *One*, that is always, as a wise philosopher among us has noted, mirrored at least twice, once by the god himself and once more by the philosopher or 'his' apprentice.[151] Let us dare to question this image of philosophy, let us use the reflected light of the moon and let us conceive of a second image of philosophy, not an imitation but a transformation of the material and natural elements, an image more difficult to obtain. So much has been lost, so much appropriated.

The pre-Hellenic Pelasgian account of creation survives only in the most fragmented manner, but the standard interpretation of even these fragments overlooks the wide-wandering goddess Eurynome and seeks to establish the patrimony of Ophion. His banishment by the Goddess does not prevent the resurrection of his myth. Let us recall again, that the hierarchy of mirroring chills the reflected light of the moon and shields us from its capacity to vary our perception of forms. No wonder, in the tales of men, Kore is abducted. How else to fill life with shadows? 'What happened in Eleusis was the separation and reunion of the dual goddess Demeter-Kore (*Deó*), she who sometimes appears as two barely differentiated figures.'[152] Kore, the reflected light of Demeter, Demeter who is the life-giving light, the photon whose energy is transmitted in diffracted light rays. Demeter-Kore is the story of the reflected, refracted and diffracted energy of that light, wandering in the world, transmitting its energy. In this cosmos, Kore returns from darkness to her origins, light and energy are conserved. Thus, even for the gods, Kore is a thing of wonder. She is divine evidence of the conservation of energy. The dark gods claim that the girl, after eating nothing for the entire period of her abduction, suddenly, forgetfully, outwitted or worse, full of secret desire, eats the seeds of the pomegranate. They claim that the fecundating light within her is the divine child – Phanes-Eros – who will force himself upon her. Let us resist the reduction of radiant light to psyche, that is, to a dark soul that sees nothing but itself in the emptiness of the eye of the Other. Let us be skeptical of the reports of the derisive 'gardener' of Hades who jubilantly proclaims the downfall of the young girl, who hoots that she has eaten the seeds of the pomegranate. What, after all, is a gardener doing in the dark caves of the snake where no flowers bloom and no moonlight gives life? Let us also then be skeptical of the scholarly claims of the new gardeners of the dark, those who argue that Demeter-Kore is the psychological manifestation of the feminine psychology. And let us be equally skeptical of the philosopher, for whom Demeter-Kore is the origin of the philosophical receptacle of all becoming, the wet-nurse of the cosmos. Let us instead propose, imagine, theorize that the Goddess, that Demeter-Kore are themselves concepts, concepts that constitute a first philosophy, a description of the nature of reality and of its creative and transformational structure. Let us not forget that energy is not lost, only transformed, constantly transformed. And let us then propose this new image of philosophy.

Notes

1. Bergson, *Creative Evolution*, pp. 304–6; Bergson, *Oeuvres*, pp. 752–4.
2. Barthes, *Camera Lucida*, p. 91 (143). Perhaps Barthes is mistaken that photographers are 'agents of death,' instead they may be agents of life, the *life* of the spectator (p. 92 (144)).
3. Bergson, *Creative Evolution*, pp. 304–6, 332 (752–4, 775–6).
4. See Chapter 2 above. See also Bergson, *Creative Evolution*, p. 299; *Oeuvres*, pp. 747–8.
5. Bergson, *Creative Evolution*, p. 300; *Oeuvres*, p. 748. Bergson's analysis of action implies the Kantian one but does not refer to it.
6. Bergson, *Creative Evolution*, 'If our existence were composed of separate states with an impassive ego to unite them, for us there would be no duration . . . that which has never been perceived . . . is necessarily unforeseeable' (pp. 4, 6 (*Oeuvres*, pp. 496, 499)).
7. Bergson, *Creative Evolution*, pp. 300–1; *Oeuvres*, pp. 749–50. This is precisely what Merleau-Ponty will protest.
8. Bergson, *Creative Evolution*, p. 302; *Oeuvres*, p. 750.
9. 'Perception of movement can be perception *of movement* and recognition of it as such, only if it is apprehension of it with its significance as movement, and with all the instants which constitute it and in particular with the identity of the object in motion' (p. 271 (314)).

10. Bergson, *Creative Evolution*, pp. 308, 279, 283; *Oeuvres*, pp. 755, 731, 734. Moreover, the nothing is implicated in desire or will since it involves a comparison between what is and what could or *ought* to be.

11. Bergson, *Creative Evolution*, p. 308; *Oeuvres*, p. 755.

12. Paraphrased from Patricia Glazebrook, 'Zeno against Mathematical Physics', p. 205. Reproduced at H. D. P. Lee, *Zeno of Elea: A Text, with Translation and Notes* (Amsterdam, 1967), p. 103; translation by Patricia Glazebrook.

13. Bergson, *Creative Evolution*, p. 307; *Oeuvres*, p. 755. See Patricia Glazebrook, 'Zeno against Mathematical Physics', p. 201. I have substituted the concept 'discontinuous' for Glazebrook's 'discrete' insofar as discrete space and time are quantum concepts, an entirely different structure from that of continuous or discontinuous space and time. Glazebrook argues that Zeno meant these paradoxes to be an indictment of mathematical physics. She cites G. S. Kirk, J. E. Raven, and M. Schofield, *The Presocratic Philosophers* (Cambridge: Cambridge University Press, 1983), p. 273, for this version of the arrow.

14. Bertrand Russell, 'The problem of infinity considered historically', in *Our Knowledge of the External World* (London, 1914), 175–8, p. 179. Henri Bergson, *Creative Evolution*, pp. 309, 306; *Oeuvres*, pp. 756, 753. Russell cited in Glazebrook, p. 202. Glazebrook also refers to Bergson but I have not utilized her reading as I am seeking greater precision.

15. Bergson, *Creative Evolution*, p. 309; *Oeuvres*, p. 756.

16. Ralph H. Abraham and Christopher D. Shaw, *Dynamics – The Geometry of Behavior, Part I: Periodic Behavior* (Santa Cruz: Aerial Press, 1984), p. 13.

17. Abraham and Shaw, *Dynamics*, p. 19.

18. Abraham and Shaw, *Dynamics*, pp. 19–20.

19. Abraham and Shaw, *Dynamics*, p. 21.

20. Gilles Deleuze, 'Preface to the French Edition', in *Cinema One, The Movement-Image*, tr. Hugh Tomlinson and Barbara Habberjam (Minneapolis: University of Minnesota Press, 1986), p. xiv, originally published in French as *Cinéma 1, L'Image-movement* (Paris: Les Éditions de Minuit, 1983), p. 7.

21. Maurice Merleau-Ponty, 'The Film and the New Psychology', in *Sense and Non-Sense*, tr. Hubert Dreyfus and Patricia Allen Dreyfus (Evanston: Northwestern University Press, 1964), pp. 51, 59, originally published in French as *Sens et non-sens* (Paris: Les Éditions Nagel, 1948).

22. Gilles Deleuze, *Cinema Two, The Time-Image*, tr. Hugh Tomlinson and Robert Galeta (Minneapolis: University of Minnesota Press, 1989), p. 280, originally published in French as *Cinéma 2, L'Image-temps* (Paris: Les Éditions de Minuit, 1985).

23. These are John Casti's wonderful explanations. I recognize that a narrative presentation of these ideas will never approximate the clarity of their mathematical expression – a point for which Alan Sokal has become infamous. See John Casti, *Complexification, Explaining a Paradoxical World Through the Science of Surprise* (New York: HarperCollins, 1994), pp. 26–8.
24. Casti, *Complexification*, pp. 28–32.
25. Merleau-Ponty, *Phenomenology of Perception*, p. 54 (66).
26. Merleau-Ponty, *Phenomenology of Perception*, pp. 54, 55 (66, 67, 68).
27. Merleau-Ponty, *Phenomenology of Perception*, p. 56 (69).
28. Casti, *Complexification*, p. 28. Although there are numerous extrinsic and intrinsic differences between the phenomenology of perception and Deleuze's philosophy of difference, nonetheless they are each drawn by the same attractor.
29. Merleau-Ponty, *Phenomenology of Perception*, pp. 56–7 (69); emphasis added.
30. Joseph Ford, 'What is chaos, that we should be mindful of it?', in *The New Physics*, ed. Paul Davis (Cambridge: Cambridge University Press, 1989), pp. 350–1.
31. Merleau-Ponty, 'The film and the new psychology', pp. 48–50 (97–103).
32. Merleau-Ponty, *Phenomenology of Perception*, p. 268 (310).
33. Merleau-Ponty, *Phenomenology of Perception*, p. 272 (314–15). With this we begin to veer wildly through an intellectual fun house.
34. Merleau-Ponty, *Phenomenology of Perception*, pp. 269–70 (311–12).
35. Merleau-Ponty, *Phenomenology of Perception*, p. 276, n. 1 (319); Deleuze, *Cinema One, The Movement-Image*, pp. 57–8 (84–5). Both readings are to me acts of violence, not because they present radically different readings of Bergson, but because each claims, without hesitation, complete authority.
36. Merleau-Ponty, *Phenomenology of Perception*, p. 271 (313). 'The arrival of movement at a point must be one with its departure from the "adjacent" point, and this takes place only if there is an object in motion which simultaneously leaves one place and occupies another.'
37. Merleau-Ponty, 'The film and the new psychology', p. 52 (107). This analysis coincides with Merleau-Ponty's critique of introspection.
38. Merleau-Ponty, 'The film and the new psychology', p. 53 (108).
39. Merleau-Ponty, 'The film and the new psychology', pp. 55–9 (112–22). These remarks are an amalgamation of the analysis given by Merleau-Ponty on these pages.
40. Deleuze, *Cinema One, The Movement-Image*, p. 57 (85). Deleuze says of both Merleau-Ponty and Bergson that for each, cinema is an ambiguous ally. While this is clearly the case for Bergson, this is not commensurate with Merleau-Ponty's own claims.

41. Merleau-Ponty, 'The film and the new psychology', pp. 57–8 (118).
42. Deleuze, *Cinema One, The Movement-Image*, p. 57 (84). Deleuze still assumes the intentional consciousness of Husserl, but the tacit cogito produces a similar if less constrained effect.
43. Deleuze, *Cinema One, The Movement-Image*, p. 56 (83).
44. Merleau-Ponty, *Phenomenology of Perception*, p. 274 (317). Merleau-Ponty comes right to the edge of insight but backs off. His faith in meaning is problematic.
45. Deleuze, *Cinema One, The Movement-Image*, p. 59 (87). The extent to which Bergson's analysis of modern science is simply not acknowledged by this view is startling.
46. Bergson, *Creative Evolution*, pp. 332, 339 (775, 781). Thus the concept of the frame as 'any moment whatever.'
47. Bergson, *Creative Evolution*, pp. 335–7 (778–80). Thus modern science is, as Bergson says, the child of astronomy, a matter of knowing the respective positions of the planets at a given moment and knowing how to calculate their positions at another moment.
48. Barthes, *Camera Lucida,* pp. 18, 20, 23 (36, 29, 44).
49. The digital process does not alter this. In place of film, an image sensor samples the light coming through the lens and converts it into electrical signals, boosted by an amplifier and sent to an analogue to digital converter that changes the signal to digits. A computer processes the digits to produce the final image data that is stored on a memory card. Ben Long, 'Framed and exposed: making sense of camera sensors', in creativepro.com archives, 25 August 2004.
50. Bergson, *Matter and Memory*, pp. 168–9; Bergson, *Oeuvres*, pp. 307–8. I have attempted to render the operations of affectivity and ontological memory in all their complexity in *Gilles Deleuze and the Ruin of Representation*, pp. 109–15.
51. Barthes, *Camera Lucida,* p. 82 (129). Barthes calls the photograph a resurrection but I am unwilling to make use of such an over-determined term.
52. See, for example, Irvin Rock, 'The intelligence of perception', in *Perception* (New York: Scientific American Library, 1984), pp. 234–5. Rock differentiates between experience and perception (rightly so) and even proposes that perception may precede conscious reasoning in evolution, making thought a modification of perception.
53. Deleuze, *Immanence, A Life*, p. 27. I am extending the Deleuzean conception outside of the field in which it was instituted.
54. I have addressed this to some extent in *Gilles Deleuze and the Ruin of Representation*. See especially ch. 5, 'Tendencies, not oppositions,' 'The dominance of action,' and 'Spiritual life.'
55. Deleuze and Guattari, *What is Philosophy?*, pp. 178, 179 (168, 169, 170). For the insufficiency of Merleau-Ponty's notion of the anonymous

body for the generation of language, see my 'Expression and inscription at the origins of language', in *Écart and Différence*, ed. M. C. Dillon (Highlands, NJ: Humanities Press, 1997).

56. Bak, *How Nature Works*, pp. 30, 31. The epistemology of combinatorial networks remains to be fully addressed, but I do not want to leave the impression that I am unaware of the difficulty or general nature of this question.

57. See R. M. Khan et al., 'Neural processing at the speed of smell', *Neuron*, 44 (2 December 2004): 744–7. Accuracy and speed remain a trade-off.

58. Deleuze and Guattari, *What is Philosophy?*, p. 164 (154).

59. Deleuze and Guattari, *What is Philosophy?*, p. 169 (160).

60. Deleuze and Guattari, *What is Philosophy?*, pp. 171, 173 (162, 164).

61. P. W. Atkins, *The Second Law* (New York: Scientific American Library, 1984), pp. 8–13.

62. Deleuze and Guattari, *What is Philosophy?*, p. 201 (189).

63. Deleuze and Guattari, *What is Philosophy?*, p. 202 (189).

64. Jack Cohen and Ian Stewart, *The Collapse of Chaos, Discovering Simplicity in a Complex World* (New York: Penguin Books, 1994), pp. 251–2. Cohen is a reproductive biologist, Stewart a mathematician.

65. Atkins, *The Second Law*, pp. 48, 62–3.

66. Deleuze and Guattari, *What is Philosophy?*, p. 202 (190).

67. The concept of a single universal wave was popular in the 1980s at the Santa Fe Institute. Conversation with Marek Grabowski, October 2005.

68. Deleuze and Guattari, *What is Philosophy?*, p. 138 (131). For logic, this empty reference is truth value.

69. Deleuze and Guattari, *What is Philosophy?*, p. 139 (132). In part, this may be in order for logic to distinguish itself from psychology and in part this may be because logical self-consistency resides in the formal non-contradiction of a proposition or between propositions (p. 137 (130)).

70. Deleuze and Guattari, *What is Philosophy?*, pp. 145–6 (138–9). Thus the pleasant or aggressive dinner conversation at Mr Rorty's house – rival opinions on the smell of cheese (pp. 144–5 (137–8)).

71. Deleuze and Guattari, *What is Philosophy?*, pp. 163–7 (154–7).

72. See James Williams, *Gilles Deleuze's 'Difference and Repetition'* (Edinburgh: Edinburgh University Press, 2003) for illuminating descriptions of affects and percepts as well as other difficult concepts in Deleuze and Guattari's work.

73. Martin Heidegger, 'The origin of the work of art', in *Poetry, Language and Thought*, tr. Albert Hofstadter (New York: Harper and Row, 1975), p. 83.

74. Cohen and Stewart, *The Collapse of Chaos*, p. 258. Perhaps herein lies the necessity for positing the system of the universe to be One-All. The question remains, is it?

75. Deleuze and Guattari, *What is Philosophy?*, pp. 178–9 (168–9).

76. Deleuze and Guattari, *What is Philosophy?*, p. 179 (170).

77. Heidegger, 'The origin of the work of art', pp. 43, 73. Art is a beginning but only a beginning for philosophers.

78. Atkins, *The Second Law*, p. 179.

79. Philosophically, this structure might be said to correspond to Nietzsche's two dice throws, one on earth affirming chance and the other in the heavens affirming the necessity of chance.

80. Atkins, *The Second Law*, p. 157.

81. Atkins, *The Second Law*, pp. 157–9.

82. Cohen and Stewart, *The Collapse of Chaos*, pp. 258–60. Thermodynamic models of independent subsystems either do not apply at the level of the formation and expansion of the universe or their effects would be so long-term as to be uninteresting.

83. Roberto Calasso, *The Marriage of Cadmus and Harmony*, tr. Tim Parks (New York: Alfred A. Knopf, 1993), p. 209.

84. 'The sovereign gods suffer from a nostalgia for the state of their forerunner, Phanes. And they try to return to it,' Calasso, *The Marriage of Cadmus and Harmony*, p. 203. This precludes the possibility, developed here, that the first-born was the goddess Eurynome.

85. Erich Neumann, *The Great Mother, Analysis of an Archetype*, tr. Ralph Manheim (Princeton: Princeton University Press, 1974), pp. 319, 262.

86. The claim that the flower is a narcissus is made in the Homeric 'Hymn to Demeter', in *Hesiod, the Homeric Hymns and Homerica*, tr. Hugh G. Evelyn-White (London and Cambridge, MA: Loeb Classical Library, 1920), p. 289; cited in Neumann, *The Great Mother*, p. 308.

87. Robert Graves reports that Ovid claims Kore was picking poppies based on several goddess images found in Crete and Mycenae; Robert Graves, *The Greek Myths: 1* (New York: Penguin Books, 1980), 24.15.

88. Graves, *The Greek Myths: 1*, pp. 287–8. It is seldom reported that Narcissus recognized himself and then killed himself in grief, mad with love for himself.

89. Graves, *The Greek Myths: 1*, 31e. Graves relates Kore's abduction to the male usurpation of female agricultural mysteries (24.3).

90. Graves, *The Greek Myths: 1*, 1.a, b, c, d; 1.1. In this archaic religion, paternity was non-existent, fatherhood being attributed to various accidents. Moreover, snakes came to be associated with the underworld.

91. Calasso, *The Marriage of Cadmus and Harmony*, p. 208. Calasso does not make this connection between Ophion and Hades, however, it is implicit in his text in the discussion of Dionysus (or Eros), child of the goddess Night and the Wind, both female and male, both snake and bull, also called Phanes (Graves, *The Greek Myths: 1*, 2b, and Homer,

Iliad, xvi, 261) whose lineage is obscure, who precedes Zeus, who initially embodies powers of creation and only later those of destruction. Thus the snake aligned with the goddess-creator becomes a snake-usurper. Hades' claim on Zeus is that 'Zeus senses the time had come for a new ring to be added to the knot of snakes' (p. 208).

92. Graves, *The Greek Myths: 1,* 1.d, 1.3. The planetary powers of the goddess Eurynome appear to correspond to the deities of Babylonian and Palestinian astrology.

93. 'The Orphics say that black-winged Night, a goddess of whom even Zeus stands in awe . . . the triple-goddess ruled the universe until her scepter passed to Uranus . . . Night's scepter passed to Uranus with the advent of patriarchialism', Graves, *The Greek Myths: 1,* 2.a, 2.2.

94. Hesiod, *Theogony,* 211–32.

95. Graves, *The Greek Myths: 1,* 4.a, 4.b, 4.c; 4.1, 4.2. Graves cites Hesiod, *Theogony,* 211–32 and Ovid, *Metamorphosis,* i–ii.

96. Plato, *Timaeus,* tr. Donald J. Zeyl in *Plato, Complete Works,* ed. John M. Cooper (Indianapolis: Hackett Publishing, 1997), 29d–e. Such self-love is said to be the effect of goodness. Also, 32b, c; 37a; 42a, b, c. Plato requires two middle terms for solid objects (for example, a cube which is represented mathematically as 2 to the power of 3), so air and water together are the middle terms for fire and earth.

97. Graves, *The Greek Myths: 1,* 24. Demeter was the general name of a tri-partite goddess: Core, Persephone, Hecate (green corn, ripe corn, harvested corn); Graves, *The Greek Myths: 1,* 24.1.

98. Plato, *Alcibiades,* tr. D. S. Hutchinson, in *Plato, Complete Works,* 133a.

99. Plato, *Timaeus,* 47a. Philosophy is the supreme good that eyesight offers.

100. Richard L. Gregory, *Eye and Brain, The Psychology of Seeing* (Princeton: Princeton University Press, 1990), p. 23. Gregory notes that only in the last 100 years has vision become the object of systematic experiments.

101. Plato, *Timaeus,* 45b, c, d, e; 46d, e. Vision and all sensations are auxiliary causes of all things because they do not possess reason or understanding.

102. Rock, *Perception,* pp. 15–16. The eye, however, is not analogous to a camera obscura and even the modern camera as an analogy 'leaves everything about perception still to be explained.'

103. 'Ballistic' is a term generally used in physics to describe any particle-like behavior.

104. Rock, *Perception,* pp. 16, 3.

105. Rock, *Perception,* p. 4. Rock also notes how different our perceptions are from what appears on the retina, thus the extent to which there is no direct perception.

106. Gregory, *Eye and Brain*, pp. 25–6. Newton, Hugens, and Foucault (the physicist) all contributed to these realizations.
107. Graves, *The Greek Myths: 1*, 1.a, b, c, d; 1.1. In this archaic cosmology, paternity was non-existent, fatherhood being attributed to various accidents. Moreover, snakes came to be associated with the underworld.
108. Neumann, *The Great Mother*, pp. 56–7; 25–33. Neumann stresses that there is both a projective worldly element and a psychic element of psychic structures and processes. Elsewhere I have argued that feminist philosophers have much to gain from letting go of the latter. See *Gilles Deleuze and the Ruin of Representation*, especially ch. 7, 'The ruin of representation.'
109. Neumann, *The Great Mother*, pp. 56–7, 314–15. The rise of a patriarchate implies the ascendancy of death. 'The . . . "pure spirit" . . . in its Appollonian-Platonic and Jewish-Christian form has lead to the abstract conceptuality of modern consciousness . . . threatening the existence of Western mankind, for the one-sidedness of masculine development has led to a hypertrophy of consciousness at the expense of the whole man' (p. 57).
110. Neumann, *The Great Mother*, p. 315.
111. Neumann, *The Great Mother*, pp. 319, 320. Often called a divine son, the moon nonetheless is a 'mere variant' of the goddess's own self.
112. Neumann, *The Great Mother*, p. 319. Neumann points to this independence of the life goddesses from any deathly masculine principle of any kind throughout his text.
113. For a clear explanation of the difference between finite and infinite, bounded and unbounded, see Rudy Rucker, *The Fourth Dimension, A Guided Tour of the Higher Universes* (Boston: Houghton Mifflin Co., 1984), pp. 91–3.
114. I am moving away from the limitations of the psychological analysis of an archetype offered by Neumann and attempting to make sense of what he calls the 'Feminine' as representative of a view of objective reality. See Neumann, *The Great Mother*, pp. 55–8.
115. Neumann, *The Great Mother*, p. 58. Neumann cites Bachoffen as the source of the thesis that what comes last will be looked upon as first and original, a hypothesis found in Aristotle, 'the later a thing comes in the formative process the earlier it comes in the order of Nature'; Johann Jakob Bachoffen, *Das Mutterrecht, Gessamelte Werke*, vol. I (Basel, 1948), p. 412, and Aristotle, *Parts of Animals*, tr. A. I. Peck (London and Cambridge, MA: Loeb Classical Library, 1937), 2.1.
116. Plato, *Timaeus*, tr. Donald J. Zeyl in *Plato, Complete Works*, 27d–28. The Greek word for 'coming-to-be' used in the text is *genesis* and its cognates whose synonyms include: alpha, birth, commencement, creation, dawn, dawning, engendering, formation, generation, inception,

opening, origin, outset, propagation, provenance, provenience, root, source, start. See Neumann, *The Great Mother*, p. 55.

117. Plato, *Timeus*, 30a, b, c, d, 31a. Neumann claims that with this, the moon principle was devalued and made into the soul, the highest material development that contrasts with the pure spirituality of the male; Neumann, *The Great Mother*, p. 57.

118. Plato, *Timaeus*, 30a–32b.

119. Plato, *Timaeus*, 42a, b, c. There would be no release from transformations until the fire-earth-water-air accretion was made to conform with the revolution of the Same, taming the turbulence.

120. Plato, *Timaeus*, 51e, 52a, b, c.

121. Plato, *Timaeus*, 47b–c. There is 'kinship' between the undisturbed orbits of the planets and our own disturbed orbits of understanding. Not quite *mimesis*.

122. Calasso, *The Marriage of Cadmus and Harmony*, p. 209.

123. Luce Irigaray, 'Kore: young virgin, pupil of the eye', in *Speculum of the Other Woman*, tr. Gillian C. Gill (Ithaca: Cornell University Press, 1985), p. 150, originally published as *Speculum de l'autre femme* (Paris: Les Éditions de Minuit, 1974).

124. Calasso, *The Marriage of Cadmus and Harmony*, p. 211. Calasso takes the bodily presence of Persphone in the realm of the dead to be a 'privilege.' Whether or not this is the case remains to be seen.

125. Calasso, *The Marriage of Cadmus and Harmony*, p. 210. The richness of Calasso's text allows the reader to draw contradictory conclusions.

126. Neumann, *The Great Mother*, pp. 325–6. Given the name 'philo-sophia' it is somewhat surprising that Sophia has been completely lost to us.

127. Calasso, *The Marriage of Cadmus and Harmony*, p. 214. Calasso seems to forget that 'revisions' of myths are the creation of poets and philosophers, not of the gods themselves.

128. Irigaray, 'Kore', p. 148.

129. Irigaray, 'Kore', p. 148. It is this shadowing function rather than mirroring that most interests me here.

130. Plato, *Republic*, 516a, 517b.

131. Plato, *Republic*, 519a, 520b.

132. Plato, *Phaedrus*, tr. Alexander Nehamas and Paul Woodruff in *Plato, Complete Works*, 246e. The gods travel through the heavens to the highest ridge, the boundary of its circular motion.

133. Plato, *Phaedrus*, 250. Human souls are continually described as twisted, crippled, engaged in wrongdoing.

134. Plato, *Phaedrus*, 248d. If this is not a discrepancy or mistranslation, then we have to take it seriously. Emphasis added.

135. Bruno Snell, *The Discovery of the Mind, The Greek Origins of European Thought*, tr. T. G. Rosenmeyer (New York: Harper and Row, 1960), pp. 8–10; Plato, *Phaedrus*, 245e; 248b, c, d.

136. Plato, *Phaedrus*, 248e–249a. Women, it appears, are entirely absent from the list of souls who may eventually glimpse truth.
137. Irigaray, 'Kore', p. 148. The relation between guileless virginity and *logos* is stated here but remains somewhat obscure in this text.
138. Kaler, *Stars*, p. 37.
139. See Richard P. Feynman, *QED, The Strange Theory of Light and Matter* (Princeton: Princeton University Press, 1985), p. 14; and Kaler, *Stars*, p. 36. Waves are characterized by the physical distance between crests (wavelength) and the number of crests passing a point per second. Multiplied, these two numbers give the speed of the wave.
140. Feynman, *QED*, pp. 38–59. Marek Grabowski provided me with this excellent little book and discussed these ideas with me on many occasions.
141. Aristotle, *Nicomachean Ethics* 8.1157a, 3–14; cited in David Halperin, 'Why is Diotima a woman?', pp. 113–51, p. 131.
142. Plato, *Republic*, 595c–596a.
143. Plato, *Republic*, 516e–517e. Such beings are unwilling to involve themselves in human affairs.
144. Irigaray, 'Kore', p. 151. See Plato, *Republic*, 596c–597b.
145. Irigaray, 'Kore', p. 148. Irigaray continues, 'light is too corruptible, too shifting and inconstant to form the basis of the relationship to the self and to the All.'
146. Rock, *Perception*, pp. 140–5.
147. Rock, *Perception*, pp. 115–18. These are the conclusions of the Gestalt psychologist Max Wertheimer. See also Wolfgang Köhler, *Gestalt Psychology* (New York: Liveright, 1929 and 1947).
148. Rock, *Perception*, pp. 128–9. These directions are not absolute, but express general principles governing perception, recognition and cognition.
149. Calasso, *The Marriage of Cadmus and Harmony*, p. 207; Plato, *Timaeus*, 29e.
150. Luce Irigaray, 'Plato's *Hystera*', in *Speculum of the Other Woman*, p. 354.
151. Irigaray, 'Plato's *Hystera*', p. 355. Irigaray's text is very dense at this point.
152. Calasso, *The Marriage of Cadmus and Harmony*, p. 210. The previous sentence is a restatement of Luce Irigaray, 'Kore', p. 149.

Bibliography

Abraham, Ralph H. and Shaw, Christopher D., *Dynamics – The Geometry of Behavior, Part I: Periodic Behavior*, Santa Cruz: Aerial Press, 1984.

Alpers, Svetlana, *The Art of Describing, Dutch Art in the Seventeenth Century*, Chicago: University of Chicago Press, 1984.

Aristotle, *Nicomachean Ethics*, tr. A. I. Peck, London and Cambridge, MA: Loeb Classical Library, 1937.

Aristotle, *Parts of Animals*, tr. A. I. Peck, London and Cambridge, MA: Loeb Classical Library, 1937.

Artaud, Antonin, 'Le pèse-nerfs', in *Oeuvres completes*, vol. 1, Paris: Gallimard, 1956.

Asia Watch Women's Rights Project, *A Modern Form of Slavery: Trafficking of Burmese Women and Girls into Brothels into Thailand*, Human Rights Watch, 1993.

Atkins, P. W., *The Second Law*, New York: Scientific American Library, 1984.

Bachoffen, Johann Jakob, *Das Mutterrecht, Gessamelte Werke*, vol. I, Basel, 1948.

Badiou, Alain, *Deleuze, The Clamor of Being*, tr. Louise Burchill, from *Theory Out of Bounds*, vol. 16, Minneapolis: University of Minnesota Press, 1999. Originally published in French as *Deleuze: La Clameur de l'Etre*, Paris: Hachette Littératures, 1997.

Badiou, Alain, *Infinite Thought, Truth and the Return to Philosophy*, tr. Oliver Feltham and Justin Clemens, London: Continuum, 2003.

Bak, Per, *How Nature Works, The Science of Self-Organized Criticality*, New York: Springer Verlag, 1996.

Balasko, Marta and Cabanac, Michel, 'Behavior of juvenile lizards (Iguana iguana) in a conflict between temperature regulation and palatable food', in *Brain, Behavior & Evolution*, vol. 52, issue 6 (1998): 257–61.

Barthes, Roland, *A Lover's Discourse, Fragments*, tr. Richard Howard, New York, Hill and Wang, 1978. Originally published in French as *Fragments d'un discours amoureux*, Paris: Éditions du Seuil, 1977.

Barthes, Roland, *Camera Lucida, Reflections on Photography*, tr. Richard Howard, New York: Hill and Wang, 1981. Originally published in French as *La Chambre Claire*, Paris: Éditions du Seuil, 1980.

Barthes, Roland, *The Pleasure of the Text*, tr. Richard Miller, New York: Farrar, Straus and Giroux, 1975. Originally published in French as *Le Plaisir du texte*, Paris: Éditions du Seuil, 1973.

Bibliography

Bassett, Louise, *Paradoxe Assurément: Michèle Le Doeuff's Philosophical Imaginary*, unpublished Ph.D. thesis, Australian National University, 2003.

Baudrillard, Jean, *America*, tr. Chris Turner, London: Verso Books, 1988. Originally published in French as *L'Amérique*, Paris: Grasset, 1986.

Bandrillard, Jean, *Simulations*, tr. Paul Foss, Paul Patton, and Philip Beitchman, New York: Semiotext(e), 1983.

Beauvoir, Simone de, *The Second Sex*, tr. and ed. H. M. Parshley, New York: Knopf, 1953. Originally published in French as *Le Deuxième Sexe*, Paris: Gallimard, 1949.

Beck, Lewis White, *A Commentary to Kant's Critique of Pure Reason*, Chicago: University of Chicago Press, 1966.

Bergoffen, Debra, *The Philosophy of Simone de Beauvoir, Gendered Phenomenologies, Erotic Generosities*, Albany: SUNY Press, 1997.

Bergson, Henri, *Bergson Oeuvres*, Paris: Presses Universitaires de France, 1963.

Bergson, Henri, *Creative Evolution*, tr. Arthur Mitchell, New York: University Press of America, 1983.

Bergson, Henri, *The Creative Mind*, tr. Mabelle L. Andison, New York: Philosophical Library, 1946.

Bergson, Henri, *Matter and Memory*, tr. N. M. Paul and W. S. Palmer, New York: Zone Books, 1988.

Bergson, Henri, *Time and Free Will, An Essay on the Immediate Data of Consciousness*, tr. F. L. Pogson, New York: Macmillan, 1959.

Bernstein, Nina, 'A mother deported, and a child left behind', *New York Times*, 24 November 2004, section A: 1.

Bersani, Leo and Dutoit, Ulysse, 'Merde alors', *October* 13 (1979): 23–35.

Cabanac, Michel, 'Pleasure, the common currency', *Journal of Theoretical Biology*, 155 (1992): 173–200.

Cabanac, Michel, 'What is sensation? *Gnoti se auton*', in *Biological Perspectives on Motivated Activities*, ed. Roderick Wong, Northwood, NJ: Ablex, 1995: 399–417.

Calasso, Roberto, *The Marriage of Cadmus and Harmony*, tr. Tim Parks, New York: Alfred A. Knopf, 1993.

Calvino, Italo, *Invisible Cities*, tr. William Weaver, New York: Harcourt Brace, 1974.

Carse, Alisa, 'Impartial principle and moral context: securing a place for the particular in ethical theory', *Journal of Medicine and Philosophy*, vol. 3. no. 2 (1998): 153–69.

Carse, Alisa, 'The liberal individual: a metaphysical or moral embarrassment?', in *Nous*, vol. 28. no. 2 (June 1994): 184–209.

Casti, John, *Complexification, Explaining a Paradoxical World Through the Science of Surprise*, New York: HarperCollins, 1994.

Cohen, Jack and Stewart, Ian, *The Collapse of Chaos, Discovering Simplicity in a Complex World*, New York: Penguin Books, 1994.

Damasio, Antonio, *Descartes' Error*, New York: Avon Books, 1994.

Damisch, Hubert, *The Origin of Perspective*, tr. John Goodman, Cambridge: MIT Press, 1995. Originally published as *L'Origine de la perspective*, Paris: Flammarion, 1987.

Davis, Mike, *City of Quartz, Excavating the Future of Los Angeles*, New York: Vintage Books, 1992.

Deleuze, Gilles, *Cinema One, The Movement-Image*, tr. Hugh Tomlinson and Barbara Habberjam, Minneapolis: University of Minnesota Press, 1986. Originally published in French as *Cinéma 1, L'Image-movement*, Paris: Les Éditions de Minuit, 1983.

Deleuze, Gilles, *Cinema Two, The Time-Image*, tr. Hugh Tomlinson and Robert Galeta, Minneapolis: University of Minnesota Press, 1989. Originally published in French as *Cinéma 2, L'Image-temps*, Paris: Les Éditions de Minuit, 1985.

Deleuze, Gilles, *Difference and Repetition*, tr. Paul Patton, New York: Columbia University Press, 1994. Originally published in French as *Différence et Répétition*, Paris: Presses Universitaires de France, 1968.

Deleuze, Gilles, *Empiricism and Subjectivity, An Essay on Hume's Theory of Human Nature*, tr. Constantin Boundas, New York: Columbia University Press, 1994. Originally published in French as *Empirisme et subjectivité: Essai sur la nature humaine selon Hume*, Paris: Presses Universitaires de France, 1953.

Deleuze, Gilles, 'Hume', in *Pure Immanence, Essays on A Life*, tr. Anne Boyman, Cambridge: MIT Press, Zone Books, 2001. Originally published in French as *La Philosophie: De Galiléé à Jean-Jacques Rousseau*, Paris: Les Éditions de Minuit, 1972.

Deleuze, Gilles, 'Immanence, a life', in *Pure Immanence, Essays on A Life*, tr. Anne Boyman, Cambridge: MIT Press, Zone Books, 2001. Originally published in French as 'L'Immanence: Une Vie', in *Philosophie 47*, Paris: Les Éditions de Minuit, 1995.

Deleuze, Gilles, *Kant's Critical Philosophy, The Doctrine of the Faculties*, tr. Hugh Tomlinson and Barbara Habberjam, Minneapolis: University of Minnesota Press, 1984. Originally published in French as *La Philosophie critique de Kant*, Paris: Presses Universitaires de France, 1963.

Deleuze, Gilles, *Masochism, An Interpretation of Coldness and Cruelty*, tr. Jean McNeil, New York: Georges Brazillier, 1971. Originally published in French as *Présentation de Sacher-Masoch, Le Froid et le Cruel*, Paris: Les Éditions de Minuit, 1967.

Deleuze, Gilles, *The Logic of Sense*, tr. Mark Lester with Charles Stivale, Constantin V. Boundas, ed. Constantin Boundas, New York: Columbia University Press, 1990. Originally published as *Logique du sens*, Paris: Les Éditions de Minuit, 1969.

Deleuze, Gilles, 'Postscript on control societies', tr. Martin Joughin, in *Negotiations*, New York: Columbia University Press, 1995. Originally published in French as '*Post-Scriptum sur les sociétés de contrôle*', in *L'Autre journal*, no. 1 (May 1990), reprinted in *Pourparlers*, Paris: Les Éditions de Minuit, 1990.

Deleuze, Gilles and Guattari, Félix, *Anti-Oedipus*, tr. Robert Hurley, Mark Seem, and Helen R. Lane, Minneapolis: University of Minnesota Press, 1987. Originally published in French as *Anti-Oedipe*, Paris: Les Éditions de Minuit, 1972.

Deleuze, Gilles and Guattari, Félix, *A Thousand Plateaus, Capitalism and Schizophrenia*, tr. Brian Massumi, Minneapolis: University of Minnesota Press, 1987. Originally published in French as *Mille Plateaux, Capitalisme et Schizophrénie*, Paris: Les Éditions de Minuit, 1980.

Deleuze, Gilles and Guattari, Félix, *What is Philosophy?*, tr. Hugh Tomlinson and Graham Burchell, New York: Columbia University Press, 1994. Originally published in French as *Qu'est-ce que la philosophie?*, Paris: Les Éditions de Minuit, 1991.

Feynman, Richard P., *QED, The Strange Theory of Light and Matter*, Princeton: Princeton University Press, 1985.

Foglia, Marc, 'Michel de Montaigne', *The Stanford Encyclopedia of Philosophy*, ed. Edward N. Zalta (Fall 2004 Edition), <http://plato.stanford.edu/archives/fall2004/entries/montaigne/>.

Ford, Joseph, 'What is chaos, that we should be mindful of it?', in *The New Physics*, ed. Paul Davis, Cambridge: Cambridge University Press, 1989.

Foucault, Michel, *Discipline and Punish, The Birth of the Prison*, tr. Alan Sheridan, New York: Vintage Books, 1979. Originally published in French as *Surveiller et punir; Naissance de la prison*, Paris: Éditions Gallimard, 1975.

French, Howard W., 'A village grows rich off its main export: its daughters', *New York Times*, section A: 4 (col. 3), 3 January 2005.

Freud, Anna, 'On adolescence', *The Writings of Anna Freud*, vol. 5, New York: International Universities Press, 1974.

Freud, Sigmund, *Beyond the Pleasure Principle*, tr. James Strachey, New York: W. W. Norton, 1966.

Freud, Sigmund, *Civilization and Its Discontents*, tr. James Strachey, New York: W. W. Norton, 1961.

Freud, Sigmund, *The Ego and the Id*, tr. Joan Riviere, New York: W. W. Norton, 1960.

Freud, Sigmund, 'Project for a scientific psychology', in *The Standard Edition of the Complete Psychological Works of Sigmund Freud*, tr. James Strachey, London: Hogarth Press, 1966.

Gibbons, Beth, 'Mysteries', in Beth Gibbons and Rustin Man, *Out of Season*, New York: Systemtactic Limited, 2003.

Glazebrook, Patricia, 'Zeno against mathematical physics', *Journal of the History of Ideas*, 62, no. 2 (April 2001): 193–210.

Goldie, Peter, *The Emotions, A Philosophical Exploration*, Oxford: Clarendon Press, 2000.

Graham, Kenneth, *The Wind in the Willows*, Avenel, NJ: Lithium Press, 1987.

Graves, Robert, *The Greek Myths: 1 & 2*, New York: Penguin Books, 1980.

Gregory, Richard L., *Eye and Brain, The Psychology of Seeing*, Princeton: Princeton University Press, 1990.

Halperin, David, 'Why is Diotima a woman?', in *One Hundred Years of Homosexuality and Other Essays on Greek Love*, ed. David Halperin, New York: Routledge Press, 1990.

Harrison, Kathryn, *The Kiss, A Memoir*, New York: Random House, 1997.

Hegel, G. W. F., *Lectures on the History of Philosophy*, vol. 3. tr. E. S. Haldane, London: Routledge and Kegan Paul, 1955.

Hesiod, *Theogony*, in Robert Graves, *The Greek Myths: 1*, New York: Penguin Books, 1980.

Hesiod and Homer, *Hesiod, the Homeric Hymns and Homerica*, tr. Hugh G. Evelyn-White, London and Cambridge, MA: Loeb Classical Library, 1920.

Hey, Tony and Walters, Patrick, *The New Quantum Universe*, Cambridge: Cambridge University Press, 2003.

Hobbes, Thomas, *Leviathan*, Baltimore: Penguin Books, 1968.

Holland, Eugene, *Deleuze and Guattari's 'Anti-Oedipus'*, London: Routledge Press, 1999.

Horkeimer, Max, and Adorno, Theodor W., *Dialectic of Enlightenment*, tr. John Coming, New York: Herder and Herder, 1972. Originally published in German as *Dialektik der Aufklärung*, New York: Social Studies Association, 1944.

Hume, David, *A Treatise of Human Nature*, Oxford: Oxford University Press, 1968.

Irigaray, Luce, *An Ethics of Sexual Difference*, tr. Caroline Burke and Gillian C. Gill, Ithaca: Cornell University Press, 1993.

Irigaray, Luce, *Speculum of the Other Woman*, tr. Gillian C. Gill, Ithaca: Cornell University Press, 1985. Originally published in French as *Speculum de l'autre femme*, Paris: Les Éditions de Minuit, 1974.

James, William, 'What is an emotion?', *Mind* 9: 188–205.

Kaler, James B., *Stars*, New York: Scientific American Library, 1992.

Kant, Immanuel, *Critique of Practical Reason*, tr. Lewis White Beck, New York: Liberal Arts Press, 1956.

Kant, Immanuel, *The Critique of Pure Reason*, tr. Norman Kemp Smith, New York: St Martin's Press, 1965.

Kemp Smith, Norman, *A Commentary to Kant's 'Critique of Pure Reason'*, New York: Humanities Press, 1962.

Khan, R. M. et al., 'Neural processing at the *speed* of smell', *Neuron*, 44 (2 December 2004): 744–7.

Kirk, G. S., Raven, J. E. and Schofield, M. (eds), *The Presocratic Philosophers*, Cambridge: Cambridge University Press, 1983.

Bibliography

Köhler, Wolfgang, *Gestalt Psychology*, New York: Liveright, 1929 and 1947.

Kristof, Nicholas D., 'Girls for sale', *New York Times*, Op-ed, 17 January 2004.

Kristof, Nicholas D., 'Loss of innocence', *New York Times*, Op-ed, 28 January 2004.

Le Doeuff, Michèle, *Hypparchia's Choice, An Essay Concerning Women and Philosophy*, tr. Trista Selous, Oxford: Blackwell, 1991. Originally published in French as *L'étude et le rouet*, Paris: Seuil, 1989.

Le Doeuff, Michèle, *Philosophical Imaginary*, tr. Colin Gordon, Stanford: Stanford University Press, 1989.

Le Doeuff, Michèle, *The Sex of Knowing*, tr. Kathryn Hammer and Lorraine Code, New York and London: Routledge Press, 2003. Originally published in French as *Le Sexe du savoir*. Paris: Aubier, 1998.

Le Doeuff, Michéle, 'Women and philosophy', in *French Feminist Thought*, ed. Toril Moi, Oxford: Blackwell, 1987.

Lee, H. D. P., *Zeno of Elea: A Text, with Translation and Notes*, Amsterdam, 1967.

Lespector, Clarice, *Family Ties*, tr. Giovanni Pontiero, Austin: University of Texas Press, 1972.

Lestienne, Rémy, *The Children of Time, Causality, Entropy, Becoming*, tr. E. C. Neher, Urbana: University of Illinois Press, 1995. Originally published in French as *Les Fils du Temps*, Paris: Presses du CNRS, 1990.

Long, Ben, 'Framed and exposed: making sense of camera sensors', at <http://*www*.creativepro.com> archives (25 August 2004).

Mallarmé, Stéphane, 'Autre éventail', tr. C. F. MacIntyre, in *French Symbolist Poetry*, Berkeley: University of California Press, 1958.

Manderson, Lenore, 'Public sex performances in Patpong and explorations of the edges of imagination', in *The Journal of Sex Research*, vol. 29, no. 4 (November 1992): 451–75.

Marin, Louis, 'Disneyland, a degenerate utopia', *Glyph 1* (1977): 50–66.

Markopoulou, Fotini, 'The internal description of a causal set: what the universe looks like from the inside', *Communications in Mathematical Physics* 211 (2000): 559–83. Available as arXiv:gr-qc/9811053 (18 November 1999).

Markopoulou, Fotini, 'Planck-scale Models of the Universe.' Available as: arXiv: gr-qc/0210086 v2 (7 November 2002).

Markopoulou, Fotini, and Smolin, Lee, 'Causal evolution of spin networks', in *Nuclear Physics* B508 (1997) 409. Available as: arXiv: gr-qc/9702025.

Massumi, Brian, *A User's Guide to Capitalism and Schizophrenia*, Cambridge: MIT Press, 1992.

Merleau-Ponty, Maurice, 'The film and the new psychology', in *Sense and Non-Sense*, tr. Hubert Dreyfus and Patricia Allen Dreyfus, Evanston: Northwestern University Press, 1964. Originally published in French as *Sens et non-sens*. Paris: Les Éditions Nagel, 1948.

261

Merleau-Ponty, Maurice, *Phenomenology of Perception*, tr. Colin Smith, rev. Forrest Williams and David Guerrière, London: Routledge Press, 1989. Originally published in French as *Phénoménologie de la perception*, Paris: Gallimard, 1945.

Merleau-Ponty, Maurice, *The Visible and the Invisible*, tr. Alphonso Lingis, Evanston: Northwestern University Press, 1968. Originally published in French as *Le Visible et l'invisible*, Paris: Gallimard, 1964.

Mohanty, Chandra, 'Under Western eyes, feminist scholarship and colonial discourses', *Feminist Review*, no. 30 (Autumn 1988): 61–85.

Murray, Alison, 'Debt-bondage and trafficking: don't believe the hype', in *Feminist Post-Colonial Theory*, ed. Reina Lewis and Sara Mills, New York: Routledge Press, 2003.

Nagel, Thomas, 'Internal difficulties with justice as fairness', in *What is Justice?*, ed. Robert C. Solomon and Mark C. Murphy, Oxford: Oxford University Press, 2000.

Neumann, Erich, *The Great Mother, Analysis of an Archetype*, tr. Ralph Manheim, Princeton: Princeton University Press, 1974.

Olkowski, Dorothea, 'Expression and inscription at the origins of language', in *Écart and Différence*, ed. M. C. Dillon, Humanities Press, 1997.

Olkowski, Dorothea, *Gilles Deleuze and the Ruin of Representation*, Berkeley: University of California Press, 1999.

Olkowski, Dorothea, 'Time lost, instantaneity and the image', in *parallax* 26 (January–March 2003): 28–38.

Olkowski, Dorothea, 'Writers are dogs, on the limits of perception for thought', in *Crossings*, no. 4 (Fall 2001).

O'Neill, Onora, 'Justice, gender, and international boundaries', in *The Quality of Life*, ed. Martha Nussbaum and S. Sen, New York: Oxford University Press, 1993.

O'Rourke, Dennis, *The Good Women of Bangkok*, prod. Dennis O' Rourke and Glenys Rowe, dir. Dennis O' Rourke (Australia, 1991, 82 mins).

Plato, *Alcibiades*, tr. D. S. Hutchinson, in *Plato, Complete Works*, ed. John M. Cooper, Indianapolis: Hackett Publishing, 1997.

Plato, *Phaedrus*, tr. Alexander Nehamas and Paul Woodruff, in *Plato, Complete Works*, ed. John M. Cooper, Indianapolis: Hackett Publishing, 1997.

Plato, *Republic*, tr. G. M. A. Grube, rev. C. D. C. Reeve, in *Plato, Complete Works*, Indianapolis: Hackett Publishing, 1997.

Plato, *Symposium*, tr. Michael Joyce in *Plato: The Collected Dialogues*, ed. Edith Hamilton and Huntington Cairnes, Princeton: Princeton University Press, 1961.

Plato, *Timaeus*, tr. Donald J. Zeyl, in *Plato, Complete Works*, ed. John M. Cooper, Indianapolis: Hackett Publishing, 1997.

Rawls, John, *A Theory of Justice*, Cambridge, MA: Harvard University Press, 1971.

Bibliography

Rawls, John, *Political Liberalism*, Cambridge, MA: Harvard University Press, 1993.

Reich, Wilhelm, *Character Analysis*, tr. Theodore P. Wolfe, New York: Farrar, Straus and Cudahy, 1961.

Robinson, Lillian S., 'Touring Thailand's sex industry', in *Materialist Feminism*, ed. Rosemary Hennesy and Chrys Ingraham, New York: Routledge Press, 1997.

Rock, Irvin, 'The intelligence of perception', in *Perception*, New York: Scientific American Library, 1984.

Rougemont, Denis de, *Love in the Western World*, tr. Montgomery Belgion, New Jersey: Princeton University Press, 1956. Originally published in French as *L'Amour et l'Occident*, Paris: Plon, 1940.

Rousseau, Jean-Jacques, *Discourse on the Origin and Foundations of Inequality*, tr. Roger G. and Judith R. Masters, New York: St Martin's Press, 1964.

Rucker, Rudy, *The Fourth Dimension, A Guided Tour of the Higher Universes*, Boston: Houghton Mifflin, 1984.

Russell, Bertrand, 'The problem of infinity considered historically', in *Our Knowledge of the External World*, London, 1914.

Sacher-Masoch, Leopold von, *Venus in Furs*, tr. John McNeil, New York: George Brazillier, 1971.

Sartre, Jean-Paul, *Being and Nothingness, An Essay in Phenomenological Ontology*, tr. Hazel Barnes, New York: Washington Square Press, 1971. Originally published in French as *L'Être et Néant, Essai d'ontologie phénoménologique*, Paris: Gallimard, 1943.

Sartre, Jean-Paul, *The Transcendence of the Ego: An Existentialist Theory of Consciousness*, tr. Forrest Williams and Robert Kirkpatrick, New York: Farrar, Straus, Giroux, 1957. Originally published in French as 'La Transcendance de L'Ego: Esquisse d'une description phénoménologique.' In *Recherches Philosophiques*, VI (1936–7).

Smolin, Lee, *Three Roads to Quantum Gravity*, New York: Basic Books, 2001.

Snell, Bruno, *The Discovery of the Mind, The Greek Origins of European Thought*, tr. T. G. Rosenmeyer, New York: Harper and Row, 1960.

Stewart, Ian, *Does God Play Dice? The Mathematics of Chaos*, London: Basil Blackwell, 1989.

Strogatz, Steven H. and Stewart, Ian, 'Coupled oscillators and biological synchronization', *Scientific American* (December 1993): 102–9.

Tuana, Nancy, 'The weaker seed, the sexist bias of reproductive theory', *Hypatia*, vol. 3, no. 1 (Spring 1988): 35–58.

Virilio, Paul, *The Virilio Reader*, ed. James Der Derian, tr. Michael Degener, James Der Derian, and Lauren Osepchk, London: Blackwell, 1998.

Weiss, Gail, *Body Images, Embodiment as Intercorporeality*, New York: Routledge Press, 1999.

Weisstein, Eric W., 'Torque', *Eric Weisstein's World of Physics*, http:// scienceworld.wolfram.com/physics/Torque.html.

Williams, James, *Gilles Deleuze's 'Difference and Repetition'*, Edinburgh: Edinburgh University Press, 2003.

Wilson, Elizabeth, *The Sphinx in the City*, Berkeley: University of California Press, 1991.

Yeóenoólu, Meyda, 'Veiled fantasies: cultural and sexual difference in the discourse of orientalism', in *Feminist Postcolonial Theory*, ed. Reina Lewis and Sara Mills, New York: Routledge Press, 2003.

Young-Bruehl, Elizabeth, 'Where do we fall when we fall in love?', *Journal for the Psychoanalysis of Culture and Society*, vol. 8, no. 2 (Fall 2003).

Index

Index